Blogging

for

dummies®

A Wiley Brand

Blogging

for
dummies®
A Wiley Brand

6th edition

by Amy Lupold Bair

Blogging For Dummies®

Published by: **John Wiley & Sons, Inc.,** 111 River Street, Hoboken, NJ 07030-5774, www.wiley.com

Copyright © 2016 by John Wiley & Sons, Inc., Hoboken, New Jersey

Published simultaneously in Canada

For general information on our other products and services, please contact our Customer Care Department within the U.S. at 877-762-2974, outside the U.S. at 317-572-3993, or fax 317-572-4002. For technical support, please visit www.wiley.com/techsupport.

Wiley publishes in a variety of print and electronic formats and by print-on-demand. Some material included with standard print versions of this book may not be included in e-books or in print-on-demand. If this book refers to media such as a CD or DVD that is not included in the version you purchased, you may download this material at http://booksupport.wiley.com. For more information about Wiley products, visit www.wiley.com.

Library of Congress Control Number is available from the publisher: 2016940948

ISBN: 978-1-119-25780-6

ISBN 978-1-119-25781-3 (ePub); ISBN 978-1-119-25782-0 (ePDF)

Manufactured in the United States of America

10 9 8 7 6 5 4 3 2 1

Contents at a Glance

Table of Contents

Introduction

Allow me to be the first to welcome you to the *blogosphere,* an exciting and energetic space online that people are using to reach out, build communities, and express themselves. *Blogging For Dummies,* 6th Edition, is designed to help you through the process of starting a blog quickly, and it gives you the tools you need to make the most of your experience in the blogosphere. The entire book is updated and includes the very latest in blogging tips and tricks. Prepare to join the world of blogging!

About This Book

This book is designed to be useful for all kinds of bloggers, whether you're the CEO of a major corporation or a hobbyist with a passion for communicating. I focus on what makes a blog work — and how a blog can work for you. Also, I realize that not everyone has the technical skills necessary to start a blog, so I provide options for all levels of experience.

This book is useful to you whether you're taking part in the conversations in the world of blogs or becoming a blogger yourself. I cover everything from technology to legal issues, so you can go forward knowing you have a resource that covers every aspect of this exciting medium.

Whether you're building a blog as a rank beginner or redesigning an existing blog to make it better, you can find everything you need in these pages. The fact that you're holding this book likely means you have some ideas about starting a blog — and I want to get you started right away!

The first part of the book gets you blogging quickly and safely. Chapter 1 introduces you to blogging, Chapter 2 walks you through the world that is the blogosphere, and Chapter 3 helps you choose the software and tools you need to get started. In Chapter 4, I show you the fastest and easiest way to get started immediately with your very own blog.

However, you don't have to memorize this book or even read it in order. Feel free to skip straight to the chapter with the information you need and come back to the beginning later. Each chapter is designed to give you easy answers and guidance, accompanied by step-by-step instructions for specific tasks.

I include sidebars that give you more information, but you don't need to read those sidebars if you're short on time. A Technical Stuff icon also indicates helpful extras that you can come back to when you have more time.

Keeping things consistent makes them easier to understand. In this book, those consistent elements are *conventions*. Notice how the word *conventions* is in italics? That's a convention I use frequently. I put new terms in italics and then define them so that you know what they mean.

URLs (web addresses) or email addresses in text look like this: `www.resourceful mommy.com`. Sometimes, however, I use the full URL, like this: `http://traction. tractionsoftware.com/traction` because the URL is unusual or lacks the www prefix.

Most web browsers today don't require the introductory http:// for web addresses, though, so you don't have to type it in.

Foolish Assumptions

Just because blogs have a funny name doesn't mean they have to be written by funny people — or even humorous ones! If you can write an email, you can write a blog. Have confidence in yourself and realize that blogs are an informal medium that forgives mistakes unless you try to hide them. In keeping with the philosophy behind the *For Dummies* series, this book is an easy-to-use guide designed for readers with a wide range of experience. Being interested in blogs is all that I expect from you.

If you're new to blogs, this book gets you started and walks you step by step through all the skills and elements you need to create a successful web log. If you've been reading and using blogs for some time now, this book is an ideal reference that can help you ensure that you're doing the best job possible with any blog that you start or manage.

That said, you don't need to know much more than how to use a web browser, open and create files on your computer, and get connected to the Internet, so you don't need to be a computer genius, either.

Icons Used in This Book

Here's a rundown of the icons I use in this book:

The Remember icon reminds you of an important concept or procedure to store away in your memory bank for future use.

The Technical Stuff icon signals technical stuff that you might find informative and interesting, but that you don't need to know to develop the blogs described in this book. Feel free to skip over these sections if you don't like the techy stuff.

Tips indicate a trick or technique that can save you time and money — or possibly a headache.

The Warning icon warns you of any potential pitfalls — and gives you the all-important information about how to avoid them.

Beyond the Book

In addition to what you're reading right now, this product also comes with a free access-anywhere Cheat Sheet that tells you how to select blogging software, guides you on what kind of blogger to be, and tells you all about the blogging software applications that are out there. To get this Cheat Sheet, simply go to www.dummies. com and search for "Blogging For Dummies Cheat Sheet" in the Search box.

Where to Go from Here

Turn to Chapter 1 to dive in and get started with an intro to blogs and an overview of why this medium is so exciting for so many people. If you just want to get started blogging today, read over Chapter 4. Otherwise, spend some time thinking about the best blog software solution for your situation — which you can read more about in Chapter 3. Already have a blog, but want to do more with it? I think Chapter 9's coverage of great content might be a great place to dive in. Good luck!

1

Getting Started with Blogging

Chapter 1

Discovering Blog Basics

B y now, you've probably heard the word *blog* tossed around by all kinds of people, seen it show up in news stories or cited on TV news broadcasts, or you may even have a child, friend, or coworker who has a blog. Bloggers are showing up inside businesses, and businesses are even using blogs to reach out to their customers. But what exactly do all these people mean when they say they have a blog? And what does a blog written by a teenager have in common with one written by a CEO?

Don't be too hard on yourself if you aren't exactly sure what a blog is. The word *blog* actually originated from a mash-up of two other words — web and log — so if it sounds made up, that's because it is. At its most basic level, a *blog* is a chronologically ordered series of website updates, written and organized much like a traditional diary, right down to the informal style of writing that characterizes personal communication. Over the years, the term *blog* has come to describe a wide variety of online communications and media. Blogging has come a long way!

In this chapter, you find out just what makes a blog bloggy and why so many people are outfitting themselves with one like it's the latest celebrity fashion trend. (Hint: It's not just that we're all narcissists!) You can get some ideas that you can use to start your own blog and become part of the *blogosphere* (the community of blogs and bloggers around the world).

Making Yourself Comfortable with Blogs

I talk to a lot of people about blogs, many of whom know that you find blogs online, but some who also have the impression that all blogs are written by extreme thinkers, cranky complainers, or fashion-obsessed teens. Some blogs really are diaries in which the blogger records the minutiae of day-to-day life — but blogs can be much more than that, and all kinds of people write them.

One of my favorite blogs (see Figure 1-1) falls into the personal diary category: The Bloggess (`http://thebloggess.com`). The personal blog of writer Jenny Lawson, The Bloggess follows everything from stories of taxidermied raccoons riding on cats to giant metal chickens left on doorsteps.

Think of a blog this way: It's a kind of website. All blogs are websites (the opposite isn't true, though), and neither the content nor the creator makes a blog a blog — the presentation does. A blog can be many things: a diary, a news source, a photo gallery, or even a corporate marketing tool. Blog content can include text, photos, audio, and even video, and bloggers talk about nearly any subject that you can imagine.

FIGURE 1-1:
The Bloggess blogs about her life — hilariously.

Source: www.thebloggess.com

TECHNICAL STUFF

One of the reasons blogs have become such a popular way of publishing a website is because they're particularly good at generating high search-engine rankings. If you have a blog, it's more likely than a standard website to come up high in lists of search results for the topics you discuss. The reason? Your posts are fresh and recent. Search engines give an extra boost to web pages that have the most recently updated or created content related to the keywords that someone is searching for. And better search-engine listings mean more visitors, more readers, more comments, and a more vibrant community. Individuals and companies have taken advantage of the blog medium to reach out to web users.

How people use blogs

With millions of blogs in the world — the blog platform Wordpress.com (`http://wordpress.com`) reports that a new Wordpress.com blog is created every six seconds — it's obvious that blogging is a popular and successful format for publishing a website. But just what are people doing with blogs? They can't all be posting pictures of their cats!

And they aren't. Bloggers are using the blog format to communicate effectively in all kinds of information spheres, from the personal to the professional. In fact, many blogs serve multiple purposes at the same time, mixing posts about activities at home with news pertaining to work. Your blog can serve many purposes in your life.

Documenting your life

A lot of folks use blogs for the same reason they might keep a diary — to chronicle their lives and activities. This urge to communicate appears in all kinds of mediums, from scrapbooking to taking digital photographs. If you're interested in sharing personal details with others, a blog gives you a fast, efficient way to do so.

If you send holiday newsletters every year or email a group of friends and family to let them know about exciting events in your life, you can have a lot of fun with a blog. You can blog as often as you want, and your readers visit when they're ready to get more information. Best of all, each blog post gives your friends and family a quick way to respond to you; they have only to leave a comment on your blog post. You might find you're talking more with your family than ever before!

Of course, not all lives come up roses every day; they can't all be wedding and travel blogs. Personal blogs can be intense when they document rough times. Amanda Henson (`http://itsmeamanda.com`), a Kentucky-based blogger, uses her blog It's Me, Amanda, shown in Figure 1-2, to document her experiences with breast cancer along with other aspects of her life from family to career. She uses her blog as a place to share insights as well as the much-needed laugh:

"Halloween is the best time to go bald. The costume options are seemingly endless! Pirate? Aye! Zombie? Braaiiinnsss! Cancer patient? Check!"

FIGURE 1-2:
Amanda Henson uses her blog It's Me, Amanda to connect with others and cope with her illness.

Source: www.itsmeamanda.com

WARNING

In your eagerness to let your friends know about what you're up to, don't forget that anyone in the world can access a blog (unlike a real diary or scrapbook), now and in the future. Don't publish anything that you might find embarrassing in the future, and have the same consideration when you talk about others or use photographs.

Exploring a hobby or passion

If you have a passion or hobby that you just love to talk about, consider doing so in a blog. Anyone who shares your interest is a potential reader and is bound to be looking for more information wherever he or she can find it.

You can detail your own experiences, offer advice to others, drum up support for whatever you like to do, or just talk about what you love. Best of all, you might be able to make connections with others who share your infatuation, making friends and finding ways to get involved with your hobby more deeply.

Bob Aycock blogs about one of his biggest passions: Disney. Magical Daddy (`www.magicaldaddy.com`) is his personal labor of love where he writes about his family and their love of all things Disney, from the parks to the movies, to the man and his mouse. Magical Daddy is also a great way for Bob to introduce readers to the Disney Parks Moms Panel, where he helped answer questions from future Disney Parks guests. Check out Magical Daddy in Figure 1-3.

FIGURE 1-3: Magical Daddy is the pixie-dust-filled online home of Bob Aycock.

Source: `www.magicaldaddy.com`

Sharing information

Sometimes a blog is all about sharing information. Journalists use blogs to report on local, national, and international news; critics and commentators use the medium to state their opinions and predictions; educators keep parents and students abreast of classroom happenings and dates; coworkers let colleagues in geographically distant offices know what's going on in relation to collaborative projects. The uses of the informational blog are really limitless.

One popular information blog is TechCrunch (`www.techcrunch.com`). This guide to all things Internet covers everything from the latest startups to the newest tech gadgets and, of course, is a frequently updated home to breaking news in the world of tech. You might not find every post useful, but if you're trying to keep up with the breakneck pace of technological innovation on the Internet, you may find TechCrunch (shown in Figure 1-4) and blogs like it invaluable resources.

FIGURE 1-4:
TechCrunch is your source for satisfying your gadget news appetite.

Making money

You have spent a lot of time producing your blog, and that time has paid off in the form of a large audience. Why not turn that influence into dollars? That's a question many a popular blogger has asked, and you can make it happen in increasingly varied ways. As the online world changes and grows, so do the ways for you to cash in!

A common and straightforward technique involves including advertisements on your blog pages. For example, Google AdSense (www.google.com/adsense) provides in-page advertising that's designed to match the content of your blog and therefore be of interest to your readers. Each time a visitor to your blog clicks one of these advertising links, you earn money from Google. I talk more about making money from advertising programs, affiliate links, sponsorships, and more in Chapter 20.

Of course, companies haven't missed out on the fact that blogs can help them drum up interest in their products and services, or inform and connect with consumers. Many companies, small and large, have added blogs to their websites, and they use the blogs to start conversations with their customers and potential customers. In many cases, use of the informal voice of the blog medium has helped customers connect with the real people who work within these organizations. This personal connection improves a company's credibility and often enhances customer recognition of its brand and values.

Southwest Airlines has taken this approach on their blog, Nuts About Southwest (www.blogsouthwest.com). On the blog's About page, Southwest says, "Our goal with the new Nuts About Southwest remains to give our readers the opportunity to take a look inside Southwest Airlines and to interact with us." Southwest tries to make sure that the blog represents many voices inside the company, from managers to captains — even the president of the company. As with personal blogs, the tone is light and conversational, making the company seem friendly and accessible.

Promoting a cause

For some, creating a blog is less about simply telling a story and more about promoting a cause or mission. Whereas many bloggers first find their voice and later use the influence of their online platform to draw attention to a favorite charity or interest, others create their online home with the express purpose of championing a cause.

Katherine Stone, the founder of the blog Postpartum Progress (www.postpartum progress.com), created her blog — which has come to include a team of contributors — with the purpose of both raising awareness of postpartum depression and providing support to pregnant and new moms. The site has developed into the most widely read blog in the world dealing with the topics of postpartum depression and maternal mental illness, and what began as Katherine's personal labor of love now includes a national nonprofit under the same name (www. postpartumprogress.org), shown in Figure 1-5.

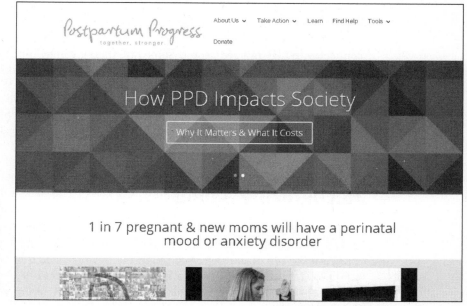

FIGURE 1-5: Postpartum Progress has gone from a cause-dedicated blog to a national non-profit organization.

Source: www.postpartumprogress.org

Flexing creative muscles

When I first began blogging, I was a stay-at-home mom with a 4-year-old and a 2-year-old. I had transformed from someone who loved writing, playing music, and drawing to someone who felt buried under the daily tasks of keeping a home running. Blogging was a welcome opportunity to flex those long-dormant creative muscles!

The world of blogging provides creatives with nearly endless opportunities to be inventive. Interested in photography? Create an image-based blog that centers around your photographs! Have a hidden hobby that you'd rather not bring into your daily life? Find your peers through your hobby-based blog and let your banner fly!

Establishing an online platform

For many bloggers, the blog itself is simply the means to an end. Creating a blog is a fabulous way to put down some roots on the Internet, build an audience, and establish an online footprint. Some bloggers do this with the hope of a future book-writing contract, whereas others use their blogs as an opportunity to highlight their expertise in a particular area.

Creating a community

The world can be a lonely place until you wake up one morning and realize that there are people interacting online 24 hours a day, 7 days a week! Although I'm certainly not encouraging checking out of the IRL — in real life — world in order to live only on the Internet, the fact is that blogs are a wonderful opportunity to connect with like-minded people. Some find their joy in helping birds of a feather flock together. A niche-blog can quickly become a place for lifelong friendships to be made and resources to be shared.

The Type-A Parent blog (http://typeaparent.com/), shown in Figure 1-6, began as a blogging community and has evolved into a blogging network and a popular social media conference.

Recognizing a blog

You've probably already encountered a blog online even if you didn't recognize it as such at the time. Because the blogger isn't required to put a big This Is a Blog! sticker at the top of the page, you might not have realized that you were looking at a blog. If you're ready to dive headfirst into the world of blogging, consider becoming familiar with typical blog elements as a way to dip your toe into the water.

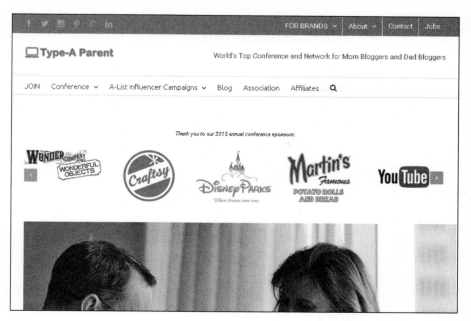

Source: www.typeaparent.com

FIGURE 1-6:
Type-A Parent has morphed from a blog to an online community to a popular social media event.

Regardless of what the blog is about or who writes it, blogs typically feature

>> **Frequent updates:** Most bloggers update their blogs a few times a week, but some bloggers even update them more than once a day. Some blogs don't have a schedule for publishing; the blogger simply updates the blog when it seems appropriate. Other blogs follow predictable editorial calendars that may include recognizable weekly themes such as Wordless Wednesday (a photo feature) or Throwback Thursday.

>> **Posts or entries:** Each time a blogger updates the blog, he or she creates a blog *post,* or entry, that he or she then adds to the blog.

>> **Permalinks:** Each time a blogger adds a post to his or her blog, that post typically appears on the blog's home page. At the same time, blog software creates a *permalink* page to contain only that blog post and its comments. (The word *permalink* is short for "permanent link.") Permalink pages are a big part of why blogs do so well with search engines — every post adds a new page to your website and provides another opportunity for your blog to come up as a search result.

>> **Reverse chronological order:** When a blogger writes a new blog post, that post typically appears at the top of the blog's first page. For blogs that follow a reverse chronological format, the next time the blogger writes a post, it shows up at the top, and the older posts move down the page.

- » **Comments:** Most (though not all) blogs allow readers to leave comments — short text messages — in response to blog posts. Comments really differentiate a blog from most websites by encouraging interaction and conversation.

- » **Search feature:** Blogs typically feature a search window, allowing readers to locate previous posts quickly by searching past content for specific keywords and topics.

- » **Social sharing icons:** Bloggers generally want readers to be able to connect with them in a variety of ways, including on social media. Most blog owners prominently display social media icons to both connect the blog to the related social media accounts and to allow blog content to be shared by readers via social media platforms.

- » **Archives:** Because blogs are updated so frequently, bloggers often sort their blogs into a date- or theme-based archive so that readers can find older information easily.

- » **Categories:** Bloggers can sort posts by subjects or categories, which allows a blogger to blog about a number of different topics and lets readers focus on the topics that most interest them.

BLOGGING THROUGH THE AGES

The concept behind a blog isn't new; after all, people have been keeping diaries and journals since the invention of the written word. Even on the web, diary websites existed long before anyone used the word *blog*.

No one really knows when the first true blog was created, but estimates put the date around 1994. The term *weblog* came into existence in 1997, and it was quickly shortened to the more colloquial *blog*. If you want to read more about the history of blogging, read author Rebecca Blood's essay on the early days of blogging at www.rebeccablood.net/essays/weblog_history.html.

No one can really measure the number of blogs in the world, for a number of technical reasons and because blogs can be short-lived (accidentally or deliberately). All studies of numbers, however, indicate that the number of blogs increases dramatically every month. For example, in May 2007, the blog search engine Technorati (www.technorati.com) was tracking 75 million blogs. By the spring of 2013, Tumblr.com alone boasted 101.7 million blogs.

Blog anatomy: Dissecting a typical blog

In this section, I give you a tour of the usual blog elements by using writer Andrea Updyke's blog, Just is a Four Letter Word (www.justisafourletterword.com). Andrea's blog has all the usual features that I discuss in this section, as shown in Figure 1-7 — and a few more bells and whistles as well.

FIGURE 1-7:
Just is a Four Letter Word is written by author and blogger Andrea Updyke.

Source: www.justisafourletterword.com

Most blogs — no matter what topic they cover — look quite similar because the elements of one blog are common to most blogs. Andrea's is no exception.

Those common elements are as follows:

» **Branding/logo header:** A *header* at the top of the blog displays the name of the blog, often including a logo or other visual element. This header is visible on every page of the blog, thereby identifying the blog even to a visitor who visits one of the interior pages without first going to the home page. In Figure 1-7, the header contains the name of the blog in a graphic as well as the blog's *navigation* — the links to the different parts of her site.

» **Most recent posts:** On many blogs, the most recent post appears at the top of the blog's home page. While you scroll down the home page, you see the next most recent post, and the next most recent post, and so on. New posts are typically at the top, making it easy to find the latest, freshest information when you visit. The number of posts displayed on the first page depends on the blog's style. Some blog home pages are organized by category and show the most recent posts in each of the categories featured. Some display the full text of a post, whereas others show only an introduction or image, requiring readers to click to read the entire post. To read older posts, you can visit the archives or utilize the search field.

>> **Post information:** Along with each entry, blog software displays information *about* the post. This sort of post information typically appears — but a blogger doesn't have to include it. A blog might be missing an element or two that I list or have others that I don't mention:

- The date and time the post was published.

- The name of the post's author. On blogs that have multiple authors, the visitor may find this info especially valuable.

- The number of comments on the post.

- A link to the permalink page, usually labeled Permalink. Sometimes, you can both read and write comments on the permalink page.

- The category in which the blogger has placed the post.

- Other links to bells and whistles unique to the blog, such as the links to share the permalink via social media or pin a post image on Pinterest.

>> **Sidebar material:** Most blogs are laid out in two or three columns, with the most real estate given to the column that contains the blog posts themselves. The second and/or third columns display organizational material for the blog and peripheral information. Some blogs don't have sidebars at all, and on some blogs, you may see elements that I don't mention in the following list of typical sidebar components:

- *Date-based archives:* Nearly every blog archives a post when the blogger publishes that post, both by date and by category. In the sidebar of a blog, you can often access both archive methods. Figure 1-8 shows the drop-down menu offering date-based archives of Andrea's blog, broken down by month. Date-based archives can also show weeks and years.

- *Categorized archives:* Figure 1-9 shows the drop-down menu category archives of Just is a Four Letter Word. By tagging each post with a category at the time that she publishes it, Andrea creates an archive organized by subject, making it easy for you to find the posts that most interest you. Clicking a category link displays only the posts in that subject area, organized in reverse chronological order.

FIGURE 1-8:
A date-based
archive.

Source: www.justisafourletterword.com

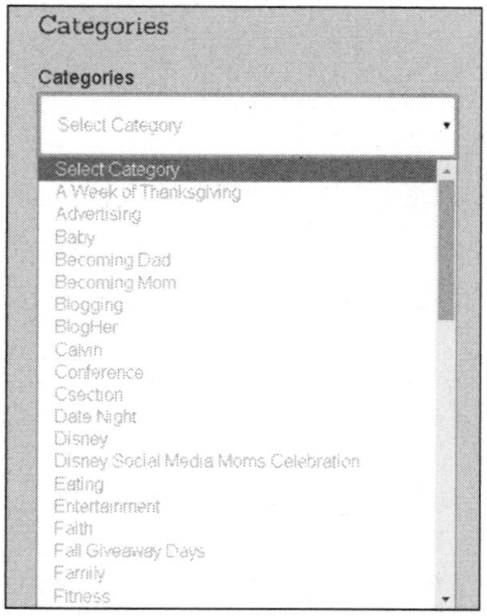

FIGURE 1-9:
A categorized
archive.

Source: www.justisafourletterword.com

- *Social media buttons:* Most bloggers use their sites to build not only a reader base, but also a social media following. This helps bloggers create more than a blog; they create an influencer platform, helping them to turn influence into income, followers into readers. As shown in Figure 1-10, Andrea's site subtly displays easy ways to click through her blog to her Facebook page, Twitter account, and Pinterest boards, among other platforms.

Social media buttons

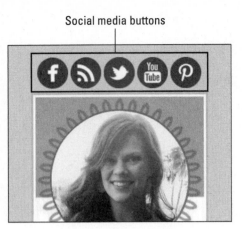

FIGURE 1-10:
Social media
buttons.

Source: www.justisafourletterword.com

- *Information about the author:* Because blogs can be so personal, sometimes you want to know more about who's writing them. Many bloggers know that their readers are curious, and those bloggers put together short bios and other information for readers. Bloggers sometimes display this information in the sidebar or link to it, as in Figure 1-11.

Welcome to Just is a four letter word. My name is Andrea! I'm a published author and blogger living in Raleigh, NC with my husband and two sons. We love many things, which is why I'm on a mission to remove the word "just" from my vocabulary and embrace my many different hats. Thanks for stopping by!

FIGURE 1-11:
A short author
biography.

Source: www.justisafourletterword.com

- *RSS feed link:* Readers can use RSS, or Really Simple Syndication, to subscribe to your blog by using a newsreader, such as Flipboard. After a reader subscribes via RSS, he or she can read the latest updates via the newsreader instead of visiting your blog. So, your readers don't have to visit your blog several times a day to see whether you've updated it. A blog often includes an RSS link (identified by an icon, as shown in Figure 1-12) in the sidebar. On Just is a Four Letter Word, Andrea includes the link to subscribe to her RSS feed with her other social media buttons. I talk more about RSS in Chapter 16.

RSS feed button

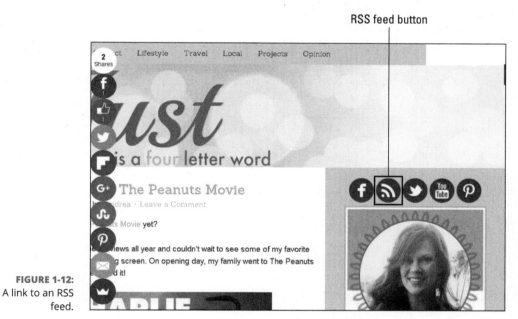

FIGURE 1-12:
A link to an RSS feed.

Source: www.justisafourletterword.com

Starting a Blog

One reason why there are so many blogs is the ease with which they can be set up and published. The early days of the Internet were full of heady talk about the democratization of publishing; people discussed how absolutely anyone would have the power to publish because of the prevalence of personal computers. In fact, that idea wasn't strictly true. Writers no longer needed a printing press and a distribution method to get their work to people, but they still needed specialized skills and technology.

Unless the wannabe publisher spent time figuring out how to write HTML, owned a computer that had an Internet connection, and understood how to put files onto a web server, he or she was still pretty much in the old can't-get-published boat. You could acquire those skills and the tools to publish, but you couldn't do so easily.

The answer, as it turns out, comes down to technology — specifically, software. I believe blogging goes a long way toward making that initial promise of the web come true. If you can write an email, you can figure out how to use the simple interfaces of blogging software without any of the muss of dealing with HTML, FTP, or any of those other awful web acronyms everyone's supposed to understand these days.

Figure 1-13 shows the publishing interface of Blogger (`www.blogger.com`), a great blogging software tool. To write a new post, you simply log into Blogger, fill in the blanks for a new post, and click the Publish button to put the entry on your blog.

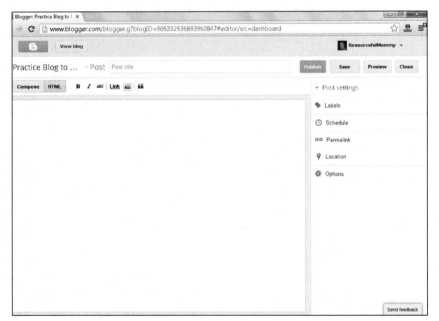

FIGURE 1-13: You can publish a blog by simply filling in a few form fields and clicking Publish.

Source: `www.blogger.com`

Different blog software offers different capabilities. As with all software, the tricky part is finding the right one to use for your situation and needs. I can assure you, however, that blogging software comes in all shapes, sizes, and price ranges — including free! In Chapter 3, I talk extensively about choosing the right software solution for your blog. Chapter 4 shows you how to start a blog in about ten minutes by using Blogger, and Chapter 5 walks you through the details of using WordPress. In Chapter 6 you can try a microblog using Tumblr; Chapter 7 takes you through starting a Squarespace blog.

Choosing What to Blog About

There is no end to the number of blog topics existing in the world today, from the common areas of finance and politics to the far more niche blogs about hairless cats with food allergies.

The blog format is exceptionally well-suited to letting you explore an idea, a hobby, or a project — but don't let that stop you from using it for other things. People have created blogs to pass along marketing expertise, sell shoes, cover the latest celebrity gossip, raise funds for charity races, and even write books. The topic or topics that you write about should excite you and hold your interest, and they can be about absolutely anything.

Having that much freedom can be a little scary and, if you're like me, can leave you with an absolute blank mind — or too many ideas! No problem; you can start a blog today about one topic, and when you actually figure out what you want to write about, change directions and go down another road. And although there are no guarantees that content you delete will disappear forever, thanks to cached copies and screenshots, you certainly have the ability to remove posts from your blog that are no longer a fit. It's a very flexible format!

TIP

Think about the following tips when you start a blog:

>> **Choose a subject that genuinely interests you.** Don't choose a topic only because you think being interested in it makes you look good or it will attract a lot of readers. You're the one who has to do the writing for the blog, and you can do that writing much more easily if you're enthusiastic about your subject. Your passion shines through to your readers and keeps them coming back.

>> **Decide whether any topics are off limits.** Bloggers who keep personal diaries for their friends and families might decide to keep certain subjects out of the public forum of the Internet. For example, do you really want your significant other reading a frank account of last night's dinner preparation argument? How about your mom or your boss?

>> **Think about your potential readers.** Who are they? How can you appeal to them and get them to keep reading your blog? Do you even care about how many readers you have? If you do, what do you want to show, explain, or ask them?

Creating a Successful Blog

Blogs are so quick and easy to set up that you can start one without having much of a plan in place for what you want to blog about, why you're blogging, or what you're trying to accomplish. Some people thrive on this kind of wide-open playing field, but others quickly become bored (or boring!).

To get your blog started on the right foot, think seriously about why you're blogging, and then make a commitment to attaining your goals. Don't get me wrong — this doesn't have to become a job! But, just as you wouldn't expect good results from a dinner prepared without paying any attention to ingredients, you can't start your blog without having a recipe for success.

Here's my recipe for a good blog:

1. Preheat the oven by setting goals.

2. Measure out several cups of good writing.

3. Mix well with frequent updates.

4. Sprinkle in a lot of interaction with your readers.

TIP

Watching how someone else blogs is a great way of finding out how to be successful yourself! Keep track of how the blogs you enjoy are keeping you interested: Take note of how often the blogger updates his or her blog, the writing style, and which posts you find most engaging and get you to leave a comment.

Setting goals

Just as you have many different reasons to blog, so do you have many ways to create a successful blog. *Don't* forget that your goals and plans might not be the same as another blogger's. *Do* think about what your goals are, and keep those goals in mind when you start your blog.

The following are ways that you might characterize a successful blog:

>> **Numbers:** Many bloggers are eager to attract readers to their blogs, and they define success by the number of people who visit every day.

>> **Comments:** Some bloggers find the interaction with readers in the comment area of the blog very gratifying. For these bloggers, getting a comment every day or on every post might mean they're successful.

>> **Personal enjoyment:** If you're starting a blog for your own personal enjoyment, you may want to occasionally assess whether it's still fun!

>> **Income:** For some bloggers, turning a hobby into an income source is a primary motivation for the creation of their blog.

>> **Results:** Many bloggers start their blog to accomplish a task (such as raising money for a charity), to sell a product, or even to get a book contract (blogs have done all these things). When these bloggers meet their goal, they know they've succeeded!

When you start your blog, take time to think about how you define success. Do you want to help your entire family keep in touch? Do you want to let your friends back home know more about your college experience? Are you starting a company and trying to get attention in the media? Consider writing your goals into your very first blog post and then returning to that post every few months to see whether your goals have changed and to remind yourself of what you're trying to accomplish.

Writing well

Some people believe that blogs are poorly written, misspelled, and full of grammatical no-no's such as incomplete sentences. Although it's true that some bloggers do write very casually, paying only cursory attention to formal writing constructs, this informality is part of the charm of the format. Many readers find the colloquial, conversational tone accessible and easy to read, and bloggers who write informally seem approachable and friendly.

With that said, there is no excuse for ignoring all the rules of writing, especially if you hope to achieve the goals you've set for your blog. Well-written and correctly spelled posts attract readers just as often (perhaps more often) as those that aren't. You can develop a friendly, personal way of writing without losing touch with the dictionary. I encourage the use of spellchecking, even for very informal blogs intended for friends and family.

WARNING

For a professional blog, don't even consider writing without paying attention to spelling and grammar. Your readers will roll their eyes, and your competitors will get a good snicker out of it.

REMEMBER

Most important, however, think through your writing and consider your readers. Take the time to practice and develop a voice that sounds personal and conversational while still qualifying as good, engaging writing. Don't let the chatty style of a blog fool you: The best bloggers spend just as much time writing a casual blog post as they would a work memo.

You can find tips on how to develop your voice in Chapter 8.

Posting frequently

Commit yourself to writing new posts on your blog frequently. Ah, *frequently* is such a deceptive little word — because really, what does it mean?

For some people, frequently means every day. For others, it means three times a day. If you want a blog that doesn't eat up every spare moment in your life but that you still update often enough to keep people interested, define the word *frequently* as at least two or three times a week. (If you want to blog more often than that, go to town.) This number of updates strikes a good balance for most blogs.

Many bloggers use a little trick to account for periods of writer's block or for when they go on vacation: They write posts ahead of time and then save them for later. Using your blog software, you can schedule a date and time for a post to go live, making it possible for you keep your readers entertained, even while you're having an appendectomy or basking on a beach in Hawaii.

You also need to pace yourself. In the first heady days of having a blog, the posts flow freely and easily, but after a few months, you might find it difficult to be creative.

Interacting with comments

Comments on blog posts are part of what makes a blog different from a website; the opportunity to interact and converse with the creator of a website and with other readers is unique to blogs.

Forums, sometimes called bulletin boards, offer one way to engage in online conversation on the web, but they aren't as directed by regular posts as blogs. Everyone in the forum community is free to chime in with a topic or question. In fact, some bloggers have chosen to add forums to their blogs as a place for free-flowing conversation. I talk more about how forums can work in Chapter 15.

Visitors to a blog have the opportunity to leave a comment on each post. Sometimes, readers leave comments in reaction to what they read; other times, they might offer a suggestion or pose a question. Because any reader can leave a comment, readers may leave comments about other comments!

Blog posts often include a link directly below each post, indicating how many comments readers have left. Clicking this link takes you to a page that displays the post, any comments that readers have left about that post, and a form that you can use to leave your own comment.

After someone makes a comment, it appears in the Comments area of the blog, usually labeled with the comment writer's name, along with the date and time that he or she left the comment. On some popular blogs, readers compete to see who can leave the first comment on a new blog post.

Not every blog allows comments. Many popular bloggers find that they're overwhelmed by the sheer volume of responses that they get and must turn off comments because they can't keep up with them. We should all be so lucky to have that problem. For most bloggers, comments are an important way to develop a dialogue with readers.

TIP

I recommend that you keep comments turned on in your blog. They're an easy way to involve your audience in your topic and to get valuable feedback about what you're doing with your blog. Most blog platforms allow you to restrict commenting on a post by post basis, so consider that option should you write a post that you'd prefer remain comment-free.

REMEMBER

Unfortunately, spammers can take advantage of comments as easily as they can send you unwanted email. If you keep comments turned on, you will get unwanted comments that have commercial messages. There are wonderfully easy ways to prevent spam comments from appearing, however. If you decide to allow comments on your blog, be sure to read them and delete inappropriate messages. Your readers will thank you. In Chapter 10, I talk at length about encouraging comments — and dealing with those comments that you don't want.

Designing for Success

Blog design is a very personal experience. The blog that you're starting is a reflection of you and your professional life. The decisions you make about how your blog looks are just as important as the technology that you choose to run your blog and what you choose to put on it. Because the web is an ever-evolving medium, no solid rules exist that tell you what you should or shouldn't do with your blog. But you can follow guidelines to keep putting your best foot forward.

If you're blogging for business reasons, either on behalf of a company or to promote yourself, make sure that both the writing and design demonstrate the proper tone. Seek advice from bloggers like you and find out from friends and family members who read blogs frequently what design elements they enjoy. Check out other blogs, especially blogs that reflect the same goals or tone you want to create. What does the design of those blogs say about the blogger and the blog content?

TIP

Regardless of the design you prefer for your blog, it is critical that your site is easy to read on a mobile device. This is called being mobile responsive and is important because of the overwhelming number of readers who prefer to enjoy blogs from smart phones and tablets rather than on their home computer or laptop.

Whether you hire a designer for your blog, use a blog template, or try to make the design yourself, seek ways to make your blog stand out from the rest. If you're a business, make sure that your logo appears on your blog. If you're creating a personal blog, add your own photos. Even if you use a default template, you can often add an identifying graphic or element on the site that differentiates your blog from others.

REMEMBER

Don't be afraid to start small and plan to redesign later. You can grow into your big ideas when you're sure that you know what you want, so take the time to look at what other blogs are doing while you make your plans.

The average blog has four very distinct areas in which to place and customize content: logos, headers, sidebars, and footers. In a blog, each of these areas has a specific purpose. As more blogs have come into existence, these areas have developed in specific ways that can help you organize your content.

Here's some detail about each of these customizable areas:

>> **Logos:** Getting a visitor's attention on the Internet is a science in itself, and clean, crisp logos can hold a visitor's interest long enough to get him or her to read some of your blog. Typically, a logo appears near the top of each blog page (but doesn't have to). Many logos include an illustrated element and a special font treatment of the blog name.

>> **Headers:** The header of any blog contains a few elements. The first element should be, of course, the name of your blog. The title should explain what your blog talks about or who you are as the main writer. You can also throw into the header some form of navigation that can help your visitors find their way around and provide them with quick links to special areas that you want highlighted on your site. On many blogs, the logo also appears in the header. As the name suggests, headers appear at the top of blog pages.

>> **Sidebars:** Sidebars usually become a major focus for a blog site. *Sidebars* are columns to the right or left (or both) of the main content area, and they contain elements such as navigational links, special graphics that point to social networking sites, lists of blogs that you read *(blogrolls),* archive links, or anything that you want to share with your visitors outside the context of a blog post. Sidebars usually appear on every page of your blog and look consistent from page to page.

>> **Footers:** Footers live at the bottom of each blog page, and sometimes they do nothing more than feature a copyright message. More advanced bloggers have expanded the use of footers to include a significant series of links to content within their sites. These links might lead to comments on the blog, recent posts, or posts that you particularly want to highlight. The footer can feature parts of your blog that you want visitors to find easily.

Chapter 2

Entering the Blogosphere

I f you put something on a public blog, *anyone* can read it. Blogs, like all public websites, are accessible anywhere in the world at any time, and anyone with unlimited access to the Internet can read it. (Many blog platforms do allow privacy settings or password protection; if you use these options, you have more assurance of privacy.)

And, as with all public websites, people can print, duplicate, and fax blog posts, tape them to lampposts, distribute them to a class, or post them on social networking websites such as Facebook. A reader of your blog can even copy and paste the text of your blog posts into a text editor or email message, sending that text buzzing around the world in the blink of an eye.

Even with available tracking software, you can't know for certain who's reading your blog, why they're reading it, or what they might do with what you post. Often bloggers believe that only their friends and family are reading their sites, so they don't worry much about what they're writing. Don't make the mistake of assuming that you know who is and isn't reading your blog! Even if you believe that your blog is seen only by friends and family, there's no way to know that for sure.

WARNING

Some blog-hosting sites require you to register to use them, and they limit readership to those who have registered. Such blogs might look as though they offer you more privacy, but don't be lulled into a false sense of security. Generally, the barriers to registering for a service are very low: You just need an email address. Those blogs might as well be public.

In rare instances, an entire blog is password-protected and therefore readable only by visitors who know the login information for the site. As long as that login information stays private, the blog is private. All the points about people being able to copy and paste or print the post still apply, however. As well, if someone shares a password or reads your blog from a public computer, you may have unwelcome guests.

In this chapter, I drive home the point that you shouldn't post anything to your blog that you don't want anyone in the world to read — and yes, that includes your best friend, your significant other, your mother, your coworkers, your boss, your landlord, your neighbor . . . you get the idea. After you've shared your thoughts in the digital space, you have no guarantees of privacy regardless of blog settings.

Assessing Your Involvement

Any productivity guru will tell you that individuals who are looking for advice think with their short-term brains. When you start a new project, you rarely think beyond the end of the calendar year — and even that can be a somewhat generous assumption. New bloggers aren't any different.

Thinking about where you want your blog to be in five years is a difficult undertaking. In fact, most bloggers will tell you that online years are a bit like dog years. The most old-school bloggers have only been around for a little more than a decade! The blogging world changes rapidly. With that said, do you hope to still actively blog five years from now, or will blogging likely be a short-term pursuit? Recognizing your level of commitment helps establish a clear vision about the resources that you should put into the blog.

TIP

Making decisions about the future of a blog can be a tricky business, but here are a few questions to answer (maybe in your new blog!) about where your blog will take you:

>> **What level of commitment are you willing to make to blogging?** Take a moment to visualize your level of commitment. On a list of your general priorities, where does blogging fall? If it's at the absolute bottom of the list, becoming a blogger may not work out well. On the other hand, if you're

thinking about how many ways you can use your blog to enhance your business visibility or to keep your family up to date about what you're doing, you might want to try blogging.

The best starting point in determining your commitment is deciding how many posts you're planning to write per day or week. Many popular bloggers tend to post about once per day, but at that stage, the blogs are usually providing a little income to the blogger. Posting once per week is typical for many personal blogs.

» **Do you like writing? How's your typing?** Being able to write is one skill, but being able to write interesting, fun prose that people actually want to read is entirely different. You can't pick up blogging overnight; you must figure out how to do it by practicing. A good way to do this is to create a test blog on a free blogging service like Blogger (`www.blogger.com`) and try posting for a period of time. If you have any fear of writing or don't know whether writing on a regular basis will work for you, you don't need to invest a lot of time and money until you know the answers to these questions. Knowing how to type is an important skill that some new bloggers might not be very good at. If you don't like to write (or type!), consider a podcast or vlogging (video blogging). I talk about those formats in Chapters 13 and 14.

» **What will the blog be about? Is your blog personal or professional?** If you think of your blog as a personal space, you should spend less time on it than you do on your paying work or occupation — and you should definitely keep your budget lower than your income! Choose a design solution and write content to suit your budget and time.

However, if you want the blog to serve a business purpose or promote your professional acumen, keep in mind that a company or consultancy needs to present a polished, professional image online with a professional-looking design — ideally, one that's integrated into any existing branding and identity. Also, rather than squeeze in time for writing the blog, designate time for blogging just as you would for a meeting, project task, or other work-related responsibility.

» **Do you think that your new blog might grow into a new career, lead to new clients and business, or help build connections with peers and colleagues?** Websites can really help you make connections (just like joining social networks and finding old classmates), and I presume that, in part, you're starting a blog to reach out to a community. If the community is a professional one or a group whose respect you must earn, your blog can send unspoken messages about who you are and what you stand for. But you don't need to get all corporate!

Most popular bloggers have developed careers based on their blogs unintentionally, all thanks to the quality of the blog. Bloggers have used blogs as starting points for book deals, television shows, and even direct sources of revenue.

Think about the needs of your audience members and how to appeal to them, even when you consider what software to use. If you want to build an empire, choose the software that has the bells and whistles necessary to make that empire possible. Chapter 3 has more information about software.

WARNING

>> **How comfortable are you with sharing information about yourself or about your business or industry?** The Internet is a public space. Don't forget that anyone, not just the people you're trying to reach, can read what you reveal about yourself on your blog. Occasionally bloggers find themselves the recipients of unwanted attention and discover that they need to blog more anonymously than they'd planned.

What Happens When You Publish?

Blogging is a very immediate medium: When you publish a post, it usually goes live on your blog right away. In fact, several things typically happen the moment you click the Publish button:

>> The post appears at the top of your blog's home page.

>> The blogging software adds the post to your blog's archive, usually by both date and subject, and to your RSS feed, which gets updated in newsreaders.

>> Anyone who signed up for email notifications receives an email about your post the next time your email is set to go out to readers.

>> If your blog software pings blog search engines and services, those search engines and services receive a notice from your blog software that you've updated your blog and put that information into their catalogs. (A *ping* is simply an electronic notification.) Users of search engine websites can then get your blog post as a result of a search.

>> A search-engine crawler indexes the post the next time it visits your blog.

All these changes happen regardless of whether you think about them. The fact that blog posts are quickly distributed with a minimum of effort on the part of the blogger is part of the beauty and effectiveness of this format. Blog software and services are designed to deliver your content quickly.

REMEMBER

Of course, you can edit your blog posts after you post them, and many bloggers make changes when necessary (see the "Making mistakes" section, later in this chapter, for some suggestions about changing your blog posts appropriately). However, editing after you post is a pretty ineffective way to control your message, because visitors might read or email the original post before you make your edits.

The content you publish on a blog or web page can live on in other unintended ways as well:

» Other bloggers might quote your post and expand on it on their blogs, creating partial copies of your deathless prose.

» Blog services might point to, and even partially excerpt, your blog post.

» Search engines might cache or otherwise archive the content temporarily or permanently.

» An Internet archive, such as the Wayback Machine (`www.archive.org/web/web.php`), might add your blog post to its permanent database.

I don't want to scare you. After all, publishing to your blog is a good thing! You want each of these processes to happen because they bring readers to your blog and present your content to potential readers. But be sure about what you're posting before you start the ball rolling.

Blogging Ethically

The best defense, as they say, is a good offense. As a blogger, you should think about what you write *before* you publish it, as well as afterwards.

What I'm about to say might shock you, so prepare yourself: Bloggers have a code of ethics.

Okay, what I really mean is that *some* bloggers have a code of ethics. This loose set of ethics and standards, to which many serious bloggers adhere, developed as blogs matured from a new medium into a more established one. For most old-school bloggers, the word to think about is *transparency*, which represents a whole range of ideas. I introduce transparency here and explain in more detail in the following sections:

» **Truth-telling and honesty:** In keeping with the diary format of a blog, being transparent on your blog has a lot to do with telling the truth about who you are, why you're blogging, and what you want to accomplish with your blog. You want to communicate openly and honestly on a blog, dealing straightforwardly with your topics and ideas, and with your readers.

>> This idea of honesty doesn't mean you need to reveal information that you're not comfortable disclosing online — quite the contrary. But it does mean that you don't intentionally mislead your readers, as I explain in the upcoming section, "Telling the truth."

>> **Admitting mistakes:** No one's perfect, and you'll eventually make a mistake. Whether you post something that you heard that turns out not to be true, or you blog while angry, the real test is how you respond to making a mistake. In the blogosphere, you need to own up to your words, apologizing if you need to and making corrections when they're necessary.

>> **Maintaining a dialogue:** A good blogger is aware of, and responsive to, his or her readers via the comments that those readers leave on blog posts. A blog isn't created in a vacuum. In fact, many bloggers feel that you can use a blog to build real relationships with people.

REMEMBER

The idea that you can use a blog for meaningful interaction is the revolutionary element in blogging. At the core, blogging is about real people talking with each other and sharing real knowledge and experiences.

Of course, a blog isn't necessarily great literature — and that's fine. But transparency comprises worthy ideas, especially if you plan to blog about personal and sensitive topics. Read on for more details.

Telling the truth

Honesty in blogging is different from honesty in real-life relationships or even journalism or advertising, because knowing who someone is or what she represents online is complex. Consider the following:

>> **Blogging anonymously:** Blogging under a pen name is okay. For many bloggers, telling the truth is first about emotional honesty and second — or perhaps not at all — about revealing who they are. For example, a personal blogger may connect with a community over a sensitive topic and thus want to use a pen name.

WARNING

The blogosphere doesn't like poseurs. If you choose to blog about your life and do so anonymously, be prepared for readers to challenge whether you're even a real person. Know that your true identity may be revealed, either publicly or among people who know you in real life. Be prepared to defend your writing as your own, especially if your anonymous blog could create conflict in your offline life or career.

A famous incident from 2001 concerning the blog of Kaycee Nicole, a young teenager who had just died of leukemia, demonstrates the kind of thing I'm talking about. People all over the world followed her blog, chatted with her online, even spoke with her on the phone during her illness. In fact, the life and death of Kaycee was the product of imagination. After some suspicious anomalies surfaced, several savvy bloggers tracked down real-world evidence that she not only hadn't died, but didn't even exist.

If you're set on blogging anonymously — and there are many reasons to choose this approach — be sure to check out Chapter 11 to learn what to watch out for.

>> **Blogging about products and services at the behest of the product or service provider:** The online community has slammed bloggers for blogging about products and services for money without revealing that they were paid to do so. A blog scandal in 2003 put Dr Pepper into the public eye for soliciting blog posts from a group of teenagers about a new product called Raging Cow. The teens received trips, samples of the product, and gift certificates, and the company asked them to promote the drink on their personal blogs. Many of the teens did so without revealing that they basically received compensation for promoting the product, and when the arrangement became public, a blogosphere boycott of the company and a lot of anger against the bloggers ensued.

Since then, the FTC has ruled that these kinds of endorsement relationships *must* be disclosed, so this is no longer simply an ethical issue. You can review the updated 2013 FTC guidelines at www.ftc.gov/os/2013/03/130312dotcomdisclosures.pdf.

>> **Blogging as a fictional character:** Interestingly, Dr Pepper also started a blog ostensibly written by the Raging Cow herself during her travels around the country, as shown in Figure 2-1. Bloggers roundly criticized this blog at the time (for being fake, of course). But the idea of creating fictional characters that write blogs has stuck around, and many bloggers have used it successfully since then. The format is still controversial, but it's also highly effective!

TIP

In general, I recommend following these rules about honesty in your blogging:

>> Explain who you are and why you're blogging.

>> If you need to hide your identity or those of people you mention, such as your children, indicate that you're doing so and why.

>> If you start a fake blog, make sure that you disclose somewhere on the site that it is, in fact, fake. (You'd think that a blog written by a bovine is obviously fake, but it doesn't hurt to say so.)

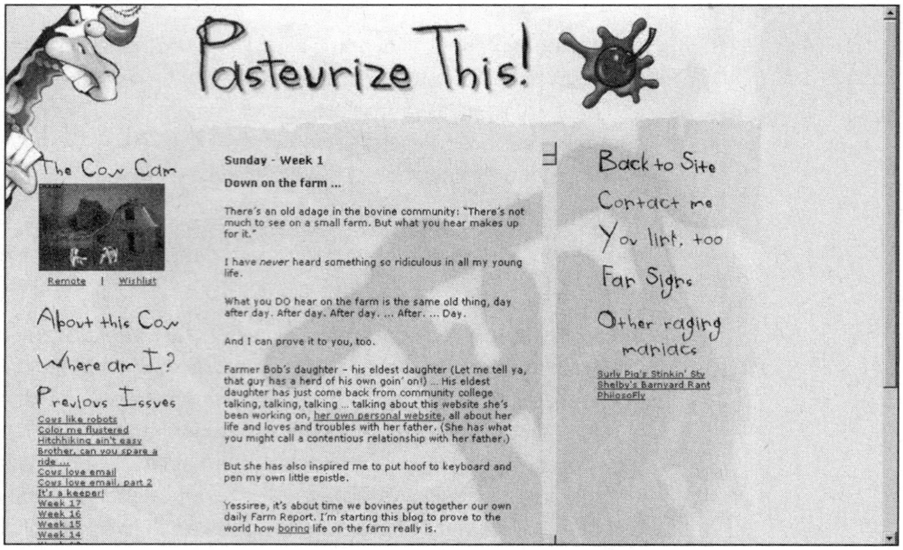

FIGURE 2-1:
The Raging Cow blog was an early example of a fake blog written by a fictional character.

Source: `http://ragingcowblog.clickhere.com/`

>> If you're making money from your blog posts, explain the arrangement and how you're allowing it to influence (or not influence) what you write. U.S.-based bloggers should review the FTC guidelines around endorsements and material considerations at `www.ftc.gov/os/2013/03/130312dotcomdisclosures.pdf`.

>> If you mention a fact or story that you got from someone else, explain who. If you can link to the source, do. Observe copyrights at all times, including copyright rules regarding images and graphics. Only use artwork and photographs that you have express permission to use!

>> Take responsibility for what's on your blog, no matter where else you might have heard or read about what you write.

WARNING

Just because other blogs or websites post and repost an image without permission does not mean that it is legal to break that artist's copyright. Be cautious when using graphics and photographs you've found online that do not give credit to an original source or indicate that the image is posted with permission!

Making mistakes

If you make a mistake on your blog, admit it. Apologize, if necessary. Above all, don't try to deny it or hide it.

Mistakes, big and little, are inevitable and upset people, but you can do a great deal to help yourself and your credibility by how you handle the mistake after you or your readers discover it.

In general, most bloggers try to avoid editing the details of a post after they publish it, which is part of the transparency I discuss earlier in the section "Blogging Ethically." Sometimes, however, you need to correct the original post when you make a factual or grammatical error. If you find the need to make a simple correction such as spelling, grammar, or word choice, it is completely acceptable to make that update with no fanfare. If you find yourself needing to change the facts of the content, however, it is best to note that change within the post itself.

Adding new content to an existing post is always more acceptable — and less suspicious — than removing content that once was present.

You can handle updates that you want to make to a blog post in two ways:

>> **Expand on your original post:** If you change your mind about something, or simply need to expand on what you first said, you may want to do so in the original blog post, instead of starting a new post. Updating the original blog post ensures that readers see your original post at the same time as the update.

For very important updates that change the intention or meaning of a post, Amy Oztan, writer at Selfish Mom (www.selfishmom.com), posts the update within the original content with the phrase "Edited to add," as shown in Figure 2-2. In this case, the update expands on the original post by pointing out new information. Some bloggers preface the new content with the acronym ETA (which stands for Edited to Add).

>> **Start a new post:** When you really mess up, you might also choose to add a new blog post that explains what went wrong and how you might be able to avoid similar mistakes in the future (assuming that's possible!) or that just clarifies the whole situation. You don't always need to go this far, but if it helps clear the air, why not? Plus, you can use the extra post to apologize if you need to.

I once accidentally sent my client kit — including my rate sheet — to my entire blog subscription list. I was able to remove it quickly from the blog itself, but there was nothing I could do about the thousands of people who received my fee list via their email inboxes or feedreaders. To address it in a comical way, I wrote a blog post titled "Hey Look! I'm Naked!" where I explained the error (see Figure 2-3). The post received dozens of comments, proving that sometimes blogging errors turn out for the best.

If you start a new post to explain a mistake, link to the old post and also go into the old post to create a link to the new one so all your readers get a chance to see all the details.

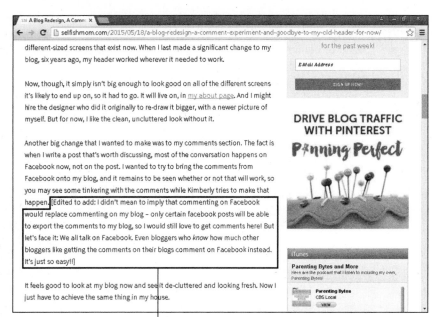

FIGURE 2-2:
When she has new information to add to a blog post, Amy Oztan adds an update to the original post.

Update to blog

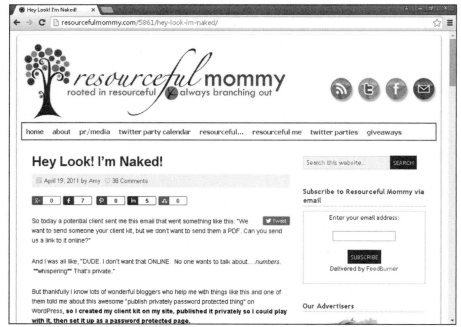

FIGURE 2-3:
Sometimes the best way to handle a blog mistake is to address it head on as I did in the post titled "Hey Look! I'm Naked!"

Handling dialogue

Most bloggers write their blogs with the hope that others will not only read their content but also respond. One mechanism for interacting with your readers is blog post comments. Comments are both a boon and a bane for bloggers: They provide a source of much interesting dialogue, but they can also likely provide an area for people to post spam and other unwanted material.

A blogger who neglects to read and respond to comments in a timely manner risks losing that community of readers as they become frustrated and feel they're not being heard. On the flip side, reading and replying to commenters helps a blogger build a larger, more engaged audience. You don't need to keep all the comments on a blog, however. Pay attention to the conversation others generate on your blog; when necessary, exercise your judgment about removing personal attacks, libel, obscenity, spam, or other undesirable content. Remember that your blog is your space. You get to decide what behavior is appropriate and what types of comments will be tolerated. You may wish to set clear guidelines for readers prior to accepting comments and use moderation tools, which differ by platform, as a way to approve comments before they appear on your site.

In Chapter 9, I cover building a strong community dialogue by using the comments on your blog. I also cover alternative ways to create engagement on your blog through comments, including social media plug-ins that bring comments from other platforms to your site.

Keeping Your Job While Blogging

Although turning blogging into a full-time job is a possibility, it is still an achievement of a small percentage of bloggers when you consider the vast number of people who blog. According to the popular blogging platform WordPress, approximately 50,000 new blogs are created each day on WordPress alone. Most bloggers must maintain a job outside of blogging in order to receive an income. Because you spend so much of your day at work, it may seem natural to include work stories in your blog. In fact, the characters and chaos you encounter every day may provide great blog fodder! However, keep in mind that blogging about work may get you in trouble, and that even blogs meant to be anonymous can't really guarantee protection or anonymity. You should also find out whether your place of work has a privacy policy that includes blogging and social media before you begin blogging, especially if you're considering including work stories on your site.

WARNING

If you choose to discuss people you work with on your blog, someone may be able to identify them even if you don't identify them by name. This could get you in trouble with both your coworkers and your boss.

Some bloggers identify both themselves and their employers on their personal blogs. Doing so is certainly transparent — after all, work is a big part of your life — but it isn't necessarily wise. As noted earlier, some places of business have policies against employee blogging and use of social media. Including information about your job and place of work may also give the wrong impression to your readers that you are blogging on behalf of your employer. It is wise to include a disclaimer on your site stating that all opinions are your own and not that of your employer. Generally speaking, employers don't want people to associate the business with the political agendas, family relationships, or dating habits of their employees.

Employers today know that blogs exist, and they're fully capable of typing your name, their name, or the company name into a search engine and finding blogs that talk about them or their company. Blogging anonymously — although a good idea if you want to criticize your employer — doesn't really guarantee that you won't get caught, particularly if other people in your office know about your blog.

TIP

I encourage you to blog about whatever floats your boat, but if you want to blog about work, you need to do so safely. Here are a few tips that you can use to stay on your employer's good side:

>> **Regardless of what you blog about, don't blog while you are at work.** Using company time and resources to write a personal blog is a clear violation of most employment contracts and can get you disciplined or fired, even if all you do on your blog is sing your boss's praises.

>> **Find out whether your workplace has a blogging policy.** If your boss doesn't know, consult with the HR department. In some cases, a policy might be in place that makes certain requests of your blogging behavior, and you can choose whether to comply with them.

>> **Ask questions about your employer's blogging policy if it's unclear or incomplete.** Find out whether certain subjects are off limits and whether you can identify yourself as an employee.

>> **Be smart about what you choose to say about your work and your colleagues.** If you wouldn't feel comfortable saying what you write in public, don't put it on your blog. Remember, anonymity is never guaranteed!

>> **Don't reveal trade secrets.** Trade secrets include confidential information about how your employer does business that can impact revenue or reputation. If you aren't sure whether you can blog about something, run it by your boss first.

>> **Review other rules and regulations that might impact what you can blog about.** For example, some employers have policies about taking photographs of the workplace or revealing addresses of buildings.

>> **Consider including a disclosure statement on your blog that says you're blogging for personal expression and not as a representative of your employer.** Sarah Pinnix makes her blogging position clear in her very thorough disclosure statement on Real Life with Sarah (`www.reallifeblog. net/about/disclosure/`), which is shown in Figure 2-4.

FIGURE 2-4: Disclosure statements, such as Sarah Pinnix's, help make it clear that you blog for yourself and not for your company.

Blogging without Embarrassing Your Mother or Losing Friends

You might think that it goes without saying that if you can lose your job over opinions that you express on your blog, you can also damage your personal relationships with friends and family. It's worth saying it anyway. Many bloggers get caught up in the confessional mood and post content that they later regret — though perhaps not as much as a friend or relative regrets it.

Understanding what's at stake

Successful blogger Heather Armstrong alienated her family early in her blogging career when she posted her views on the religion in which she was raised. Her parents, who were still firm believers in that religion, read the post and were hurt, as was her extended family and the community in which they lived. (I'm sure she also received plenty of emails from people outside of family who also felt strongly about their religion.) Heather calls herself a poster child for what not to do on a blog, though, in fact, the process has resulted in Dooce (www.dooce.com), a blog that's both well-known and profitable today.

In an interview with Rebecca Blood (who studies blogs), Heather cautions that criticizing others might make great posts, but the chances are good that the person you criticize will read what you've written and feel hurt. You can read the full interview on Rebecca Blood's website at www.rebeccablood.net/bloggerson/heatherarmstrong.html. Even if you never criticize others, you might possibly reveal information about others — their conversations with you or their interactions in your life. It is nearly impossible to blog about your personal life without at least vaguely referencing others.

Protecting others in your life

Some bloggers choose to apply the Mom Test to a post before clicking Publish: Will your mom approve of your post? Although this approach works for many bloggers, I quite frankly worry more about local friends and work clients when deciding to publish a post. Decide what appropriateness litmus test works for you before you begin blogging, or even decide that you're willing to take a no-holds-barred approach to blogging and put it all out there. If you'd like to consider others before creating content on your blog, think about the following:

>> Don't blog about topics that you think might hurt others.

>> Don't blog about others without their permission, even about topics that you consider inconsequential. Don't identify friends, family, and romantic interests by name without their permission.

>> Remember that your blog software archives your blog posts, so someone might read what you say today at a later time. For instance, if you write a report on an unsuccessful relationship, the next person you want to date might read it.

TIP

Before you hit the Publish button, stop for a second and put yourself in the shoes of your reader: Are you writing for the reader, or are you writing for yourself? If your answer is the latter, you might be better off keeping a real diary in a format that the entire world can't publicly access.

Protecting Your Privacy and Reputation

Your blog might not reflect your employer's viewpoints or your family's, but it certainly reflects your own. Don't forget that what you put on your blog today might stick around for a long time to come and that the reader might not always have your best interests at heart.

WARNING

Never put any personal identifying information online that exposes you to possible identity theft or physical confrontation. Don't post your Social Security number, home address, birthdate or place, mother's maiden name, passwords, bank account numbers, or any information that you use as password reminders or identifying information with financial institutions. Most bloggers prefer to keep phone numbers private, as well. Don't reveal this information about the people you blog about, either.

Many bloggers solve the issues discussed in this chapter by choosing to blog anonymously or by using a *handle* — a phrase or moniker that doesn't personally identify the writer.

Don't forget that many of your online identities are linked. For example, if you use a nickname when you leave comments on other blogs, and then use that same nickname on a bulletin board or when you sign up for a social-networking service, people can easily connect the dots. In fact, many of these services already work together. Most social media platforms are now connected. For example, posts on Instagram can also appear simultaneously on Facebook and Twitter. If you identify yourself on any of these sites or tools and then tie them together in some way, others can easily follow the trail to figure out who you are.

Anonymity gives you a great way to protect yourself on your own blog, but it doesn't keep you from showing up on other people's blogs or Flickr photo streams. If your friends and family have blogs, consider setting ground rules with them about situations and topics that you want excluded as subjects on their blogs. Be willing to accept the same kinds of requests about your own blog writing.

TIP

One of the best ways to take charge of your own online identity is to start a website or blog yourself. If other people are mentioning you online, having an official website that contains accurate information can help supplant or downplay less desirable material.

If you want to find out more about controlling your online identity or protecting your privacy, review some of these great online resources:

» Visit the Electronic Frontier Foundation's (EFF) guide "How to Blog Safely (About Work or Anything Else)" at www.eff.org/wp/blog-safely for advice on blogging anonymously, and be sure to read Chapter 10 of *this book.*

» The EFF's "Legal Guide for Bloggers" is a great resource on a number of issues, including defamation, privacy rights, and legal liability: www.eff.org/issues/bloggers/legal.

» Reputation.com (www.reputation.com) is the first business dedicated to online reputation management and provides a variety of resources for those concerned with how they appear online.

» Wikipedia's entry on Online Identity is informative and useful, and covers more than just blogging: http://en.wikipedia.org/wiki/Online_identity.

Chapter 3

Choosing and Hosting Blog Software

I f you're serious about turning your blog into a visual masterpiece, you're likely to choose a blog software package that you install on your own web server. Hosted solutions are great, but you run up against the limits of customization quite quickly.

In this chapter, you can find information about choosing the right software for your situation. If you pick blog software that you need to install, you also need to purchase a domain name and web-hosting platform where you will install your software.

Prepare yourself for strange new technology jargon while you explore what makes blogging exciting, frustrating, confusing, and rewarding — blogging software.

Having Your Own Domain Name

Clearly you are reading this book because you want to start a blog. But before you get too much further, you need to deal with the single most important decision of your blogging career: the name of your blog!

Your blog's name should tie closely into the *domain name,* or web address, that your visitors use to access your blog. If possible, your blog's name and URL, or domain name, should match exactly so that it's easy for readers to find you. For example, my personal blog is called Resourceful Mommy and the domain name I purchased is `www.ResourcefulMommy.com`.

While purchasing a domain name from a URL registration service, you may choose to also pay for web hosting so that your blog software has a place to live on the Internet. Other options are to pay for web hosting with a different hosting company, or redirect your domain name to a free blogging service. The option of redirecting your domain name is covered in depth in Chapter 4. In the following sections of this chapter, I walk you through the basic details of a purchased domain name and web-hosting service.

As mentioned previously, a *domain* is the address (or main URL) that people type in their web browsers to get to your website. Think of a blog's domain as functioning much the same as an address of a house. Each house on a street has an individual address. When someone searches for your home address on Google, he or she finds a specific number and street name that defines your home's location. If you search for a website by using a search engine, the website address you find is the domain name or URL.

Picking a domain name

You can use any available, or not currently owned, word or phrase as your domain name. You can make your domain name a company name, a nickname, or your favorite food group. For years, professional web designers and developers have been saying that all the good domains are gone, which is far from the truth. After all, new websites and blogs are launched all the time, and many of them have great, memorable domains!

TIP

Even if a domain name is available, that doesn't necessarily mean that it is safe to choose that name for your blog and purchase that domain. You should also check to see whether that blog name has already been registered as a trademark so that you can avoid accidentally infringing on someone else's mark. You can search registered trademarks for free at `www.uspto.gov`.

For an example of a great domain name, check out the blog She Buys Cars (`www.shebuyscars.com`), a name that perfectly describes the online web community for women who influence car purchasing decisions (see Figure 3-1).

Source: `www.shebuyscars.com`

FIGURE 3-1: Think creatively to find a blog name and domain that is perfect for the goal of your site, like SheBuysCars.com

Think up a phrase or sentence that says something about you and your blog as a starting place. Write your topic keywords on sticky notes and then move them around. That trick may lead to something great.

What exactly does a domain do for you? It has several plusses:

>> Your readers can easily remember your site.

>> Having a domain of your own looks professional; it's a nice marketing benefit at a small cost.

>> You can change web hosts or hosted blog solutions with impunity because your address is actually a separate service. If — or when — you move your blog, your web host can help you use the same domain to get to your new server on the web.

Your domain should represent your blog's name and purpose, although at the end of the day, there are no hard and fast rules. Here are a few quick guidelines that you might want to follow. Try to choose a domain that

» Matches your blog name

» Is based on your topic keywords

» Is a play on words or slang based around your topic

» Is humorous or otherwise memorable

TIP

If you're having trouble coming up with a name idea, consider using your name. In fact, even if you ultimately want to use another domain for your blog address, owning the domain for your own name is a good idea. You can use several domain names to reach the same website or blog, too, so using your own name as a domain might help people find you in search engines.

TIP

Many online tools can help you choose a domain name if you're having trouble. Domain-name-choosing websites help by suggesting word combinations and coming up with randomly generated choices. One good site to use for this purpose is Bust a Name (www.bustaname.com), which is shown in Figure 3-2.

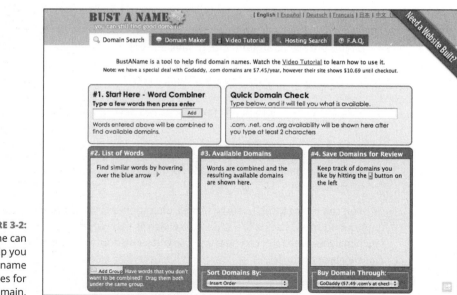

FIGURE 3-2:
Bust a Name can help you brainstorm name possibilities for your domain.

Source: www.bustaname.com

Even if you end up using a hosted blog solution and therefore don't need to get web hosting, you can buy a domain and forward the address to your blog. This is handy to do because it makes your blog's address easier to remember. After you register your domain, check the Help text of the registrar to find out how to forward the domain to your blog's web address (URL). Instructions vary by registrar.

Registering a domain

Registering a domain is a straightforward process. First, use a domain registrar to buy your name. After you own the name, you just need to point your new domain at your web host. This process basically involves telling your domain registrar which web server your website is on; your web-hosting company or domain registrar gives you the information and tools to make it all work.

You can use many domain registration services. The choice really comes down to the domain management interface — the tools that you get to manage your domain. Some management screens are incredibly difficult to work with. Finding a host that has a clean and easy-to-use interface makes a world of difference when you're updating or making changes to your web domain. Be sure to shop around, as well. The annual fee for domain registration varies widely, and for the most part, the price differences don't equal a difference in what you get.

Domain registration services often offer coupon codes. Be sure to use your favorite search engine to locate applicable codes before purchasing your desired domain names.

You can choose to register for your domain for a single year or for multiple years at a time. Typically, registering for multiple years earns you a small discount. If you choose to register for only a year, you need to renew the domain in a year (assuming that you want to keep your website going). Registration services also allow you to choose an auto-renew option. Many domain registration companies also offer web-hosting and email packages.

Make sure that you keep your domain registration up to date. If you have any changes to your domain or contact information, including your email address, update your domain information immediately. If your information isn't current, you can lose access to your domain or miss email reminders to renew your domain. Print a copy of the login information and store it safely.

Visit any of the domain registrars in the following sections to check whether your domain is available, and then register it.

GoDaddy

www.godaddy.com

GoDaddy is a popular web host and domain registrar that provides a long list of web services, including domain hosting, web hosting, and email address hosting. It has a good reputation and is easy to contact if you require assistance. Domain prices vary, but typically start at $14.99 for a year's registration.

To register a domain with GoDaddy, follow these steps:

1. **Point your web browser to** www.godaddy.com.

2. **Type the domain you're interested in into the Find your perfect domain name text box.**

3. **Click the Search Domain button.**

   GoDaddy returns a page indicating whether your domain is available.

4. **If your domain is available and you want to complete your purchase, click the Select button to move forward with the purchasing process.**

   If your domain is unavailable, use the Search Again text box to try a new name.

5. **Continue shopping for other domains on GoDaddy or follow the instructions for completing the credit card purchase of the domain you select.**

Network Solutions

www.networksolutions.com

Network Solutions is one of the granddaddies of all registrars. At one time, it was one of the few places you could register a domain. Services are varied and flexible, with a variety of available options. Domains are available for as little as $19.99 for one year of registration.

Namecheap

www.namecheap.com

This domain registrar offers domains starting at the low price of $10.69 per year and provides customers with a variety of payment options, including PayPal. Namecheap has grown in popularity owing to low pricing and good customer service.

Hover

www.hover.com

Hover promises to simplify the domain registration process for users and is known for its highly accessible customer service team. Domains start at $12.99 per year and include domain privacy, a great option for those hoping to blog as anonymously as possible.

Panabee

www.panabee.com

Panabee promises to help users select the best domain name for them, offering a variety of options based around keywords, and vowing to not buy the domains themselves if you choose to leave and come back later. There will be no idea-stealing from Panabee! Prices begin at just $0.99.

TIP

Be prepared for a laundry list of add-on offers when purchasing a domain name. I typically decline all offers and proceed to check out, but be prepared to make a decision about the following offers:

>> **Additional, related domains:** If purchasing a .com, for example, you will be asked to also purchase that domain name with additional suffixes such as .co, .net, and .org. Buy these additional domains only if you believe it is necessary to protect the blog name you've created.

>> **Private domain registration:** If you're planning to blog anonymously, you need to purchase this additional service so that readers can't see the name and address of the person who purchased your blog's URL.

>> **Certified domain seal:** Some website owners choose to pay for this seal with the intent of turning their site into an e-commerce site. This add-on is not necessary for a blog.

>> **Web hosting:** Select your preferred web host prior to purchasing your URL. If you choose to host with your registrar service, you may be able to save money by purchasing both services at the same time.

>> **Upgraded email:** You will receive access to domain-related email addresses when you register your domain, so unless you need an upgraded service for business reasons, you likely want to decline this offer.

Finding Web Hosting

With a domain in hand, you can turn your attention to web hosting.

If the domain is your address, *web hosting* is your actual house on the web. Your web host provides an online location for your blog's software, graphics, and other files. This location is known as your blog's web server. When people type your URL into their web browser, the web server provides them with access to your blog.

Doing your research

Your primary concern when selecting a web host for your self-hosted blog is to find a web host that meets all the requirements of your blog software. Most blog software uses a LAMP (Linux/Apache/MySQL/PHP) web server, a mix of several kinds of web server technology that is ideal for running dynamic websites such as blogs:

>> **Linux:** A very common web server operating system. It's very stable and considered a standard for web servers. As a blogger, you probably don't need to make too many changes to the operating system, as long as it's in place for you.

>> **Apache:** Apache is *web-page-serving software,* which means it looks at what web page is requested and then feeds the browser the appropriate file. It does most of the hard work of serving web pages to visitors coming to your website.

>> **MySQL:** MySQL is the most popular database software for blogs. For any blogging package, you need some kind of database system to store all your blog posts and run the other functionality of the blog software. MySQL is the standard database tool for most blog software.

>> **PHP:** PHP is the programming language that a lot of blogging and content management systems use. It sits between the blogging software and the database, making sure all the parts work together.

The preceding four technologies are considered the bare minimum that most blogging packages need to function. But you should consider these requirements, as well:

>> **Disk space:** For blogging, disk space is important if you decide to store a lot of images on your blog or upload audio and video files. Uploading images is relatively easy to do, but you need the space to store those images. For the average blog that has a few photos, you most likely want about 500 megabytes (MB). Blogs that have a lot of photos require several gigabytes (GB) of disk space. Video blogs need a whole lot more disk space (unless you use an online video-sharing service) than text or photo blogs, so you want more than 10GB. Those files do take up a lot of space!

Running out of disk space is an easily solved problem: Most web hosts allow you to add disk space when you need it for an additional cost. Check with your web host to find out what it charges for additional storage.

>> **Email management:** You probably want an email address with your new domain. If you want to use your blog for business purposes, having an email address that matches your domain looks more professional. Some web hosts allow you to create multiple email addresses under one domain, which is ideal if you would like to segregate contact inquiries from personal emails, for example.

>> **Backups:** Consider how you plan to back up your data (including your database content) and whether the web host will also back up the files on your web-hosting account. Knowing this information can save you from disaster and data loss in the future. Daily backups aren't a bad idea!

>> **Bandwidth and CPU resources:** Computers and networks can take only so many visitors and downloads, and hosts usually set a quota on how much bandwidth you can use for the particular web-hosting package that you buy. Ask about what happens if you exceed your monthly allowance of bandwidth. (Usually, you have to pay for the extra resources.) For most bloggers, this won't be an issue, but if you develop a very popular blog with lots of visitors, or are serving very large files like videos, bandwidth can become an additional cost.

Buying web hosting

After you purchase your domain, you *should* be able to pick a web host just as easily. But the reality is that web host offerings are all over the map, so you need to do your research, ask for recommendations from friends and colleagues who have websites, and compare the details of what different hosts offer. Remember to also look into the web hosting provided by your domain registration site. This may save you money and will also streamline the management of your blog.

When comparing web hosts, always confirm the numbers provided in sales materials. Here are the top questions to ask a prospective web host about its web-hosting packages:

>> What's your reliability and uptime guarantee? Most web hosts will tell you the amount of time in a given month that they guarantee your website to be available given normal traffic loads. None of them, however, can absolutely guarantee 100 percent uptime.

>> What's your data transfer limit, and how much do you charge for additional bandwidth? Bandwidth/data transfer is used as visitors visit your website and download pages from your site to view them. If you have a lot of files being transferred, or a single file that thousands of visitors download, you may hit your limit and need to buy more.

>> How much disk space does the package include, and what do you charge for additional space?

>> What kind of technical support do you offer? What are your telephone hours? How do you handle email support?

When you find a web host that interests you, check out the packages offered. Many web hosts provide a handy comparison chart that you can use to quickly compare pricing and features, as Nexcess.net (www.nexcess.net) does in Figure 3-3.

FIGURE 3-3:
Check the web host for package comparison charts to help make your decision.

Source: www.nexcess.net

The following sections help you get started with your web-hosting search by discussing three top web-hosting services.

Siteground

www.siteground.com

Siteground is a critically acclaimed hosting solution that allows bloggers to easily install the popular blogging software, WordPress. Plans begin as low as $9.95 per month and can be tailored to meet your exact needs in the event that an existing plan is not a fit for you. If you wait to purchase your domain name until you've selected a hosting plan, keep in mind that one domain name registration is included in the price of hosting with Siteground.

Doteasy

www.doteasy.com

Doteasy offers a wide range of web-hosting solutions for bloggers, including hosting. Doteasy offers 24-hour email technical support. Blog-friendly web-hosting options start at $4.75 a month — the cost of the Starter Hosting package, which includes 1GB of disk space and 10 email accounts. Upgrade to the Unlimited plan for $10.95 a month and get unlimited disk space and bandwidth.

Hostgator

www.hostgator.com

Hostgator is one of the most popular web hosts used by bloggers. Even its smallest plan includes unmetered disk space and bandwidth and begins at $4.86 per month when you register for 36 months. Hostgator also offers an included web builder, making it easier for new bloggers to get started quickly.

Bluehost

www.bluehost.com

Another web host that is popular with the blogging community, Bluehost plans also offer unlimited resources and site builder software, and they start at just $7.99 a month. Technical support is available via both phone and live chat, and dedicated server upgrades are available should your blog traffic grow to need this feature.

TIP

Want even more info about web hosting? Check out Peter Pollock's *Web Hosting For Dummies* (John Wiley & Sons, Inc.)!

Deciding on the Right Blogging Software

After you've made the decision to host your blog on a self-hosted web platform (alternatives are discussed in Chapter 4), you need to choose the blog software that you'd like to use. Choose wisely, grasshopper, and watch your blog software grow while you add more bells and whistles. Pick poorly, and be faced with the ultimate chore: migrating your blog from one blog software package to a better one. You can do this transfer, but you can't do it easily. Spend the time to find out about the available blogging tools and the functionality they provide now so that you can save yourself a lot of headaches later.

First, you need to recognize that all blogging platforms aren't created equal. Of course, blogging software packages, whether they're managed by you or by paid web-hosting technical staff, all share the same or similar functionality that you need for a typical blog. But each software package was designed with very different goals in mind.

Unlike software that you install on a desktop or laptop computer, blogging software requires a server environment to function. This server is provided by the web host you selected earlier in the chapter.

Bloggers can use either of two kinds of blogging platforms:

>> **Hosted blogs:** *Hosted* blog services provide a unique situation in which you don't need to worry about the software technology at all. You can concentrate on worrying about what your next blog post will be about, rather than how to configure a web server. To use hosted blogging software, you log into the editing tool, write a post, click the Publish button, and log out.

You don't need to think about *how* the software is managed, just as long as it's there the next time you want to post something. Many bloggers consider this setup the deal of the century. One popular hosted solution is Blogger (www.blogger.com), which I discuss in detail in Chapter 4.

Extra bonus: If you choose hosted software, you don't have to worry about web hosting — the software company is providing that service for you! See the section "Understanding Hosted Blog Software," later in this chapter, for a more in-depth discussion of this option.

But beware! The content on hosted blogs is technically owned by the hosting site and not by the blog author . . . you. If content ownership is more important to you than ease of use, hosted blogs are not the right option for you.

TIP

Social networks allow you to connect with current friends and make new ones while sharing photos, videos, and text. They've exploded in popularity in the last few years, and many of them have added a blogging tool. I cover how blogging fits into social networking in Chapter 18.

>> **Non-hosted blogs:** You might want to run your own blogging system right from the beginning. This type of setup is known as *non-hosted* or *installable* blogging software. By installing blog software on your own web server, you take on all responsibilities related to maintaining the blogging software and the data created when you blog. Strictly from a technical point of view, this type of setup for a new blog might be a little on the difficult side and cause more stress — especially for the nontechnical folks who are figuring things out while they go — but you ultimately get more flexibility when you use a non-hosted setup.

Although hosting your blog through your own web host is a bit more difficult than creating a blog on a hosted platform, available blog software (that is often free!) can make the process nearly as easy to manage. If you love a challenge or want all the bells and whistles, consider hosting your blog yourself. Later in this chapter, the section "Understanding Blog Software That You Install on Your Own Server" explains the details of how non-hosted blog software works.

Budgeting for software

Many of the hosted services available to bloggers offer a basic blogging package at no cost. A great number of the non–hosted blogging software packages are also free, but the web server that you need to install them on most definitely isn't. How much money you can commit to your new blog can help you figure out what platform you should acquire.

TIP

Consider how much financial commitment you want to dedicate to your new blogging life. Costs can be associated with

>> **Blogging software:** Some packages are free; others aren't. In some cases, the blogging software might be free for personal use but can cost money if you use it for commercial purposes.

>> **Upgrades:** When you choose a software package that has a price tag, be sure to note the costs for upgrading that software down the line. Blog software is in flux, and you'll need updates!

>> **A domain name:** Regardless of whether you choose a hosted or non-hosted solution, you can buy a domain name (also called a *web address*) and point it at your blog.

>> **Web hosting:** If you choose a blogging software package that needs to be installed on a web server, you need to find web hosting.

>> **Support costs:** If you have questions about your blog software or web hosting, getting answers might cost you. Find out what the support policies are for both software and hosting before you buy.

>> **Web designers:** If you choose to hire a web designer or developer to produce a design, install the software, and get your blog started, you have to pay those folks.

>> **Special bells and whistles:** You might find that you can purchase and use extra add-ons with your blog, from cool functionality to exciting designs.

It *is* possible to start a blog completely for free by opting for a hosted blog with a free basic package and choosing not to buy a custom URL.

Making sure you get the basics

Most blogging packages include a variety of options. Some options are designed to trick out your ride, making your blog into a thing of beauty and delight. Some options are really less optional by definition and more a necessity. Good blogging software *must* have the following five features:

>> **A usable publishing interface or control panel:** Check out how the control panel looks before you commit yourself. A good user interface is important, and if you can't make sense of what you see, chances are good that you won't enjoy using the software.

>> **Comments:** A blog isn't a blog unless your readers can leave comments on your posts. You don't have to use the comments, but blogging software without comments takes away a vital element of blogging — allowing your readers to cultivate discussions.

>> **Spam deterrents:** Spam comments are a part of every blog, but that doesn't mean you have to live with them. Like email spam, comment spam tends to be an automated process that posts on your blog useless information and includes links to all kinds of other sites. Look for blogging software that has functionalities in place to help you moderate and block spam or is, at the very least, compatible with anti-spam tools you can install later.

>> **Media tools:** The Internet has evolved from a focus on the written word to a focus on visual media. Although it is still possible to catch the attention of readers through quality writing, nearly all blog posts do — or at least should — feature a photograph or two. Be certain to choose software that makes uploading media to posts an easy task. Many software options even allow you to edit images within your posts.

>> **Search Engine Optimized:** With millions of blogs filling cyberspace, it is critical that the posts you write can be easily optimized for indexing within search engines. Although you may certainly add plug-ins down the road, it's ideal to select blogging software that helps search engines such as Google and Bing see your blog.

I highly recommend two other features, although not all bloggers use them:

» **Categories:** Blogs often jump from topic to topic. Categorizing your posts gives your readers a quick and easy way to sort through your content, focusing on what most interests them. The Finer Things in Life (www.amys finerthings.com) uses categories, called topics here, to sort blog posts; Figure 3-4 shows the categories in the horizontal navigation bar above the blog posts.

Categories are high-level organizational tools. For example, a food blog might have posts sorted into categories like Vegetarian, Dessert, Main Dish, and so on.

FIGURE 3-4: The Finer Things in Life organizes blog posts by category or by topic.

Source: www.amysfinerthings.com

» **Tags:** A *tag* is a term associated with a blog post. For example, when I write a blog post about a trip to Disneyland Park in California, I tag that entry "Disneyland." Tagging has proven to be one of the best ways to sort through blog data quickly.

Tags are like keywords that you might use when doing a search on a search engine website, and they tend to be more specific than categories. A blog post on a food blog might use categories as I describe in the preceding bullet, and then tag individual posts with more specific terms, such as *chocolate, hazelnut,* and *brownie.* To differentiate between categories and tags, think of categories as describing a group of blog posts, and tags as describing individual posts.

TIP

According to the Pew Research Center (`www.pewinternet.org/fact-sheets/ mobile-technology-fact-sheet/`), 34 percent of smartphone users access the Internet via their smartphone the majority of the time. Do you want people to read your blog? Be sure that your blogging design is mobile responsive, meaning that your blog's appearance and interaction experience changes when viewed on a phone, making it easier for smartphone and other mobile device users to read and respond to your writing.

Upgrading with bells and whistles

You can implement a number of cool toys on your blog:

>> **Backup:** The last thing you want to do is create a blog that you love, populate that blog with weeks, months, years of content, then lose the whole shebang because of a technical disaster outside your control. Backup tools automatically back up your site — including everything from the words in your posts to the graphics in your sidebars — on a schedule that you can choose. These backups can be sent to a cloud storage system, your email, or even your computer's hard drive. Backing up your blog is a great way to buy peace of mind for little or no cost!

>> **Spam blacklist:** Most blogging packages have some kind of blacklist protection against spam comments. These blacklists are often centralized lists of email addresses, URLs, and IP addresses that spammers use, which the blog software prevents from commenting in any blog post on your blog. With an up-to-date blacklist, you can stop a lot of spam before it becomes a comment.

>> **Contact forms:** Chances are that at some point, you will want to allow readers to contact you. Although some bloggers post an email address on their blog contact page, many prefer to keep their email address private and instead use a contact form. Most contact forms require that the users prove they are not a spamming system before allowing them to send a message to your inbox.

>> **CAPTCHAs:** *CAPTCHAs* are images that display letters and/or numbers that a person can read but a machine can't. When someone wants to leave a comment on a post, he or she must correctly type these letter/number combinations into a text box, which proves to the blog software that the commenter is indeed a human and not a computer spam system. This process blocks out the comment spam and lets through the valuable feedback. Variations on CAPTCHAs include simple math problems that a user needs to solve in order to post a comment.

TIP

You can tie together more and more web services these days, from your pins on Pinterest, to your Twitter updates, to your . . . well, you have a lot of possibilities. Some blog software allows you to automate those kinds of connections, so if that interests you, keep an eye out for software with these features. I walk you through some possibilities in Chapter 18.

Understanding Hosted Blog Software

Hosted services take a whole lot of responsibility off the blogger. The blog software company manages the data, software, and web hosting; the blogger manages the content. Some services, such as Blogger, do it all for free, whereas other services, such as TypePad, charge a monthly fee to run your blog. Yet other services, such as WordPress, offer a level of free service with the option to upgrade when your blogging requires a little more power. Hosted blog software allows you to make someone responsible for the entire gauntlet of technical tasks that don't excite you.

TIP

Seasoned blogging veterans may recommend that new bloggers start by using a hosted service that's free. The reason is simple: If you find the idea of having a blog appealing, but you have never tried blogging or played with blogging software, you might not like it all that much in reality. A free blogging service allows you to test drive blogging before making a huge time or monetary commitment. A word of warning: Free blogging platforms come with pitfalls and restrictions such as a ban on paid ads on your site. Be sure to read terms of service documents carefully!

TIP

Remember those bells and whistles I mentioned earlier in this chapter? If you choose to begin blogging on one type of hosting service but want to change to another type of service in your blogging future, there are tools available — often for free! — that will help you move all your content, comments, graphics, and more from one blog platform to another.

Reaping the benefits

An upfront cost of zero is very attractive to new bloggers. If you want access to blog technology and have a limited budget, free looks just about perfect. Not all hosted software is free, but most of them generally have quite reasonable costs. A hosted blog that charges a monthly fee is still a minimal investment, on par with other inexpensive hobbies.

But free or inexpensive isn't the only upside to hosted blog services. They really take the complication out of starting a blog. For the technophobe, a hosted solution is ideal because you have very few technical issues to worry about. Hosted services take care of

>> Web domains

>> Software maintenance and updates

>> Data storage and backup

>> Template design and management

Hosted solutions are also generally quicker to set up than is software you have to install on your own server, so you can start blogging sooner when you choose one of these solutions. Plus, as mentioned earlier, should you choose to migrate your blog to a self-hosted server in the future, free software is available to make this process possible.

Updates on hosted blogs are generally free, and the software is available to the end user 24 hours a day, 7 days a week. Sounds like a really good deal, huh?

Living with the limitations

Before you sign yourself up, be sure you understand the tradeoffs that come with using a hosted blog service. Ultimately, you don't control your own blog. If the company goes out of business, takes servers down for maintenance, or decides to change its offerings, you're pretty much stuck with the results.

A free hosted solution, for example, might suddenly decide that it should start charging; one that already charges can always raise its rates.

REMEMBER

Despite limitations, there are multiple hosted blogging platforms that have been around for what, in the blogging world, feels like a lifetime. These platforms are owned by reputable companies such as Google and offer stability that comes from years and years of working out the kinks. If you're leaning towards diving into blogging by creating a site with a hosted blog service, don't let the limitations of this type of platform hold you back!

Most hosted solutions let users make some modifications and tweaks, but some only allow you to install a limited selection of plug-ins and extras. In some cases, the level of customization is quite limited. With hosted blog software, that ubiquitous WYSIWYG (what you see is what you get) acronym is a double-edged sword: You can't actually always do more with less. On the other hand, should you begin to feel adventurous, some hosts allow users to play around with the backend of their blog without the danger of breaking the entire site. Others, such as Word-Press, offer nearly endless and often free upgrades thanks to the open-source developer community they've fostered.

TIP

If you blog on behalf of a company or business, you might want to cross a hosted solution off your list for a couple of reasons:

>> You probably need to make your blog part of an existing website, integrated into the look and feel of the company brand. Hosted blogs don't allow this customization or integration.

>> With a business blog, you need control of the data. Putting the blog on your own server removes any doubts about security or data ownership.

WARNING

When you think about whether to use a hosted solution, be sure you understand the terms of service of that host. Some hosts reserve the right to cancel or remove your blog or blog posts.

Make sure to read all the fine print for the host that you want to use! You don't want to run into legal restrictions that mean you can't actually use your blog the way you want to, and you definitely don't want to suddenly find your blog missing if the hosted software company decides you're in violation of its rules.

Choosing hosted software

In the following sections, you can take a look at some of the most popular hosted platforms to see which might be the best fit for you and your new blog. These blogging software packages have been around for quite a while and are regarded as some of the best that the blogging community has to offer.

Blogger

www.blogger.com

Blogger is the quintessential hosted blogging platform. Started in 1999 at Pyra Labs, Blogger weathered the rough Internet waters at the turn of the century to become the most well-known hosted blogging platform. The Blogger service became incredibly popular, and eventually, Google purchased it. Since then, Blogger has introduced many new features and remained one of the premier blogging platforms. Blogger has many features that allow bloggers to publish multiple blogs:

>> All blogs are free and hosted for you, with no hassles and no mess.

>> Blogger offers a wide variety of free templates to get you going, which you can customize in a number of ways.

>> The publishing tool includes Google AdSense (a blog advertising program) and other neat elements, such as polls and lists, integrated into it, allowing you to add functionality to your blog.

>> Because it is owned by Google, Blogger links seamlessly with your other Google accounts, including Gmail and Google+.

>> Blogger's Android app allows users to blog easily from their phone or tablet.

>> If you don't want Blogger to host your files, you can save all your blogging files to another server.

TIP

I show you how to get Blogger set up in Chapter 4. Because you can use it so easily and set it up quickly (and because it's free), I encourage all new bloggers to use Blogger as a learning tool, even if you plan to use other blog software for your real blog.

WordPress.com

www.wordpress.com

In 2005, the popular WordPress blogging platform launched a hosted service, in addition to software that you can install on your own server. WordPress.com, shown in Figure 3-5, offers a clean, easy-to-use interface, and bloggers tend to see it as more flexible than anything else on the market.

In short, WordPress.com

>> Is free to use (although some premium levels are available with additional functionality)

>> Has many options for design templates, letting you choose a look that suits your content

>> Includes features such as tags and categories, permitting easy organization of your posts

>> Offers spellchecking, rich-text editing, and photo uploading

>> Lets you measure your site traffic and statistics to help gauge your popularity

>> Is optimized for SEO, making it easier for your blog to be found by search engines such as Google and Bing

>> Provides a WYSIWYG (what you see is what you get) posting and editing environment, which means you don't need to know HTML

>> Includes tools that allow you to insert photos, videos, and audio files into your blog posts

>> Gives users access to hundreds of thousands of plug-ins and provides ways to upgrade your blog and add additional features and tools

>> Integrates an excellent spam-fighting tool, Akismet

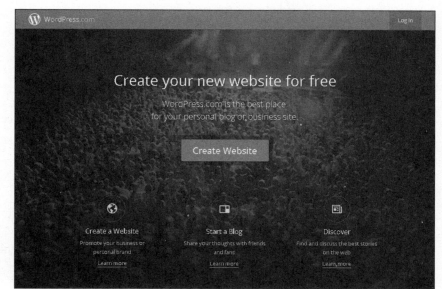

FIGURE 3-5:
Use WordPress.
com to get a free
but powerful
blog.

TIP

On WordPress.org, you can get software to install WordPress on your own website. I talk more about WordPress.org later in this chapter, and in Chapter 5, you can find out more about both versions in detail.

TypePad

www.typepad.com

TypePad was launched in 2003 to great fanfare and used to be one of the most popular domains in the world. It allows you to do more than just blog; it was one of the first blogging platforms to offer the capability to create static content pages. TypePad pricing starts at $8.95 a month and ranges upward, depending on the services that you include. TypePad also offers a 14-day free trial for new users.

TypePad offers

>> A WYSIWYG (what you see is what you get) posting and editing environment, which means you don't need to know HTML

>> Built-in tools to track your blog analytics, such as traffic to your site

>> Tools that allow you to insert photos into your posts quickly, automatically resizing them and adding thumbnails to blog posts

>> Tools that allow you to quickly place videos and podcasts into your blog posts

Squarespace

www.squarespace.com

Unlike Blogger and Wordpress.com, Squarespace is a fee-for-service blogging platform that begins at $8.00 a month. Also unlike Blogger and Wordpress, Squarespace uses a completely unique drag-and-drop interface. This platform allows for easy blog customization, among other features.

Squarespace offers

>> A large selection of visual themes

>> Mobile publishing capabilities through apps

>> E-commerce options for bloggers interested in including an online storefront

>> Drag-and-drop image managing and organization

>> Social media integration

>> Static pages

Tumblr

www.tumblr.com

Tumblr, which was purchased by Yahoo! in 2013, is a fun and really easy-to-use hosted blogging service — and it's free. Tumblr blogs are a little different from other major blogging platforms in that it is really easy to re-post material from another Tumblr blog to your own blog, so sharing is a big part of the Tumblr experience.

Tumblr offers:

>> The ability to run several blogs from a single dashboard interface

>> The ability to quickly post text, photos, quotes, links, music, and videos from your browser, phone, desktop, or email

>> A mobile-friendly interface, including dedicated mobile apps

>> Mobile publishing capability, including through text and email

>> Many different themes that let you customize the way your blog looks so that it's personal to you

TIP

Discover more about using Tumblr in Chapter 6, where I cover everything from signing up to posting content on a Tumblr blog.

Remember to read the terms of service carefully when selecting a hosted blog platform. You may not actually own the rights to the content you are posting!

Understanding Blog Software That You Install on Your Own Server

If you're interested in joining the blogging world but technology freaks you out, you can make life easier by using hosted solutions. However, bloggers who require more flexibility than what hosted solutions offer or are simply concerned with issues such as content ownership may choose non-hosted blogging packages. Configuring software to your own tastes and requirements can really improve the overall quality of your blog, making it more attractive to readers and ultimately more successful.

Flexibility can take your blog to the next level. If you have the money and the skills to install your own blog software, doing so can give you better tools and control over your blog, enabling you to do things like customize the design, add third-party widgets for serving ads, or dabble in customizing the publishing interface.

Choosing a non-hosted blog isn't a plug-and-play solution. Unfortunately, choosing to install blog software, rather than to use a hosted service, means that you need a whole bunch of other technical services to make it all work. However, you may find that it is worth the additional work and cost!

Reaping the benefits

If you use non-hosted blog software, you're in full control. You can do just about anything to the software after you install it:

>> **Personalize the design:** For those who have web design skills, stand-alone blogs generally are very adaptable. Some blogs have incredibly diverse and clever designs, many created by the author of the blog to match the style and topic of the blog. Installing the software on your web server gives you access to every part of the blog software's innards, from templates to graphics, so you can make your blog look exactly as you like.

>> **Customize functionality:** A lot of the blogging software available is *open source* (meaning the code for the software package is available to developers so that they can manipulate it). Programmers can add, remove, update, and improve functionality for each package. Some packages offer many different options, and independent programmers might also offer additional functionality either for free or at a low cost.

>> **Look smart:** The blogging world, like any other world, has social divisions, and at the top of the blogging heap, you find geeks. If you want to play with the cool nerds, you need to install your own blog software. Technical bloggers will recognize your prowess and give you props.

Living with the limitations

The first stumbling block you discover when installing your own blogging software is . . . installing your own blogging software. Somehow, you have to get the software files onto your server, run the scripts, modify the code, and generally muck about in the ugly innards of the software. This process can either be simple or a complete nightmare, depending on your technical savvy and the complexity of the blog software package that you choose.

TIP

You can shortcut this issue by choosing a web-hosting company that offers blogging software. Most blogging software companies provide a list of web hosts who have in-house expertise in handling their software; just browse around on the software company's website to find that list. You can also have the blogging software company install the software for you. For a fairly reasonable fee, you can put that job into the hands of an expert. This solution makes sense for one big reason: You need to install the software only once. If you don't already know how to do it yourself, you don't have to spend hours beating your head against a wall to obtain knowledge you'll probably never need again.

Of course, all software requires some level of maintenance, and most web hosts don't handle software upgrades and tweaks. Be prepared to handle those requirements when they come up by doing them yourself or finding an expert who can handle them for you.

Using non-hosted software has some other downsides as well:

>> **Design personalization and code customization:** Making your blog look pretty sounds great, but you need a cornucopia of associated skills to make that happen — everything from graphic design to HTML coding. If you don't have these skills yourself or access to someone who does, you don't actually have the ability to customize your blog, despite your software. The good news is that online resources are nearly unlimited if you want to learn these skills!

>> **Domain registration and Web hosting:** Unlike the hosted systems, you can't avoid spending money to host your own blog software. Several costs automatically kick in, such as domain name registration and web hosting (explained in the sections "Registering a domain" and "Finding Web Hosting," earlier in this chapter).

>> **Technical support:** Even if you pay to get the blog software installed for you or sign up with a web host that does it automatically, if the software breaks (and doesn't all software break at some point?), many web hosts can't or won't fix it.

>> **Backing up:** If you install your own software, you're responsible for making sure that the software and data get backed up or for finding a web host that includes backups as part of the hosting package.

Choosing non-hosted blogging software

If you're ready to make the leap into the deep end of the blogging pool, the following sections give you recommendations for a range of well-respected non-hosted blogging tools.

WordPress

www.wordpress.org

Since 2003, WordPress has provided a solid platform for new and experienced bloggers who want the control of installing blog software on their own computers. Many bloggers say that WordPress is the easiest blogging platform (aside from hosted blogging software) to set up and configure. I cover installing and using WordPress in Chapter 5.

TIP

The interface acts exactly the way the hosted WordPress.com system works. That said, if you're considering using WordPress, sign up for a test blog on WordPress.com to get a good preview of how WordPress works.

Here are some of the highlights:

>> WordPress is free!

>> It offers many, many user-submitted and user-prepared designs, ready for use.

>> It includes tags and categories, allowing you to organize your posts easily.

>> It has editing tools (such as spell checking), offers common text styles, and gives you easy ways to include photos, videos, and other media.

>> It displays statistics about your visitors to help you understand the traffic to your blog.

>> It fights spam with a range of anti-spam tools.

Movable Type

www.movabletype.com

Movable Type is the grandfather of all installable blogging platforms. Released in 2001, it quickly became one of the most popular blogging software packages, for geeks and pundits alike. Movable Type was the first blogging software that permitted contributions by multiple authors, and bloggers highly regard it for the many ways that you can leverage it to create easily updateable websites and blogs.

If you're serious about looking at hosting your own installation, Moveable Type is a strong contender. Movable Type offers

>> A WYSIWYG (what you see is what you get) editing environment that saves you time and effort

>> Easy tools for categorizing your posts, inserting photos and multimedia, and spell checking

>> Automatic generation of RSS feeds to give your blog longevity

>> Searchable content, tags, and other cool tools

>> A range of licensing options for personal, commercial, and educational use

Pricing varies, but the basic commercial installation is $499, and you may qualify to use the free Blogger license if you are an individual blogger and not setting up a blog for an organization or business.

ExpressionEngine

www.expressionengine.com

Back in 2001, a company called pMachine released a blogging software package called pMachine Pro. pMachine Pro quietly hatched a following based on clean interface, solid performance, and flexibility in both design and layout. From that success, pMachine built the content management system and blogging software ExpressionEngine, an exceptionally powerful platform.

Today, pMachine (now known as EllisLab) supports all kinds of sites by using ExpressionEngine, which it offers in both commercial and personal flavors. As is Movable Type, ExpressionEngine is highly regarded by web developers because it offers great blogging tools, but it's flexible enough to be used to develop all kinds of websites — not just blogs.

ExpressionEngine users have

>> The capability to run multiple blogs that have many contributors

>> A powerful templating engine

>> Additional modules and community plug-ins, including mailing lists, forums, and photo galleries

>> Strong comment moderation and prevention tools

>> Different levels of user access, allowing administrators to control what blogs and templates users can edit

ExpressionEngine's commercial license runs you $299.

Installing blog software

After you purchase your domain and web hosting, you can get into the nitty-gritty technical task: installing your blog software. To get started, look for installation instructions on your blog software company's website. Each blogging package has a set of instructions for doing the job yourself and details about hiring company technical support to do the job for you.

REMEMBER

Keep in mind that installing blog software is a one-time task! When you finish, you never need to do it again, and you probably don't need the skills necessary to install the software in order to use your blog.

Unfortunately, the steps that you need to take to install a particular blog application vary dramatically from software to software, so I can't give you detailed step-by-step directions. Each blog software package has its own particular requirements for installation, but the general process follows these steps:

1. Download the latest version of your blogging software.

2. Uncompress the package and upload it to your new web host by using FTP (file transfer protocol).

3. Execute the installation application associated with your software.

To make your installation experience as trouble-free as possible, watch out for the following common problems:

>> **File location:** When you upload your blog package, make sure that you upload it to the correct location. All web hosts tell you where to place your web files and software so that visitors can find your blog. If you put your files in the wrong place, no one can access your blog.

>> **Database requirements:** Sometimes, you need to create a database prior to installing your blog software. Each web host has a different procedure for creating a database, so if your installation instructions mention this requirement, consult the web host documentation or support materials to find out how to set things up properly.

Sound like gibberish? The truth is that almost anyone can use blogging software, but only quite technically advanced computer users can install it themselves. If you're a web designer or developer, you may be able to install the software yourself. If you aren't technical but want to be, this project gives you the chance to really get your hands dirty.

However, if tech stuff makes you cringe, you can investigate having someone else install the software. My main advice is to find a professional, which you can find among the following:

>> **Bloggers:** Many bloggers make a living with the skills they've developed while blogging rather than through blogging itself. Ask around the blogging community to find someone who may be able to help install and set up your site.

>> **Web designers:** Many people who build websites for a living can help would-be bloggers get blogging software installed and running. Of course, you need to pay these folks for their time, so shop around for several quotes to get the best deal.

>> **Blogging software companies:** The best blogging software companies offer inexpensive solutions to this problem: They install the software for you on your own website. Check with the blogging software company to see whether it offers this service.

>> **Web-hosting companies:** Some web hosts install software for you if you ask (and pay them), and some even offer a one-click installation. These one-click installations can save bloggers from headaches, pain, and midnight crying sessions. You just click a button to install the desired blogging software on your web server. If this option sounds appealing, check with the web host you're eyeing before you sign up to see whether it offers one-click blog software installations.

TIP

Many blogging software companies have figured out that installing blog software creates a real barrier to the nontechnical customer. As a result, you can often go to a blogging software company's website and find a list of web–hosting companies that offer one–click installation for a particular blogging platform.

2

Setting Up Your Blog

Chapter 4

Starting a Blogger Blog

P art of the beauty of a blog is how quickly and easily you can get going. You can go from zero to blog in about ten minutes by using good blog software, especially if you go with hosted blog software. As mentioned in previous chapters, one such blogging option is Blogger, which is the focus of this chapter. I show you how to set up a blog with Blogger, write and publish blog posts by using its interface, manage your settings, and customize your template to make your space on the web unique.

If you're unfamiliar with hosted blog software versus server-based software, flip to Chapter 3 for an introduction to blog software. In Chapter 5, you can find an introduction to WordPress, which offers both hosted and server-based blogging software. In Chapter 6, you discover Tumblr, a short form of blogging called micro blogging. And in Chapter 7, you can learn about launching a Squarespace blog.

Starting a Blog with Blogger

You can't find a better place to test the blogging waters than Blogger (www.blogger. com). It's free, fast, and easy to use. Because you can get started so easily, you can use Blogger to play with code and discover how blogging works without having to invest a lot of time and energy in web servers and complicated installation processes.

Blogger promises to get you blogging in three steps: Create an account, name your blog, and choose a template.

Each hosted blog software platform has a different process for getting started, but each one requires the same kind of information: your contact information and a name for your blog.

Creating an account

In order to sign up with Blogger, you must first have a Google account.

To sign up for Blogger while also creating a Google account, follow these steps:

1. **Direct your web browser to www.blogger.com.**

2. **Click Create account as shown in Figure 4-1.**

3. **Fill in the requested new account information, including selecting a username.**

   Take note that your username is not necessarily the same as your blog name.

4. **Agree to the Google Terms of Service and Privacy Policy.**

5. **Click Next step.**

6. **Return to www.blogger.com and complete the following steps.**

To sign up for Blogger by using an existing Google account, follow these steps:

1. **Type your Google account associated email address into the appropriate text box on the Blogger home page** (www.blogger.com).

2. **Click Next.**

   A password field appears.

3. **Fill in your Google account password and click Sign in.**

4. **Click the New Blog link in the Dashboard, and then check out the following section in this chapter.**

Naming your blog

When you have a Blogger account set up, you can choose a name for your blog. If you're creating a blog that you plan to actually use (rather than just test, a topic that I discuss in Chapter 3), give a lot of thought to the name that you choose. Your blog name needs to accurately portray your blog's tone and content. If you plan to use this blog as a test space, don't worry too much about choosing a name that has a lot of meaning, but be sure you choose something that you can remember!

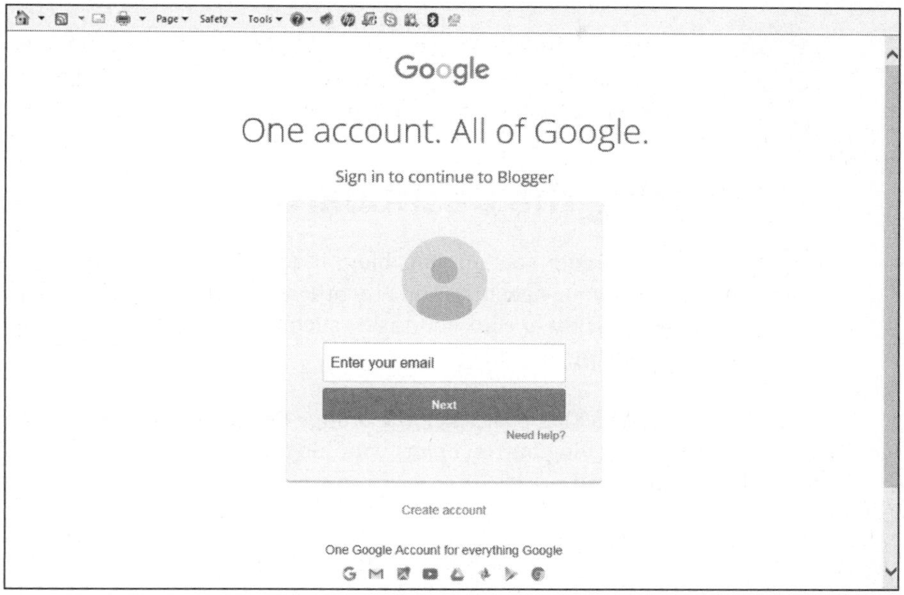

FIGURE 4-1: Creating a Google account is the first step to blogging on Blogger.

Source: www.blogger.com

To name your Blogger blog, follow these steps:

1. **Type the name of the blog in the Title text box.**

2. **Decide what phrase you want to use in your URL and type it in the Blog Address text box.**

   A *URL* (uniform resource locator) is better known as a web address. To open your blog, visitors type this address into the address bar of their web browsers. You can use any word or phrase that you want as a URL, as long as someone else isn't using it, but you probably want to keep it short, sweet, and memorable so that others can get to your blog quickly and easily. You can't use spaces or punctuation, except dashes, in your URL.

   There doesn't seem to be a limit to the number of characters you can type in this box, but that doesn't mean that you should use all that space. Try to keep your blog name short enough to remember!

   As you type, Google checks to see whether your URL is available and displays the status of that check below the text box.

3. **Select one of the Template styles shown by clicking the image.**

   You can change this selection later.

4. **Click the Create Blog button.**

   Blogger sets up your new blog and takes you to the Dashboard.

REMEMBER

After you complete this setup process, you don't need to repeat it when you want to add a post to your blog. The next time you come to Blogger, simply use the login boxes on the home page to log in and get started posting to your blog.

Using the Dashboard

When Blogger sets up your blog, it adds it to a Dashboard (see Figure 4-2) that displays your new blog and any others you may have. You can use the Dashboard to get quickly to common tasks, such as writing a new post, checking your stats, and viewing your blog.

To write a blog post, click the orange Pencil button next to the name of your blog. The View blog button opens your blog, allowing you to view it the same way your visitors will see it.

FIGURE 4-2:
Use the Blogger Dashboard to get started writing blog posts for any blog you maintain using Google.

Source: www.blogger.com

The Posts drop-down list gives you access to all your past posts, pages, comments, stats, earnings information, layout, template, and blog settings. Simply click the arrow in the Posts drop-down list to view all the options, as shown in Figure 4-2.

Writing a Post

You officially join the blogosphere by writing your very first blog post, an *entry*, for your new blog. (The *blogosphere*, by the way, is the semi-ironic way that bloggers refer to themselves, their blogs, and the phenomena that is blogging today. You're a member of the blogosphere when you have a blog. Welcome!

The mechanics of writing a blog post aren't much different from writing an email. Bloggers often make most posts quite short, and they write those posts directly and conversationally. Of course, you might decide to use your blog to write the next Great American Novel, in which case your posts might be quite a bit longer than what's standard! That's fine, too. Every blog takes on a personality and life of its own. If you want to find your own narrative voice for your blog, go to Chapter 8.

TIP

If you've used a web-based email service such as Gmail, Hotmail, or Yahoo!, the Blogger software feels very familiar. To create the post, you simply have to fill in the appropriate text boxes in a form, format the text, and then send it off to its destination — in this case, to your blog, rather than a friend's email inbox.

Follow these steps to write a blog post on Blogger:

1. **From the Blogger home screen, click the orange Pencil button next to your blog's name.**

   Blogger opens the Publish entry screen, as shown in Figure 4-3.

2. **Enter a title for your post in the Post title text box.**

   Titles are a lot like newspaper headlines: They should be catchy and informative, and they should encourage visitors to your blog to continue reading the rest of the post.

3. **Write your post in the large text box.**

TIP

   Consider writing your blog posts in a standard word-processing program, such as Notepad or Microsoft Word — and then saving that post. Too many bloggers have spent hours composing right in the entry box of their blog software, only to find that their Internet connection has failed or another technical problem has occurred — which results in a lost post. You don't want to lose all your carefully considered prose just because your cat pulled the cable modem out of the wall! It's safer to compose offline and then simply copy and paste the text into the blog software.

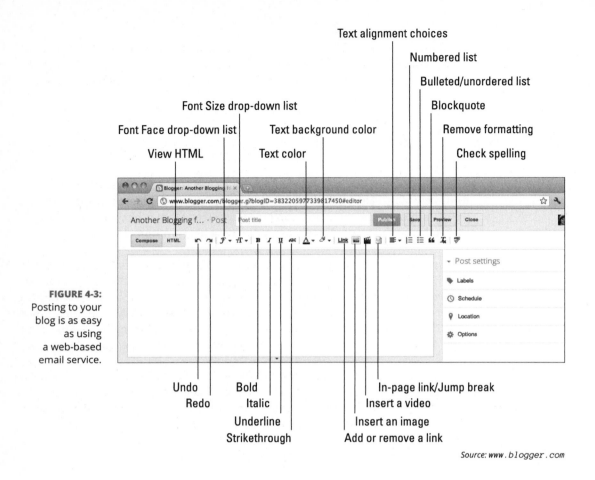

Text alignment choices

Numbered list

Bulleted/unordered list

Font Size drop-down list

Blockquote

Font Face drop-down list

Text background color

Remove formatting

View HTML

Text color

Check spelling

FIGURE 4-3:
Posting to your
blog is as easy
as using
a web-based
email service.

Undo — Bold — In-page link/Jump break

Redo — Italic — Insert a video

Underline — Insert an image

Strikethrough — Add or remove a link

Source: www.blogger.com

4. **Format your post.**

   Blogger's entry box includes icons across the top that let you change the font
   style and font size, apply bold and italic to text, and create common formatting
   styles such as lists. To use these features, select the text that you want to
   modify by clicking and dragging over the text; then click the appropriate icon or
   select an option from the desired drop-down list.

**TECHNICAL
STUFF**

If you know how to write HTML code, you can also try composing your post in the
HTML mode. Click the HTML button and include HTML tags in your text, as needed.
If you want to find out more about coding HTML, check out the discussion of com-
mon tags in the bonus content found at www.dummies.com/extras/blogging.

Adding a link

The Link icon deserves special attention. You use this icon whenever you want to
link to another blog, a news story, or any other page on the web.

When you want to create a clickable link in your blog post, follow these steps:

1. **Highlight the text that you want to make clickable by clicking and dragging.**

2. **Click the word Link.**

   A pop-up window appears, as shown in Figure 4-4.

3. **Select Open This Link in a New Window and/or Add 'rel=nofollow' Attribute.**

4. **Enter the URL of the website to which you want to link and click OK.**

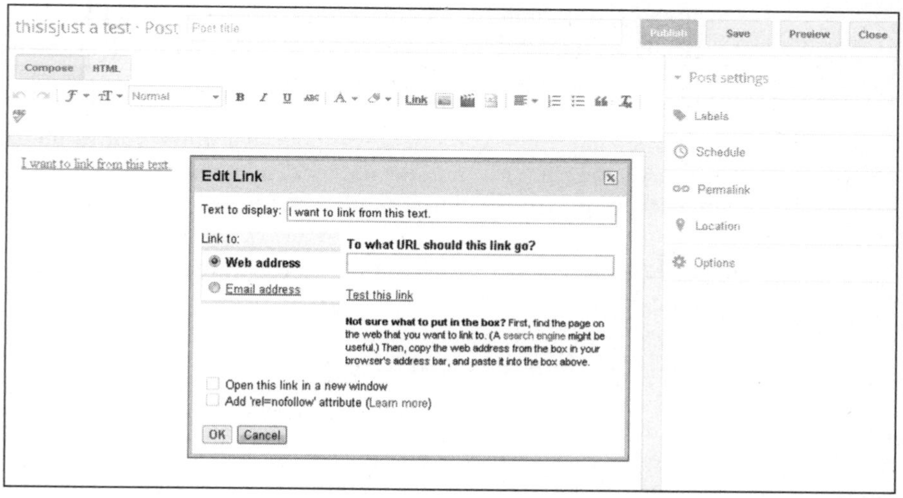

FIGURE 4-4: Use the Link icon to create clickable text in your blog post.

Source: www.blogger.com

You can most easily make sure that you have the right link by going to the web page to which you want to link. Then copy the URL from the address bar. (Press Ctrl+C to copy and then Ctrl+V to paste; on a Mac, use ⌘ rather than Ctrl.) To make sure that the link is going to the right page, you can click the Test This Link link in the Edit Link window to preview the page.

After you click OK, the linked text appears as underlined blue text in your post. It doesn't become clickable until you publish it.

TECHNICAL STUFF

Don't forget that if you know HTML and would prefer to create the link manually by using HTML code, you can do so on the HTML tab.

Spellchecking your text

Blogger provides a handy tool for anyone who needs help with spelling (and who doesn't?). After you finish writing your post, click the Check Spelling icon. It's the icon that shows the letters ABC with a checkmark below them (refer to Figure 4-3).

Blogger highlights incorrectly spelled words in yellow. Click any misspelled word to see a list of suggested alternatives. Select any suggestion from the list or simply type your own correction.

Including an image

In the age of Pinterest and Instagram, adding an image to every blog post is practically a requirement. Without an eye-catching image, how will your Pinterest-savvy readers share your amazing post?

Blogger has some good built-in tools that allow you to upload an image that's already the right size and format for displaying on the web. For help in formatting photographs from a digital camera or another source, see Chapter 12.

Follow these steps to upload an image from your computer and add it to your blog post:

1. **Click the Insert Image icon.**

   It looks like a photograph (refer to Figure 4-3).

   The Upload window opens.

2. **Click the Choose Files button to upload an image on your computer.**

   A File Upload dialog box opens.

3. **Locate the image that you want to upload from your computer and select it.**

4. **Click Open.**

   The image is uploaded to Blogger.

5. **Click Add Selected from the lower-left corner of the Upload screen.**

   The image is placed in your blog post.

6. **Select the image and then choose your image formatting options (see Figure 4-5):**

   - *Image Size:* Determines how large the display of the image is in your blog post, regardless of the dimensions of the source image. You can choose Small, Medium, or Large.

- *Alignment:* Determines how text wraps around the image. You can choose None, Left, Center, or Right.

- *Caption:* Places text directly under the image.

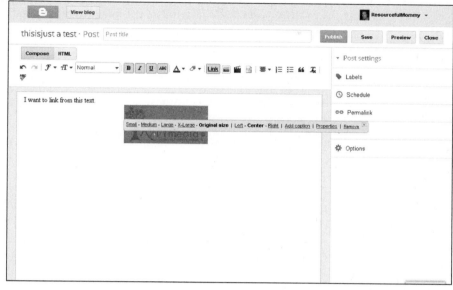

TIP

You can also add an image to your post from another website, as long as you have permission to use the image or it's in the public domain. (Read more about copyright in Chapter 9.) You can add an image from a site easily by using Blogger. Just follow these steps:

1. **Find an image or photo on the web that you want to use.**

Make sure that you're allowed to use it by checking the website for copyright permission or asking the creator.

2. **Right-click the image and select Copy Image Location from the menu that opens.**

The phrasing of this option may differ from one browser to another. If you don't see anything that looks right, choose Properties from the menu. A window opens that shows you the URL address, which you can then click and drag to highlight. Press Ctrl+C to copy the address (⌘+C on a Mac).

3. **Head back to Blogger and start a new post, or open one that you've already created.**

FIGURE 4-5: Selecting an image you have uploaded allows you to size and align it, as well as add a caption.

4. **Click the Add Image icon.**

   It looks like a photograph (refer to Figure 4-2).

   The Upload window opens.

5. **From the More drop-down menu, choose the From a URL link and press Ctrl+V (⌘+V on the Mac) to paste the image address into the image URL text box on the right of the window.**

   Blogger loads a preview of your image.

6. **Click the Add Selected button to insert the photo in your post.**

7. **Select the image and then choose your image formatting options (refer to Figure 4-5):**

   - *Image Size:* Determines how large the display of the image is in your blog post, regardless of the dimensions of the source image. You can choose Small, Medium, or Large.

   - *Alignment:* Determines how text wraps around the image. You can choose None, Left, Center, or Right.

   - *Properties:* Allows you to provide your image with a title.

   - *Caption*: Places text directly under the image.

One final way to add an image to a Blogger post is to drag and drop a photo directly from another window open on your desktop, such as Facebook or your computer's media viewing gallery!

Publishing Your Post

When you're satisfied with your blog post, you can publish it so that the world can admire your erudition. Publishing a post isn't hard: Click the orange Publish button at the top of the page. Your post appears on your blog, making it available for others to read.

Before you publish, you can take advantage of three areas of the Blogger Publish page that I find very helpful: previewing, saving as a draft, and selecting post options.

Previewing your post

Before you publish, you can preview what you've created by clicking the Preview button (found at the top-right of the browser window). This preview is WYSIWYG (what you see is what you get), which means that it shows you the post exactly as you formatted it, including links, text colors, embedded images, and so on. The Preview is shown in a new browser window.

TIP

I like to preview my post before I publish because I can more easily read for meaning and content at this point. Think of the preview as a last chance to catch grammar problems or even to think twice about what you're posting if it's controversial. Of course, you can also see how the text and content flow around any images that you've added.

If you see changes that you want to make, simply switch back to the editing screen, make your changes, and click the Preview button again.

Configuring post settings

To the right of your blog post, you see the post settings links. These let you decide on a number of important ways your post is handled by Blogger, from when the post is published to whether you allow comments.

Scheduling your post

Many bloggers like to create posts in advance of when they plan to publish them. For example, if you're planning a vacation, you can write several posts before you leave. When you put them into Blogger, click the Schedule link to the right of the post box before you publish your post. Set the date and time you want your post to go live, click Done, and when you click Publish, Blogger will hold your post until that point.

By default, Blogger sets the publication date and time of the entry to the date and time that you began writing that entry. You might choose to change the date or time for a number of reasons:

>> **Social or professional reasons:**

- Create a blog post for a friend's birthday and make the date match the time your friend was born.

- If you're blogging at work, you might want to set your date and time to a period when you weren't supposed to also be at your desk (ahem) *working*. Chapter 2 discusses blogging and workplace issues in detail (and recommends that you don't blog at work, unless that's part of your job responsibility).

>> **To work around your schedule:**

- If you take a long time to write a post, by the time you're ready to publish it, you might need to put a more realistic time on the entry.

- If you save your post as a draft and publish it later, you can update the date and time to accurately reflect the real publication date.

Allowing comments

You can choose whether you want readers to be able to comment on your blog post by selecting the Options link under Post settings. There are two options for new posts: Allow and Don't Allow.

TIP

You can make the decision to turn off comments at any time, so if you decide later that you don't want to receive further comments, you can always edit the entry and turn off this option while keeping existing comments.

Most of the time, you want to allow comments; after all, part of what makes a blog exciting to read is the opportunity to interact with the blogger. Sometimes, though, you might write an entry that you don't want to read discussion about, perhaps because you don't want to start a long argument or because the entry has become a target of spammers. You can find more about interacting with your reading community and preventing spam in Chapter 10.

Launching your post

After you have the text and photos laid out nicely and you've chosen your settings, it's time to publish! This is pretty hard, so get ready:

1. Click the Publish button at the top of your blog post.

2. Ha ha, just kidding. There is no Step 2! Your post is on your blog. Go take a look. You're a blogger! Congratulations!

Viewing Your Blog Post

After you hit publish, you can see how your post looks on the blog. You may find this step rewarding — and you definitely don't want to skip it. Even if you preview your post before publishing, you haven't seen your post in the way that your read-ers see it. You can do that only by actually going to your blog as it appears to everyone on the web and taking a look.

Computers can still make errors or fail between the moment you click Publish and when the entry shows up on the blog. I like to look at my blog every time I post a new entry to make sure that it actually looks right on the page and that the blog software successfully processed it.

When you click Blogger's Publish button, the system provides you with a handy link to view your blog. Click View Blog to head over to your blog and see your handiwork.

Of course, if you prefer taking the long way, you can always type the web address (the one that you chose when you set up your blog) into the web browser to see your blog without going through the Blogger Dashboard.

REMEMBER

While you look at your blog, make sure that the formatting, images, and text look the way that you want them to, and click any links that you created. If anything doesn't work quite properly, go back into Blogger and make changes to your entry.

Selecting the Dashboard Settings

Blog software, as a rule, is quite customizable. As the owner of the blog, you can decide a number of things about the way your blog looks and works, and you can control those elements from the control panel — called the Dashboard in Blogger — of your blog software.

Most blog software packages work quite similarly, and if you know how Blogger works, you can make the most of any other software.

Blogger divides its settings into several areas: Basic, Posts and Comments, Mobile and Email, Language and Formatting, Search Preferences, and Other as shown in Figure 4-6. I cover important highlights from the settings in the following sections.

You access all the Blogger settings via the tool icon on the Blogger Dashboard. (In other blog software packages, this area is called the control panel, the admin panel, and so on.) To reach the Dashboard, just log in to the Blogger website. If you're already logged in, look for a link to the Dashboard in the upper-left corner of any page and click it. This link is the Blogger icon. My Dashboard is shown back in Figure 4-2.

The Dashboard shows all the blogs that you've started with Blogger. For each blog, you can quickly start a new post, view your blog, or jump into other areas. A single click takes you into the blog settings, or to the template or layout that you're using.

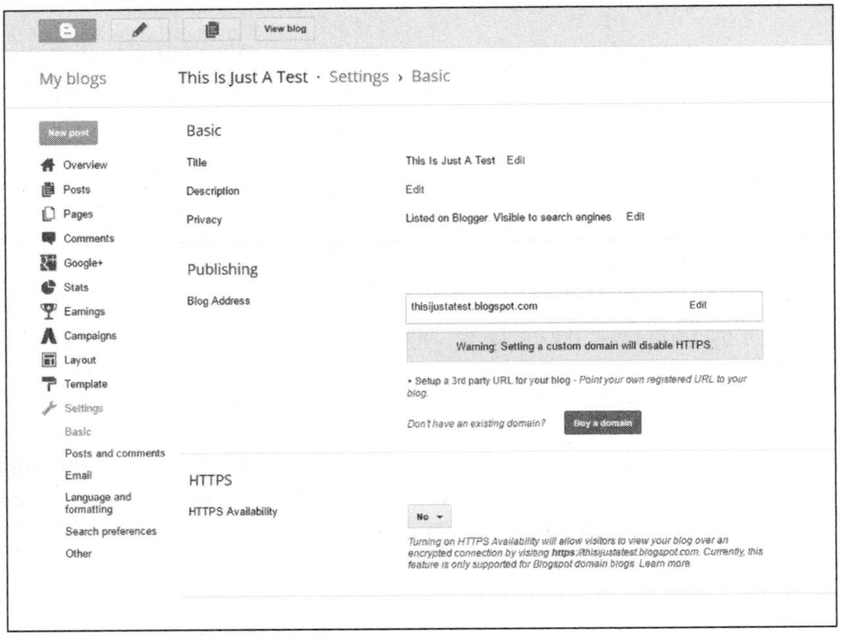

FIGURE 4-6:
The Blogger
Settings area
allows you to edit
a variety of
aspects of your
Blogger blog.

TIP

You can access all the Blogger settings for your blog from the Dashboard. Look for the Posts drop-down list (it looks like two pieces of paper) next to the blog you want to configure, and click the arrow to open the menu. Selecting the Settings option (refer to Figure 4-2) takes you into the right area to do everything discussed in this section.

Making basic changes

From the Basic Settings area, you can change the name of your blog (Blogger refers to this name as the blog title) as well as give it a short description. Most of the Blogger templates display the description near the top of the page. Even if you change the title on your blog page, the URL that readers type into a browser to visit your blog stays the same, but you can also change the URL.

You can also add authors to your blog — people who can also contribute blog posts, creating a group blog. To add someone as an author, you simply need that person's email address. If the person you're adding has a Blogger or Google account, I recommend using that address so that all his or her Blogger and Google account services are tied together.

If you aren't happy with the web address for your blog, you can edit the address by changing the Blog Address setting. For instance, if you start a blog called My New Kitten, Maggie, and your cat grows up (they do that, I hear), you might want to edit both the name and the location of your blog. (You have to make the name change on the Basic Settings tab, which I describe in the preceding section.) Use the Publishing tab to change the URL. For example, you can change

```
http://mynewkittenmaggie.blogspot.com
```

into

```
http://mygrownupcatmaggie.blogspot.com
```

REMEMBER You can change your address only to one that another Blogger member isn't already using, so you may have to make several tries before you find one that's available. Although you can make changes to the URL of your blog, remember that doing so means that no one can access your blog from the previous address, so anyone who has bookmarked your blog or memorized the address can't reach you after you make the change.

TIP If you own a URL and would like it to point to your Blogger blog, you can set this up under the Publishing section as well.

Making comment changes

Comments are both strengths and weaknesses of the blog medium. Both readers and bloggers enjoy the capability to leave a comment, which lets you interact or converse with a blogger.

WARNING Commenting has a downside: Spammers have discovered the comment technology, as well. Just as with email, you can expect some commenters to tell you about fabulous mortgage opportunities, Mexican pharmaceuticals, and other less-than-savory possibilities — information neither you nor your readers want.

The Posts and Comments settings help you reduce spam on your blog. One of the best ways to reduce spam is to specify who can comment on your blog. From the Posts and Comments screen, select an option from the Who Can Comment options:

>> **Anyone:** This option allows the widest possible audience, with no limitations on who can comment. It provides no spam prevention, but it also imposes no barriers to leaving a comment to genuine commenters.

>> **Registered Users:** Sets your blog to accept comments only from registered members of Blogger or OpenID so that you can cut down on some spam. Don't forget that not everyone has a Blogger or OpenID account — or wants one — so you might lose some real comments.

>> **Users with Google Accounts:** Because Google validates the accounts it creates, letting users who have Google accounts leave comments can help ensure that you get comments from humans rather than spammers.

>> **Only Members of the Blog:** Prevents anyone who isn't a member of your blog from leaving a comment. No one you haven't personally authorized as a member can leave a comment. This option creates a lot of work for you because you have to maintain the list of authorized members, but you don't get any spam.

TIP

You can add members to your blog from the Basic Settings page.

Also on the Posts and Comments page, you can specify your comment moderation options. Change the Comment Moderation setting to Always. Turning on comment moderation prevents anyone from posting a comment that you haven't approved. When someone leaves a comment, you get an email that lets you know about the comment. From the Dashboard, you can authorize or reject the publication of the comment. You can also moderate comments via email.

REMEMBER

Moderating comments is a lot of work for you, but it improves the quality and readability of comments on your blog for your readers, and it discourages spammers in the future.

Making email changes

On the Email settings page, you can turn on a cool feature that allows you to post to your blog by sending an email message. When it's configured, you can simply send an email to the address from any device capable of sending email (such as your smartphone!). The subject of the email becomes the title of the blog post, and the text of the email is the entry body. It's a very quick, easy way to publish to your blog, which makes it great for when you're traveling.

To set up an email address to be used to send a post to your Blogger blog, click the Email Settings link and fill out the Posting Using Email text box. Be sure to save the settings and test to make sure that it works!

TIP

In the Email page, you can enter an email address in the Comment Notification text box at which you want to receive notification when someone leaves a comment on your blog. This setting helps you keep track of comments left on your blog, especially when you have a lot of old posts on which you might not see comments when you view your blog.

Customizing Your Blog

The look that you picked when you started your blog might be just fine, but many bloggers want to tweak and customize the look and feel of their blogs — I know I did when I started working on my blog. I was using personal words and pictures, and I wanted to make the rest of the site look more like my own website rather than a Blogger design.

Blogger differentiates between the *template* and *layout* of your blog. The template dictates the look of the blog; the layout is the placement of the elements of the blog.

When you start your Blogger blog, you choose a template, and that template determines the look and feel of your blog as well as the placement of the elements and what those elements are. However, you should think of the template and the layout it comes with as a starting point; it's not set in stone.

You can change the look of a Blogger blog in four ways:

>> Change the template you are using completely.

>> Customize an existing template using the Template Designer.

>> Create your own template in HTML (see the "Editing templates old-skool: Using code" sidebar).

>> Edit the layout of your template to move, add, and remove elements.

TECHNICAL STUFF

EDITING TEMPLATES OLD-SKOOL: USING CODE

If you're a web designer or coder and you want to sink your teeth into the Blogger template itself, you can do so. To get to the code from the Blogger Dashboard, select Template from the blog's Dashboard and click Edit HTML for the template you're using.

From here, you can edit the HTML and save as you go. Blogger recommends that only advanced users use this tool. You should be proficient with HTML and CSS and know a certain amount of Blogger's own coding language to successfully edit these files.

Blogger suggests that using the Template Designer gives you good options without as much risk of breaking your blog.

Choosing a new template

One of the fun features of Blogger is the ability to choose from a number of templates for your blog. The template determines both the look and feel of your blog as well as how the blog elements appear on the page. Blogger has many templates to choose from, and don't forget that you can customize or change the template later if your first choice no longer looks as fresh in six months. (For more info, see the "Using the Template Designer" section, later in this chapter.)

To choose a template, follow these steps:

1. **From the Dashboard, select Template from the Posts drop-down list.**

2. **Use the scrollbar to browse through the available templates in the Template screen.**

   The previews on this page give you an idea of how your blog would look both on a computer and on mobile if you used the various templates.

3. **When you find something intriguing, click the thumbnail image.**

   A larger image of the template opens in the window so that you can take a closer look, as shown in Figure 4-7.

TIP

   You can preview as many or as few templates as you want. To close a preview without implementing the template, click the X in the upper-right corner of the preview window.

FIGURE 4-7: You can preview the Blogger templates when you start a new blog.

Source: www.blogger.com

4. **After you decide on a template, click the Apply to Blog button on the preview window or click the Apply to Blog link under the template thumbnail.**

   Blogger displays a confirmation message that the template has been implemented on your blog.

Using the Template Designer

Don't know any HTML but still want to tweak certain elements of your blog's design just a little? You're in luck — the Blogger Template Designer gives you some excellent tools to do just that. In fact, I think you'll be pleasantly surprised to discover just how many things you can change easily.

The Template Designer gives you the capability to change:

>> The font face, size, and color of text, links, navigation elements, and sidebar elements

>> The background color, image, or both

>> Widths of the columns on your blog

>> Layouts of your blog to use one, two, three, four, or even five columns

TIP

In fact, you can even use the Template Designer to insert some of your own custom styles, if you're up to date with HTML and CSS.

To use the Blogger Template Designer, follow these steps:

1. **From the Dashboard, select Template from the Posts drop-down list.**

2. **Click the Customize button under the Template you're currently using.**

   The Template Designer opens.

3. **Click the Background link in the left column and click the thumbnail in the Background Image box.**

   The Select Background Image window opens.

4. **Browse the available backgrounds and select one to preview it, as shown in Figure 4-8.**

   Looking for something specific? Choose one of the image categories in the left side of the window to see topically selected images, such as Shopping, Technology, or Nature.

   You can upload an image from your computer to use as a background by selecting Upload image.

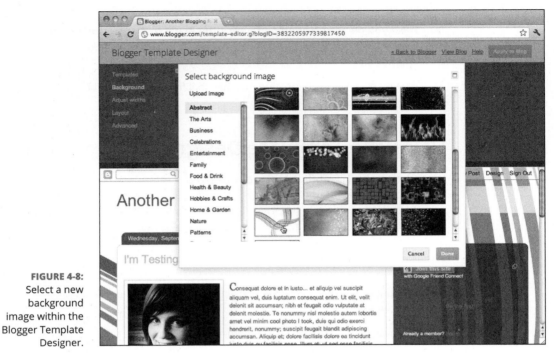

FIGURE 4-8:
Select a new background image within the Blogger Template Designer.

Source: www.blogger.com

5. **Click Done.**

6. **If desired, choose a new color theme from the options in the Background page of the Template Designer.**

The themes set background, link, text, and other element colors.

7. **Click the Layout link from the left side of the Template Designer.**

This opens the layout page.

8. **Select the thumbnail that uses the number of columns you want your blog to have.**

You can also select the layout to use in the footer — that's the bottom area of your blog.

Selecting a thumbnail implements that layout on your blog.

9. **Click the Advanced link on the left side of the Template Designer.**

10. **Select an element to customize from the available list.**

In Figure 4-9, I customize the Blog Title.

You may customize each element in the following ways:

Font Face: Choose from the standard web fonts, such as Arial, Times New Roman, and many fancier web fonts.

Font Style and Size: Bold, italicize, and make text larger or smaller that the template's initial settings.

Color: Select a color for the element by using the following selection suggestions:

- *Hexadecimal Code:* If you know the hexadecimal code for the color that you want to use, you can type it into this text box. *Hexadecimal code* is a code that contains letters and numbers that equate to a color. Primarily graphic and web designers use hexadecimal codes, so don't worry if this seems like gibberish to you.

- *Color Picker:* Click the drop-down list on the color picker to really fine-tune an exact color choice (see Figure 4-9).

- *Colors from This Template:* These colors are already in use in your template.

- *Suggested Colors:* This palette shows colors that Blogger thinks fit well with the colors already in use.

- *Background Color:* Choose a color for the background of the element you are customizing. The ways you can select a color are the same as for the font color choices.

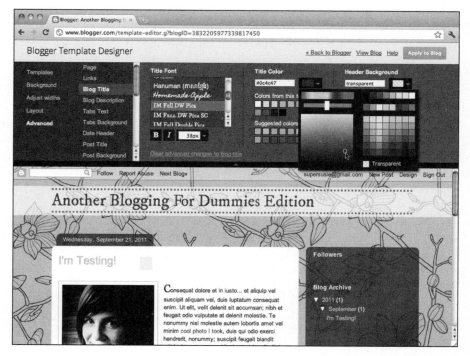

FIGURE 4-9:
Select new colors for many elements with the Blogger Template Designer.

Source: www.blogger.com

When you click a color, Blogger shows a preview of how it looks on your blog in the lower half of the screen.

11. **After you make your edits, click Apply to Blog.**

A Blogger page opens, displaying a confirmation that it has saved your edits. You can return to the Blogger home page or continue making changes in the Template Designer.

Editing page elements

The Layout area of Blogger (see Figure 4-10) gives you, the blogger, a groundbreaking tool that allows you to have detailed control over the layout and look of your blog without requiring you to become an HTML guru and stay up late figuring out the intricacies of web publishing. This kind of editing control reflects the growing do-it-yourself attitude found in the blogosphere: Bloggers want sites that reflect their own sensibilities, but not everyone has the time to become an expert or the budget to hire one.

This access also reflects the growing expertise of many computer users who can edit photographs and create graphics, and it gives them the capability to make the most of those skills.

In the Layout screen (refer to Figure 4-10), a wireframe of your blog template appears. A *wireframe* is a visual representation of the template layout that uses only outlines, or boxes, of the elements.

The following list explains how you can use the wireframe features to customize your page:

>> **Edit page elements.** Click the Edit link for any page element that is already being used to change its formatting. What you can change depends on what kind of element it is and the features Blogger has given you access to. For example, clicking Edit on the Blog Posts area lets you edit:

- The number of posts on the page

- The date style

- Wording of the byline, labels, and comments areas

- Social networking sharing tools such as Twitter, Facebook, and Google+

- Ad placement in your page

- The order of elements in a blog post

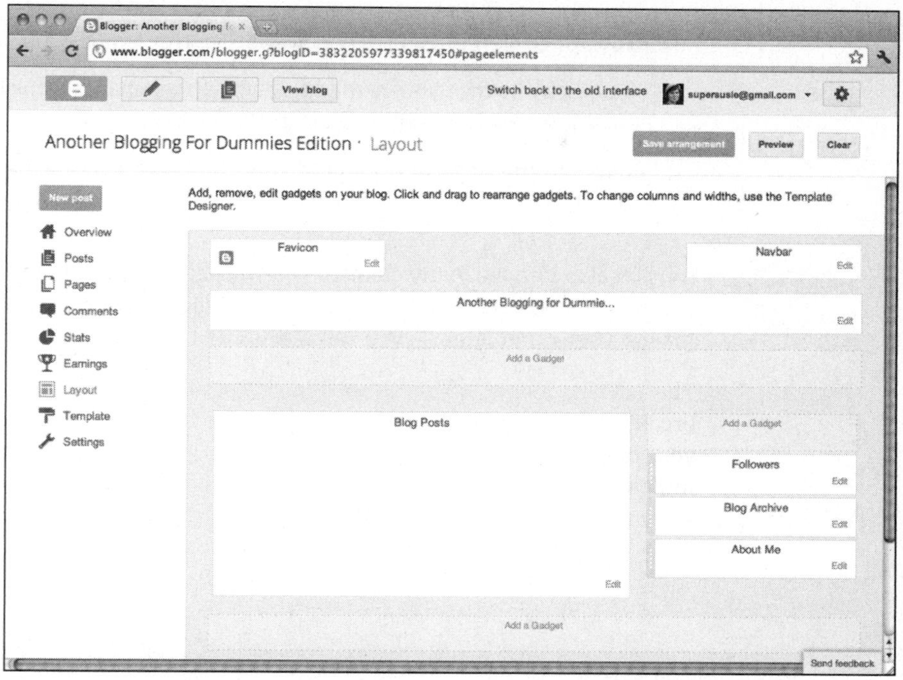

FIGURE 4-10: Use the Layout page in Blogger to customize your blog layout.

Source: `www.blogger.com`

» **Add a gadget.** Click the Add a Gadget link to place in your sidebar polls, images, lists, advertising, and more from a library of Blogger-provided elements. You have many to choose from, but here's a quick list to give you a feel for the options:

- Poll
- List
- Link List
- Image
- Google AdSense (see Chapter 20)
- Text
- HTML/third-party functionality
- RSS or Atom feed (see more about RSS in Chapter 16)
- Video clips
- Logo
- Your profile
- Newsreel

>> **Move page elements.** Click and drag them to a new position.

>> **Preview edits that you've made.** See how your changes look before you save them to your blog by clicking the Preview button.

>> **Revert to the original version of your template.** Click the Clear Edits button.

TIP

You can also remove many elements on the page. Click Edit and look for a Remove button for anything you don't want to include on your blog. Don't worry if you change your mind later — you can always add them back in.

Chapter 5

Starting a WordPress Blog

I f you spend much time looking at blogs or talking to bloggers, you can't miss references to WordPress, one of the best-known and well-liked blogging software options available today. WordPress comes in two flavors — hosted and installable. In this chapter, I focus on working with the installable version that you place on your own web server.

This chapter runs through an overview of how to install WordPress on your server, use the administration panel, play with themes and widgets, and find out where to connect with other WordPress users in your local community and online.

TIP

I can cover only so much detail in a single chapter, so if you want to dive into greater detail about WordPress and find out how you can keep your software installation healthy for a long time to come, invest in a copy of *WordPress For Dummies*, 7th Edition, by Lisa Sabin-Wilson (John Wiley & Sons, Inc.).

Choosing between WordPress.com and WordPress.org

Some blog software is available as both a hosted service and a version that you can download and install. WordPress is one of those packages. (For a refresher on hosted versus server-based blogging software, see Chapter 3).

References to WordPress (Figure 5-1) are uniformly about the version of the software that you download and install on your own server. You can check it out online at www.wordpress.org. However, the option at WordPress.com is a hosted version. Fortunately, you can use both types of WordPress for free.

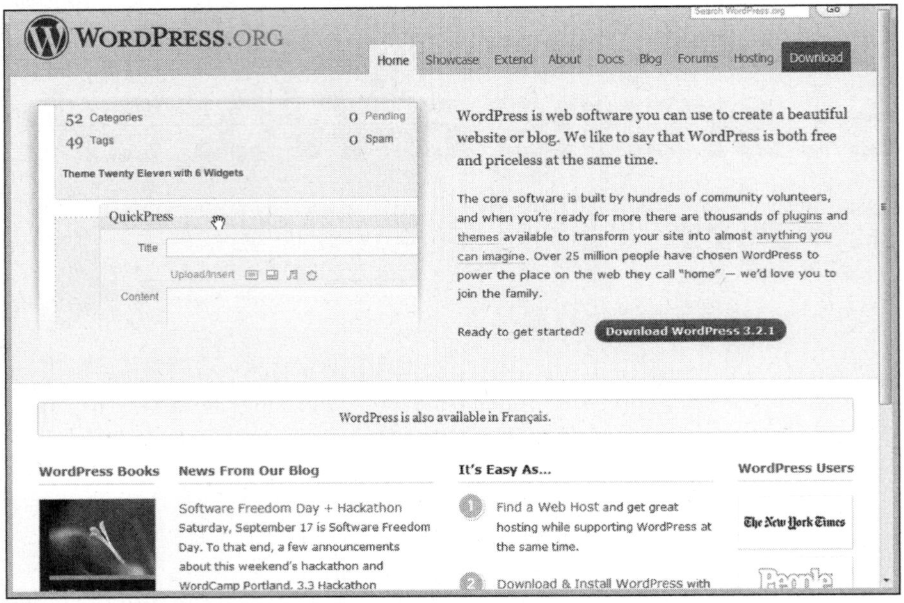

FIGURE 5-1: WordPress.org is the open source release of the WordPress platform.

When WordPress.com was launched, many bloggers rejoiced because WordPress had reached the blogging mainstream. Bloggers could now create blogs with ease and use the tools that they had come to love without having to tinker in the background or stress over how to maintain those blogs.

Table 5-1 breaks down the pros and cons of each version of WordPress.

TABLE 5-1

WordPress.com versus WordPress

Flavor	Pros	Cons
WordPress.com	A free and hosted service. The WordPress.com service deals with daily maintenance, such as backups and software updates.	Customization of features such as theme and design come at an additional cost.
	Security is a little better than some hosting services: Your blogs are replicated in three different locations, thus keeping your blog posts safe.	In order to remove WordPress.com ads from your site, you have to pay a fee.
	You gain the benefits of the WordPress.com community's featured blog postings and shared content.	The ability to include eCommerce on your blog is only possible after a paid upgrade to your site.
WordPress	It's free.	You must install and maintain the software yourself.
	You can fully customize the WordPress software; you can also use any theme you like or create your own.	Needing your own domain and web hosting adds to your costs.

Although choosing a version of WordPress may seem daunting, it really isn't. You just need to ask yourself these questions: How much control do you want to have over your site? Do you worry about not owning your content? Do you prefer freedom over ease? If your answers are positive, you should continue reading this chapter! If not, WordPress.com may be the WordPress for you.

TIP

Still stuck? You can find additional information about the two options at `http://support.wordpress.com/com-vs-org`.

OPEN SOURCE SOFTWARE

WordPress is open source software, which means that its *source code* — the programming that runs the application — is freely accessible to developers who want to customize it or create new software from or for it.

Also, you can freely distribute open source software, and no one places restrictions on how you (or anyone else) can use it. In fact, one of the few terms of using open source software is that you can't place restrictions on the use or distribution of what you create from it.

Installing WordPress

In this chapter, I focus on installing and using WordPress on your own web server. (If you think the hosted version is what you need, just point your web browser to www.wordpress.com and follow the simple sign-up instructions to get started.)

You can get your WordPress installation up and running without a huge amount of difficulty, but in order to get your site going, you need to follow some very important steps.

TECHNICAL STUFF

Although this chapter walks you through the process, you can also follow along with WordPress's instructions, located at http://codex.wordpress.org/Installing_WordPress.

Registering a domain

Have you already chosen a name for your blog? Have you purchased the related domain? When you're itching to get your blog online and want to control every aspect, the domain is the first thing that you need.

As explained in Chapter 3, a domain is the name and brand of your blog, and the web address (or URL). It gives visitors an idea of what your blog is about and who you are. You can have some fun getting creative with your blog name! Before committing to a blog name, why not see what others have done? The following list gives you five examples of some of the world's top blogs and their domains:

>> **Mashable** (www.mashable.com): A news aggregation site with the purpose of informing and entertaining.

>> **TechCrunch** (www.techcrunch.com): A technology-industry blog.

>> **Gizmodo** (www.gizmodo.com): A blog that talks about almost anything.

>> **Lifehacker** (www.lifehacker.com): A site that suggests ways that you can make your life better and more efficient.

>> **Gawker** (www.gawker.com): A site featuring the most-talked-about stories on the Internet.

The domains in the preceding list make quite an impression despite the fact that, at first glance, they don't necessarily tell the visitor much about the content. If you find and bookmark a blog that you like, you keep going back for the great content, not the domain name. In Chapter 3, I talk about acquiring domains in detail, in case you need a refresher about how to do so.

Selecting web hosting

After you choose an appropriate domain for your blog, you need somewhere for your WordPress install to live. In Chapter 3, I tell you what to look for in web hosting and make some recommendations. Don't forget that you can also ask other bloggers what host they use and what their experience has been.

If you've read Chapter 3 of this book, you already know that web software such as WordPress has certain technical requirements. The requirements for WordPress are

>> PHP 5.6 or greater

>> MySQL 5.6 or greater

>> The mod_rewrite Apache module

Most web hosts have similar configurations and should be able to handle what you need, but you can review the official WordPress requirements page at `http://wordpress.org/about/requirements`. WordPress also has a handy bit of text that you can copy and send to potential web hosts to see whether their services can handle WordPress. How cool is that?

TIP

Although the web hosting field changes from time to time with new hosting companies popping up, the following are some of the industry's top picks for providing everything that you need for WordPress:

>> Bluehost (`www.bluehost.com`)

>> DreamHost (`www.dreamhost.com`)

>> HostGator (`www.hostgator.com`)

>> Media Temple (`www.mediatemple.net`)

>> GoDaddy (`www.godaddy.com`)

>> SiteGround (`www.siteground.com`)

>> 1&1 (`www.1and1.com`)

Each of these companies offers well-known, quality web hosting, but if you want to continue looking, compare notes with other bloggers and refer to Chapter 3 for good advice about choosing a web host.

Getting the software

After you sort out your web host and site domain, you next need to download and extract the WordPress files from WordPress.org and put them on your computer. Choose a place you'll remember, such as a Documents or Download directory. Follow these steps:

1. **Point your web browser to `www.wordpress.org`.**

The main WordPress page appears.

2. **Click the blue Download WordPress tab in the top-right corner.**

The site takes you to a short instructional page that has download information on it.

3. **Click the Download WordPress plus version number button.**

Your web browser may ask you to select a location to place the files that are downloading. If it does, choose a place on your computer that you will remember. Your Desktop or Documents folder are decent choices.

4. **After the compressed file downloads, double-click it to expand (or *unzip*) the files it contains on your computer.**

The files are saved on your computer, as shown in Figure 5-2.

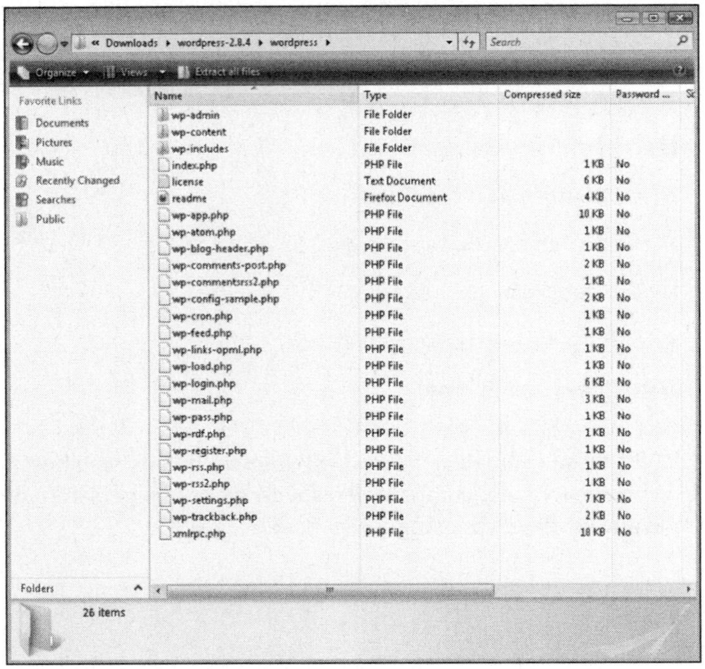

FIGURE 5-2:
After you extract the WordPress files to your hard drive, you should see a folder structure similar to this.

TECHNICAL STUFF

WordPress.org provides the downloadable file in two compressed formats: GZip (.tar.gz) and ZIP (.zip) format. These days, most computer systems recognize the ZIP format, and you should be able to open it without installing any additional software. After you expand the .zip file, you can delete it from your computer.

TIP

Many host companies walk you through the downloading and installing of Word-Press on your site via your cPanel (control panel) as shown in Figure 5-3. Ask your web host whether it offers packages that include WordPress installation as part of the setup.

The Install WordPress button

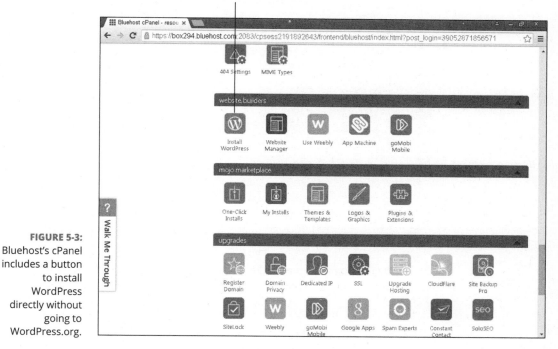

FIGURE 5-3: Bluehost's cPanel includes a button to install WordPress directly without going to WordPress.org.

Uploading the WordPress files

Do you have your files unzipped? Great! Now, the installation process gets a little more technical. You need to upload these unzipped files to your web hosting space by using an FTP (file transfer protocol) client. If you don't have an FTP client installed on your computer, you have plenty of free options that you can download and install.

The following are my two favorite FTP clients:

>> **FileZilla** (www.filezilla-project.org): Available for all computer platforms (see Figure 5-4)

>> **Cyberduck** (www.cyberduck.ch): Available only for Macintosh computers

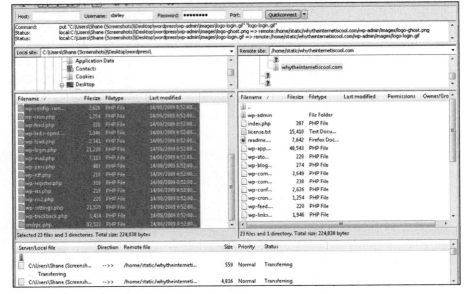

FIGURE 5-4:
This FileZilla interface, which has the hard drive on the left and the web server on the right, is similar to most other FTP client interfaces.

Both of these programs have the capability to connect and transfer files to your new web host. To place the WordPress files on your web host, follow these steps:

1. **Download and install the FTP client of your choice.**

Look for installation instructions on the FTP software website.

2. **Start your FTP client.**

3. **Connect to your web server by using the details that your web host provided you for FTP access.**

These details usually include a URL, username, and password.

The directory in which you store the WordPress files is normally the main directory that you see when you connect via FTP. Check with your web host if you're confused.

4. **Using the FTP software, upload the WordPress files from your computer to the server.**

In some FTP clients, you can drag and drop the WordPress files to the location on the web host. Others use arrow interfaces.

5. **When the files finish uploading, close your FTP client.**

REMEMBER

At some point in the future, you may need to upload additional files (although WordPress is fairly good at doing most of its updates directly through the interface). That said, make sure to retain the information that you used to connect to your web host.

Setting up the database

You're doing great! But don't rest on your laurels; this next step is probably the most technical. Take a deep breath and prepare to set up a database for your WordPress blog. You can do it!

Arguably, setting up a database isn't actually terribly difficult. However, each web host handles databases in different ways, so I can't give you straightforward instructions for accomplishing this task.

REMEMBER

Your web host is in the business of handling technical issues, and of course, it sets up the environment in the first place. Don't hesitate to request assistance with your database setup.

TECHNICAL
STUFF

The database system that you need to use is called MySQL. (Without MySQL, you can't use WordPress.) *MySQL* is a relational database management system. It can store all kinds of data for WordPress — from your blog posts to sidebar widget links, as well as all your WordPress settings. So, MySQL stores the blog posts that you write inside a database that's fast, efficient, and flexible.

If you want to know more about MySQL, pick up a copy of *PHP & MySQL For Dummies*, 4th Edition, by Janet Valade (John Wiley & Sons, Inc.). But take my word for it that after you set up your database, you won't need to know anymore about MySQL for the purposes of using WordPress.

After you know how to access your database setup tool, follow these steps:

1. **Log into your web host.**

2. **Create the database.**

   You need to name your database something that makes sense. If you have a blog called Joe Smith's Wondrous Adventures, you can name the database joesmith. The length of database names and database usernames are normally limited, and you can't include special characters in the names.

3. **Create a database user.**

   You can make the username anything, except the name that you used for your database. The same length and special character restrictions apply, though.

4. **Assign a password to that user.**

Don't forget to write this information down so that you can use it when you run the WordPress install script.

Because web hosting companies can choose for themselves which MySQL database system to include in their hosting packages, I don't know which of the following applies to your situation. But web hosts commonly use one of the following management systems:

» **phpMyAdmin:** A database management tool (shown in Figure 5-5) that a lot of web hosts provide to their clients. You can create and delete databases, manage database users, and (depending on what permissions the web host gives you) manipulate the data itself.

» **cPanel:** A common web host interface that generally enables users to create and delete databases. You normally do any additional manipulation by using phpMyAdmin.

» **Plesk:** Yet another web host interface that allows users to create and delete databases and manage database users. You do any data manipulation by using phpMyAdmin.

The web host that you choose probably uses one of the interfaces in the preceding list. You can figure them out and use them fairly easily. If you're running only one blog, you need only a single database. If you're thinking of running more than one, you need to find out how to keep your databases healthy and separate by using tools that your web host provides.

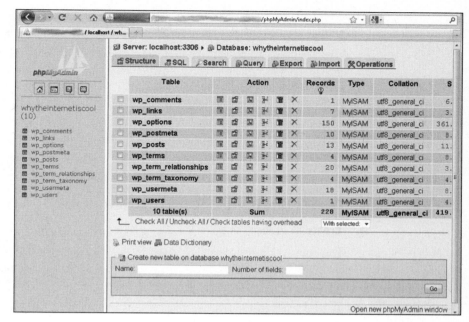

FIGURE 5-5:
phpMyAdmin is a tool that you can use to manage and create databases.

Running the install script

After you put the WordPress files in the directory your web host recommends and write down the database information, you only have to run the WordPress installer. The installer is super simple. Things can go wrong, of course, but if the installer gets stuck, it does a very good job of letting you know exactly what you need to do.

Follow these steps to install WordPress:

1. **To run the installer, point your Internet browser to**

www.yourwebdomain.com/wp–admin/install.php

Remember to replace www.yourwebdomain.com with your domain name!

The installer checks to see whether you've created or edited the configuration file. If it doesn't find one, it will create it for you.

2. **Click Create a Configuration File.**

This creates your WordPress configuration file. Now all you need to do is enter the information the configuration file needs.

3. **Make sure you have the database name, username, password, and hostname. If you do, click Let's Go!**

4. Enter the database information (see Figure 5-6).

You can usually leave the database host as localhost because most web hosting environments use that host without complaint. You don't have to change the table prefix, either.

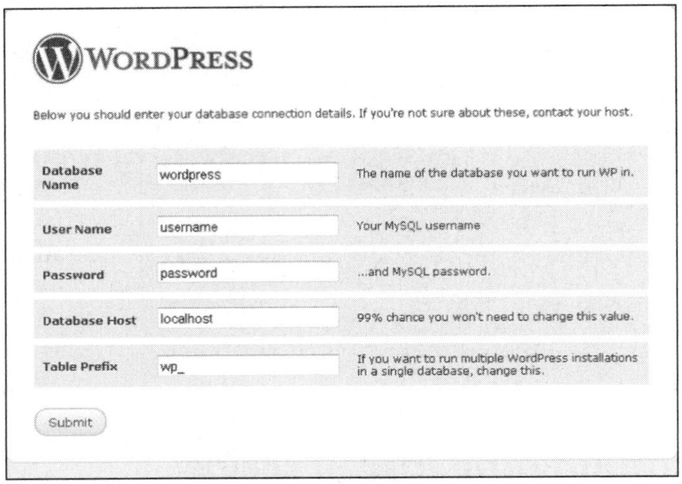

WORDPRESS

Below you should enter your database connection details. If you're not sure about these, contact your host.

Database Name	wordpress	The name of the database you want to run WP in.
User Name	username	Your MySQL username
Password	password	...and MySQL password.
Database Host	localhost	99% chance you won't need to change this value.
Table Prefix	wp_	If you want to run multiple WordPress installations in a single database, change this.

Submit

FIGURE 5-6:
Provide the database information to the WordPress installer.

5. Click Submit.

6. Click Run the Install.

7. Enter a blog title and your email address in the text boxes provided.

8. Click Install WordPress.

If everything goes well, the installer displays the word Success on the screen. The username and password of the administration user also appear on the screen. Keep a record of this information in a safe location because if your blog experiences any problems or you need to conduct any WordPress configuration or management, you will need to log in using the admin account.

9. Click Log In.

The log-in page appears, where you can log into your new installation.

That's it! You've done it! You can now log into your new WordPress installation and get busy publishing.

TECHNICAL STUFF

The configuration file is named wp-config.php. If your installer can't create the configuration file automatically, follow the instructions that WordPress provides at http://codex.wordpress.org/Installing_WordPress#Setup_configuration_file to create the file by hand.

Getting Familiar with Settings

After you have your new blog software installed and running, you can log into your WordPress admin account and take a look around. The WordPress software does a lot right out of the box to make your blogging life as simple as possible. You have the ability to create blog posts; create static pages; add images and multimedia files; connect to social networking sites, such as Instagram and Pinterest; and chat with blog visitors by using the commenting system.

Either these functions come with the WordPress install, or you can add them by using a plug-in that you download and install. Each of these plug-ins typically has an administration page.

In the following sections, I introduce you to the administration section of the blog itself.

Logging in

Before you can start posting, you need to head on over to the Log In page and enter the username and password that were provided to you during the installation process.

To log into your new website, you may want to bookmark the following link:

`www.yourdomain.com/wp-admin/wp-login.php`

Remember to replace `www.yourwebdomain.com` with your domain name!

Setting up an Editor account

WordPress allows you to set up and maintain several levels of user accounts in addition to the administrative account created during the setup process. These account types are called *roles*. They are as follows:

>> **Administrator:** Administrators have access to all features and areas of the blog software, from technical configuration to user accounts to content tools. This is the most powerful level of access on your blog; handle with care!

>> **Editor:** This is a user who can publish posts, manage posts, and manage other account posts.

>> **Author:** This is a user who can publish and manage his or her own posts.

>> **Contributor:** This is a user role that allows someone to write and manage posts but not publish them live to the blog.

>> **Subscriber:** This is a user who can read comments, post comments, and receive other private information.

TIP

If you are the only person blogging on your website, you should still go ahead and set up an Editor user account for creating blog posts. I recommend that you don't use the administrative account created during installation as the account you use when you author blog posts; it's a bit like driving a car by opening the hood and manipulating the engine directly. Instead, use the perfectly good steering wheel that comes with WordPress by setting up an Editor account. Reserve the administrative account for administrative tasks like installing new themes, plug-ins, and any other general maintenance.

Set up your Editor account by following these steps:

1. **Log into your WordPress installation.**

2. **From the Dashboard, click Users.**

   You see the full list of users and their roles.

3. **Click Add New.**

   WordPress loads the Add New User screen.

4. **Fill out the user fields.**

   You see a listing of text boxes: username, first name, last name, email, website, and password. Only three are required: username, password, and email address. I recommend filling in the first and last names as well.

5. **Select the Editor role.**

6. **Click Add User.**

   The user is created.

TIP

When you set up a new user, you can choose to send the account information to the new user's email address. In this case, the account is for yourself, so you don't need to select this check box. If you want to have additional writers on your blog, consider setting them up as Authors — instead of Editors — and notifying them as you set up their accounts.

REMEMBER

After you create your new Editor account, don't forget to log out of the administrative account and then log in again as an Editor!

Using the Dashboard

Each time you log into your WordPress blog, you end up on the Dashboard page. Get to know this page well because you spend most of your blogging time here. You can configure the front Dashboard to your liking by moving panels around and turning panels on or off. You can see the Dashboard in Figure 5-7.

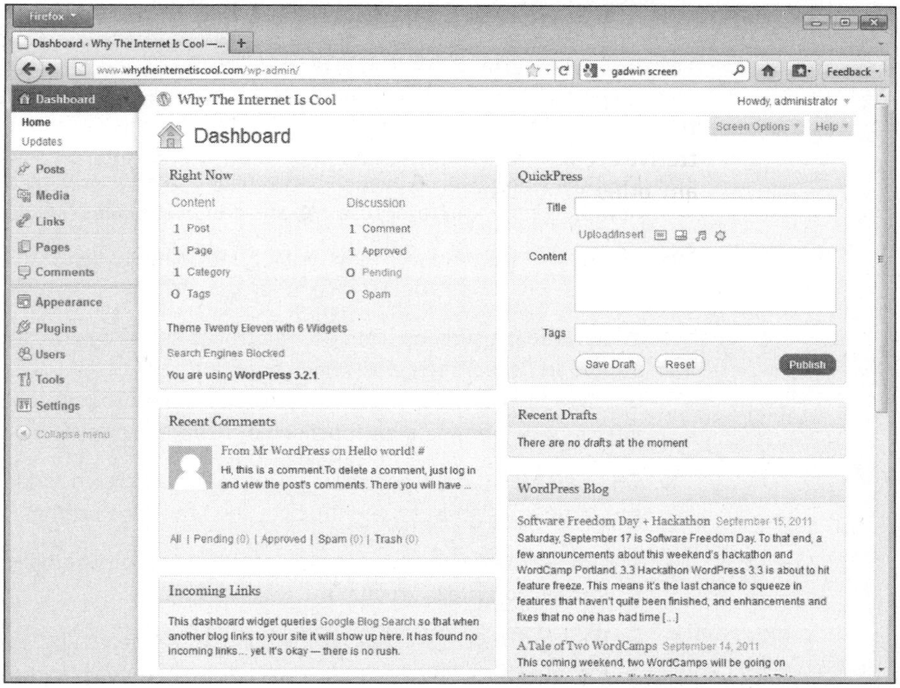

FIGURE 5-7: Prepare to spend a lot of time with the WordPress Dashboard.

On the left side of the Dashboard, a series of menus points you to the various sections of the administration panel. You likely visit some of these menus on a daily basis and some only once in a while:

>> **Posts:** Find links that allow you to edit posts, add new posts, and manage categories and tags.

>> **Media:** Get a link to upload new media files to your media library or manage previously uploaded media.

>> **Links:** Manage lists of links on your website. For example, group links together into categories and post them in sidebars as link lists.

>> **Pages:** Click to go to the Page Administration section. Pages in WordPress are considered *static* pieces of content (pages that change only once in a while) and aren't blog posts. Use them for pretty much any section of your website, such as a bio page or contact page. You can then link to these pages from a sidebar menu or via another blog post. Some themes may also provide you with menus that you can use to link to different sections of your blog.

>> **Comments:** Post, delete, and respond to comments that readers have added to blog posts on your website.

>> **Appearance:** View installed themes, activate new themes, edit existing themes, and search for additional themes from the online WordPress theme catalog.

>> **Plugins:** View installed plug-ins, activate and deactivate plug-ins, search for new plug-ins from WordPress.org, and edit plug-in files right in the interface.

>> **Users:** Manage the users for your blog, including readers and additional authors.

>> **Tools:** Manage additional tools for improved speed by using Google Gears, import and export blog posts and comments, and conduct WordPress upgrades. Google Gears is an optional plug-in for browsers like Firefox and Internet Explorer and adds functionality to your browser.

>> **Settings:** Make all the general changes to the blog, such as the name of the site, your email address, and the date and time-zone settings.

- *General*: Contains basic account information such as email address, time format, and site language.

- *Writing:* Contains settings for the editor interface, as well as default settings for categories, RSS, and tags. You can also access settings to set up remote email.

- *Reading:* Choose the number of blog posts that appear on the front page of your blog and the number of postings available in your RSS feed.

- *Discussion Settings:* Control what kinds of communication your blog sends out. For example, you can get the blog to notify you by email when someone adds a new comment.

- *Media:* Upload and manage any of your media files. You can add titles and descriptions, organize images and audio, add captions to images, and make minor changes to image sizes.

- *Permalinks: Permalinks* are the permanent links to your individual posts. You can configure the format of the post URLs so that they contain both date information and keywords, or keywords only. You can also set default categories for posts and tags.

Checking out the panels

On the right side of the Dashboard, you see a series of panels. Each panel gives you access to parts of the administrative interface for WordPress. The default panels are

» **At a Glance:** Contains a quick overview of what's happening on your blog. The panel displays

- The number of posts on the blog

- The number of comments

- The spam count

- The number of categories and tags currently in use on the site

» **Activity:** Lists the most recent comment activity on your blog and provides links that allow you to moderate and respond to comments without leaving the Dashboard.

» **Quick Draft:** Allows you to post a quick note on your blog right from the administration panel.

» **WordPress News:** Contains a listing of blog posts from other WordPress blogs that talk about WordPress.

Creating a Post

I'm sure you're bursting at the seams to get your first blog post online. The process is quite simple in terms of using WordPress. The real challenge is coming up with good stuff to blog about! Jump to Chapter 9 for a lot of tips and ideas on writing for your blog.

To start a new blog post, follow these steps:

1. **Click the Posts menu in the Dashboard and select Add New.**

   WordPress opens the Add New Post page, shown in Figure 5-8.

2. **Give your post a title by entering it in the text box below Add New Post.**

3. **Add some text in the body text box.**

   Use the formatting buttons if you want to change the style of your text, create a list, or otherwise add elements.

FIGURE 5-8:
Adding a new
post using
WordPress.

4. **Use any of the other options that you want for this post.**

WordPress gives you the following options:

- *Excerpt:* If you want, you can write a short summary of your post for the Excerpt field.

- *Post Tags: Tags* are keywords that describe the topic of your post. Tagging your posts lets search engines easily identify the subject material you discuss and means your post is likely to rank higher in search engine listings.

- *Categories:* Use the Add New Category link in the Categories box if you need to create a new category for your post. Categories are general groups that you can sort your blog posts into so that readers can easily locate the content most interesting to them.

- *Discussion:* You can choose whether you want to allow readers to post comments on this posting and whether you want to permit trackbacks. Trackbacks link two or more blog posts together.

- *Custom Fields:* You can add custom fields to your posts, which you fully control. *Custom fields* are simply fields that appear in each blog post that you can display by altering the template for your blog. For example, if your blog is a restaurant-review blog, you might choose to add custom fields for the location or rating of each restaurant that you review.

5. **Click Publish to save your blog post and check out your blog to see how it looks!**

   If you're not ready to post your blog entry to the public, you can save your posting as a draft or preview it before you post it. Also, you can set a particular date if you want to schedule your post for publication in the future.

   Look for a Visit Site link at the top of the Dashboard; the link takes you right to your blog.

Customizing Your Design

After you've played around with a few of the WordPress features, you may be thinking, "How do I make this new blog pretty?" The answer is as simple as a menu click. Just follow these steps:

1. **From the menus on the left side of the Dashboard, click Appearance.**

   The Themes tab opens, displaying a list of themes that you can install and allowing you to install new themes.

2. **Select Add New to search for themes based on color, keyword, columns, width, features, or subject, make your selections, and then click Find Themes.**

   WordPress returns a list of themes based on your search query.

3. **Click Live Preview to see how a particular theme looks.**

4. **After you find a theme that you like, click Install to load the theme onto your server.**

5. **Click Activate to apply the theme to your blog.**

You can install several themes all at the same time and then take time to test which theme best suits your blog.

Now, do you want to get into the code even more? If so, get ready to dive into HTML. Only the brave venture into this territory because it requires knowledge of HTML, CSS, PHP, and WordPress's own markup language. The code editing for WordPress includes a little more than just plain old HTML.

Some bloggers love playing with HTML code; others run away as fast as they can. If you have the chops, however, the developers of WordPress have made accessing and modifying the theme files a fairly easy task.

Select Editor from the Appearance menu to get at the editing interface for the currently installed theme. The editor is simply a text editor in which you can manipulate the files in your theme without using any other technology (such as FTP) to access the files. It's simple to use and doesn't have too many frills.

The drawback to using the editor is that you really need to know your stuff when it comes to HTML code, CSS, and a little PHP thrown in for good measure. If you don't know what these technologies do, I don't recommend touching your theme without a little practice beforehand. Make backups!

Finding Out More about WordPress

You could spend a lot of time figuring out WordPress, and I just can't fit it all into a single chapter. (I tried!) But you're far from alone in your search for a better understanding of your new WordPress blog. A great many websites and blogs can help you further your WordPress education. Here are a few handy resources:

>> *WordPress For Dummies,* 7th Edition, by Lisa Sabin-Wilson (John Wiley & Sons, Inc.): You knew that *For Dummies* had a book on this topic, right? Of course you did! Why not pick up a copy? You can dig deeper into the ins and outs of WordPress code, themes, and widgets. This book can be your one-stop resource. Tell Lisa Sabin-Wilson that *Blogging For Dummies* sent you!

>> **WordPress Community:** The official WordPress documentation is available online and updated regularly. You can find out about the latest functionality as well as see what's coming up in the future. The community offers a Frequently Asked Questions (FAQ) section, and you can get involved in this large and active web community.

    https://wordpress.org/support/

>> **WordCamp:** Over the last couple of years, camps have been popping up everywhere. *Camps* (also known as *unconferences*) are informal gatherings of people who love to get together and talk about their interests. If you love WordPress, you need to go to a WordCamp in your area soon because you can find out a lot of things not covered anywhere else. What could be better than a bunch of people getting together to talk about everything WordPress? Maybe a bunch of people getting together to talk about everything WordPress who also have cupcakes? Visit the website to see whether a WordCamp is coming to your community. If not, you can start one!

    http://central.wordcamp.org

Chapter 6

Starting a Tumblr Blog

D o you think blogging might just be too much work? Before you dismiss my question as sarcastic, consider this: Orbit Media's 2015 study (www. orbitmedia.com/blog/blogger-research/) of bloggers' habits found that bloggers are spending more time per post than ever, with the majority of bloggers spending two or more hours on each post they write. That's not an insignificant amount of time, and not everyone has that kind of time to devote to blogging.

So, if you're interested in blogging but worried about time, a micro blog might be an alternative you should consider. *Micro blogging* is pretty much what it sounds like — creating very short blog posts. But the micro blog may have all the other usual trappings of a blog, such as comments, RSS feeds, and so on.

In this chapter, I introduce you to micro blogging options and walk you through starting a micro blog using Tumblr.

Introducing Micro Blogging

Micro blogging is characterized by very short, quick, and frequent blog posts, often produced from some nontraditional publishing tools such as mobile phones, email, instant messages, and text messages. However, you can still use a web interface to produce a micro blog!

Some micro bloggers use their blogs as mechanisms to collect and archive interesting tidbits of information that they come across while they surf the web. Many micro blogs contain very little personal content in the form of writing but do have a lot of photos, video snippets, and links. In fact, many micro bloggers don't explain why they choose to include something in their blogs at all, and in this way, micro blogs can be much more idiosyncratic to the individual blogger than a regular blog.

2 Kinds of People (2kindsofpeople.tumblr.com) is a micro blog created on Tumblr, a platform which is covered in depth in this chapter. The premise of the blog (see Figure 6-1) is that there are only two kinds of people in this world, a concept presented over and over again with brief, visual posts.

FIGURE 6-1:
2 Kinds of People is a good example of a micro blog.

Other micro blogging tools act a little differently. Facebook, LinkedIn, Google+, Twitter, and MySpace — or any social network that allows you to post status updates — are technically micro blogging tools, as well. I spend more time covering the Twitter phenomenon in Chapter 18.

Status updates are very short text posts that are generally used to let others know what you're thinking or doing.

Some popular tools for micro blogging include

>> Tumblr (www.tumblr.com)

>> Twitter (www.twitter.com)

>> Plurk (www.plurk.com)

>> Ello (www.ello.co)

Starting a Micro Blog with Tumblr

In this section, I walk you through starting a micro blog by using Tumblr, one of the most popular micro blogging services out there.

Tumblr (www.tumblr.com) is hosted blog software, which means that you don't need to have web hosting, a domain name, or anything more than the capability to access the website in order to get started.

TIP

I cover the differences between hosted and installable blog software in Chapter 3.

Signing up and getting started are simple processes. Feel free to skip past nonessential requests such as following five blogs to get you started in your Tumblr experience. To begin blogging on Tumblr, just follow these steps:

1. **Point your web browser to** www.tumblr.com.

   The main Tumblr page opens.

2. **Type your email address into the Email Address text box.**

3. **Type a password of your choice into the Password text box.**

4. **Type a username.**

5. **Click the Sign up button, as shown in Figure 6-2.**

6. **Provide your age and accept the Tumblr terms of service.**

7. **Verify that you are not a robot by clicking the box.**

Creating a Text Post

Tumblr allows you to create blog posts by using text, photos, quotes, links, chat excerpts, audio files, and video. I show you how to post entries that include some of these different elements in the following sections. For more on including audio, such as podcasts, and video in your blog posts on other platforms, jump to Chapters 12, 13, and 14.

Create a quick text post in your Tumblr blog by following these steps:

1. **Click the Text Post icon (a capital and lowercase letter A) on your Tumblr dashboard.**

   Tumblr displays the Add a Text Post page.

2. **(Optional) Give your blog post a title in the Title field.**

3. **Type the text of your blog post in the Post field.**

   Use as much or as little text as you want.

If you're ready, you can post to your blog right now by clicking Publish, or you can spend a little time making your post fancy. In the following section, you can find out about the options.

Formatting your blog post

Tumblr, like most blog software, gives you the ability to format your blog post while you create it. The icons appear above the content field, shown in Figure 6-3, when you highlight the content, enabling you to format what you've written.

Formatting tools

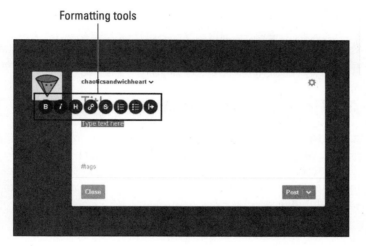

FIGURE 6-3:
Use the formatting tools in Tumblr to format your blog posts.

Tumblr uses a WYSIWG (what you see is what you get) interface, which shows you the effect of a tool in your blog post right when you apply it. This list describes each of the available tools (following the order of the icons from left to right):

>> **Bold:** Make any text in your blog post bold by clicking and dragging over the text that you want to affect and then clicking the Bold icon. The selected text is made **bold.**

>> **Italic:** Italicize any text in your blog post by clicking and dragging over the text that you want to affect and then clicking the Italic icon. The selected text is then shown in *italics*.

>> **Heading:** This transforms your content into a larger font, appropriate for a section heading within your post.

>> **Insert/Edit Link:** Make any text or image in your blog a clickable link to any website. I give you step-by-step instructions for adding a link in the section "Adding links to your post," later in this chapter.

- » **Strikethrough:** This style is commonly applied to text that you need to correct. Click and drag over the text that you want to affect and then click the Strikethrough icon. The selected text is then made ~~strikethrough~~.

- » **Ordered List:** In web browsers, ordered lists usually appear as numbered lists. You can most easily use this tool by typing each list item into your blog post on a separate line. Click and drag to select all the items; then click the Ordered List icon.

- » **Unordered List:** In web browsers, unordered lists are usually displayed as bulleted lists (like this list you're reading right now). You can most easily use this tool by typing each list item into your blog post on a separate line. Click and drag to select all the items; then click the Unordered List icon.

Use the tools described in the preceding list to format your text, and when you're ready, read the following section to see how to add an image to your text blog post.

Adding an image to your post

Blog posts are more fun with photos! If you want to add an image to a text blog post on your Tumblr blog, you can upload a digital image directly from your computer. Simply click the plus sign next to your Text Post window (see Figure 6-4) to make the toolbar appear. Click the camera icon and select an image file from your computer.

The plus sign icon

FIGURE 6-4:
The plus sign icon allows you to add media to your Tumblr text.

Uploading pictures that don't belong to you? Don't forget to respect copyright law! Hop to Chapter 12 for more information about copyright and images on your blog.

Adding links to your post

Links add a lot of value to a blog post by giving your readers the resources to explore a topic further or find more information about your discussion or idea. As long as you link to useful information, don't hesitate to add links to your posts.

You can add links to both text and images. Follow these steps:

1. **Select text or click an image in your blog post.**

2. **Click the Link tool (it's a small piece of chain).**

   Tumblr opens the Insert/Edit Link window.

3. **Type or paste a URL into the Link URL text box.**

4. **Click the Done button to add the link to the text or photo in your blog post (see Figure 6-5).**

Quickly create a link.

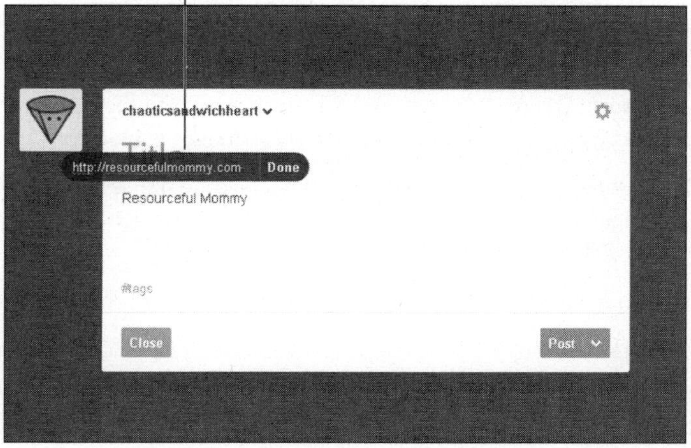

FIGURE 6-5:
Quickly create a link in your blog post by using Tumblr.

If you want to remove a link that you've created, you can easily do it. Simply click the text or photo on which you placed a link, and then click the Link tool.

Publishing your post

When you finish everything that you want to do to your blog post, it's time to publish! Simply click the Post button (refer to Figure 6-3), and your post appears on your blog for others to view.

TECHNICAL STUFF

Click the Publish drop-down list to save your post without publishing it or to set a date in the future to launch it.

TIP

You don't need to be sitting in front of a computer in order to post to your Tumblr blog! You can also post via email, app, and even phone call.

Creating Non-Text Tumblr Posts

Loving the idea of diving into the blogging world without spending huge amounts of time on content creation? Want to share your creativity with the world without writing a ton of text? One of the best-loved features of Tumblr is the ability for users to create quick content that requires little time and little-to-no writing whatsoever! Figure 6-6 shows the Tumblr posting menu where you can select from the seven types of posts available to your Tumblr blog. These seven types include the following:

>> **Text:** As covered in previous sections, text posts on Tumblr are very similar to traditional blog posts both in creation and in appearance to readers.

>> **Photo:** The perfect post style for the budding photographer, photo posts allow you to post one photo or a set of images in blog post form.

>> **Quote:** Want to share a quote from a favorite movie or book? Publish an original poem? Inspired by a famous quote? The quote post style is often used for these very reasons.

>> **Link:** It is possible to simply share a URL with the Tumblr-reading world!

>> **Chat:** Although this post type is called Chat, it is not actually a place for Tumblr users to engage in conversation. The purpose of this type of post is to copy and paste a chat that you had online via another platform.

>> **Audio:** Have something to say to the world and don't feel like typing it? Tumblr audio posts are a way to do just that.

>> **Video:** Have something to say to the world, don't feel like typing it, and don't mind if the world sees you? Tumblr video posts allow you to share your favorite videos with your readers — or viewers!

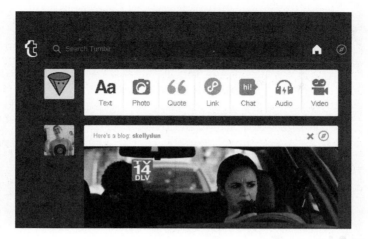

FIGURE 6-6:
The Tumblr
posting menu
allows users to
choose from
seven types
of posts.

TIP

Love something that you see on another Tumblr blog? Unlike traditional blogging where you should never consider grabbing another blogger's content and posting it on your site, Tumblr users often reblog each other's content. Every Tumblr blog post has a reblog button in the bottom right-hand corner, which you can use to place that content on your blog. Reblog away!

Customizing How Your Blog Looks

This section introduces you to the customization options for your Tumblr blog. You can change the look and feel of the blog, as well as some of the functionality. Adding your own touches really personalizes a blog and makes it feel more like home.

Get to the appearance customization options by clicking your blog's avatar to the left of your post creation taskbar (see Figure 6-7).

Your blog is now in edit mode. Click Edit appearance to do the following:

>> **Blog Avatar:** Change or hide your blog's avatar.

>> **Accent color:** Change the accent color on your Tumblr blog.

>> **Background color:** Change the background color of your blog's posts.

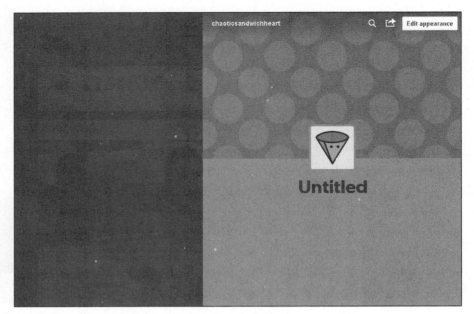

Want to make additional changes? To customize additional appearance settings by selecting a new theme, follow these steps:

1. **Select the person icon on your Tumblr blog's taskbar as shown in Figure 6-8.**

2. **Select the blog you would like to customize.**

3. **Click Edit appearance. A new window will appear as shown in Figure 6-9.**

4. **Click Edit theme.**

Within this setting, you can change everything from your header image to your font style. Get started changing the appearance of your blog by choosing one of the design themes that Tumblr automatically provides. Tumblr offers nearly hundreds of free options. If you're good with HTML, you can also create your own custom theme.

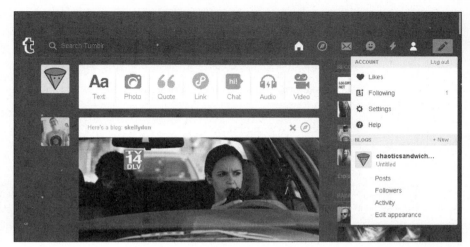

FIGURE 6-8:
Access the customization section of your Tumblr blog.

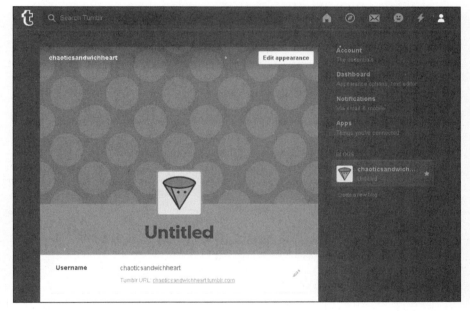

FIGURE 6-9:
The Edit appearance section of your Tumblr blog allows you to change your selected theme.

Configuring Your Settings

As mentioned earlier, there are some macro-level settings for your Tumblr blog that you might want to consider customizing as well. You can access these settings by clicking the person icon in your Tumblr Dashboard and then clicking the gear icon in the menu.

The settings you can tweak include the following:

>> **Email:** Change the email associated with your blog.

>> **Password:** Change your account's password.

>> **Dial-a-post:** Associate a phone number with your account in order to call in posts from your phone.

>> **Language:** Select the language for your blog.

TIP

Want to learn even more about Tumblr? Check out *Tumblr For Dummies* by Sue Jenkins (John Wiley & Sons).

Chapter 7

Creating a Squarespace Blog

In a blogging world that for a time was dominated by Blogger and WordPress, Squarespace (www.squarespace.com) has made a splash as another viable blogging platform option. Squarespace blogs come with many of the features that bloggers on other platforms are required to add with special themes or additional plug-ins. For example, your Squarespace account provides you with website analytics (see Chapter 19 to learn more about blog analytics), social media integration, and automatically mobile-ready designs.

If you would like to customize the look of your blog by editing the *Cascading Style Sheets (CSS)*, which are your blog template's style sheets, you can do that with Squarespace. If you just want to select a blog template and get right to blogging, you can do that with Squarespace. And because Squarespace allows bloggers to try its platform for free for 14 days, there's no real danger in giving this platform a try if you read through this chapter and feel that it might be right for you.

Creating a Squarespace Account

Like test driving a vehicle before purchase or dating before marriage, the best way to begin your Squarespace blogging experience is through the 14-day free trial offered by this blogging platform. Should you choose to stay with Squarespace for the long term, however, you should know that unlike Blogger and Tumblr, this platform does not remain free. Prices begin at $8 per month when billed annually and go up to $26 per month for business sites.

To begin the creation of your Squarespace account, visit the platform at www.squarespace.com and click Get Started, as shown in Figure 7-1.

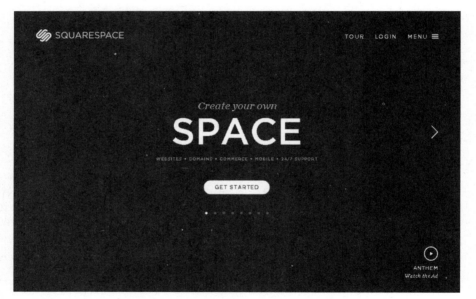

FIGURE 7-1:
To create your Squarespace account, click Get Started.

Selecting a template

TIP

Because of the way Squarespace presents template options, I suggest that you narrow down the focus of your blog before selecting a template. For our purposes, let's assume that you've chosen to create a website for the purposes of blogging. Once you select the "Website" option, you will be able to select a template for your new Squarespace blog.

Choose a template to begin the creation of your Squarespace blog. Although you may select any template you like, Squarespace categorizes templates that might specifically suit the following categories:

>> Businesses

>> Portfolios

>> Personal

>> Musicians

>> Restaurants

>> Weddings

Before selecting a template, you may choose to view that template both as a screenshot and as a live preview, which allows you to dive deeper into the features of the template before making a selection. To choose the template you'd like to use, simply click that design and then click "Start with (*design name*)," as shown in Figure 7-2.

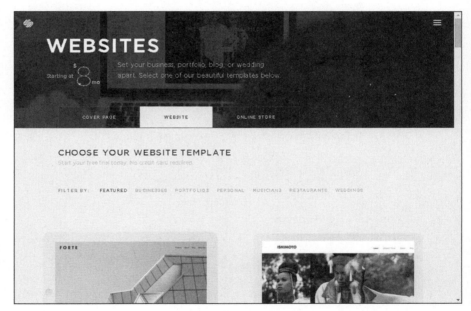

FIGURE 7-2:
Select a site template to begin blogging on Squarespace.

It's time to create your account! Provide the following information and select Finish & Create Site to finish your initial account setup:

>> First name

>> Last name

>> Email address

>> Password

Choosing a site name

Congratulations, you have a Squarespace blog account! Before you can begin blogging on your new Squarespace website, you'll be asked to answer a few questions to help get you started, as shown in Figure 7-3.

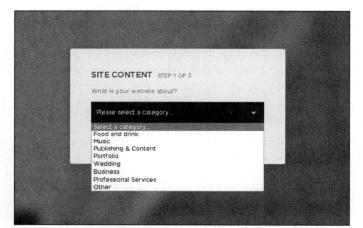

FIGURE 7-3:
Squarespace helps you create your new site by asking a series of questions.

Information collected by Squarespace includes

>> Site purpose

- Business

- Personal

- Ecommerce

- Non-Profit

>> Your site title

It's now time to select a name for your blog and dive into creating content.

REMEMBER

Deciding on the best name for your Squarespace site? Now is a great time to visit or revisit Chapter 3 to learn more about selecting and registering a domain name. Squarespace can also help you with this process!

Now that you've selected a Squarespace blog template and a blog title, it is time to customize your site. The left sidebar of your new blog, as shown in Figure 7-4, offers the following menu items:

- » Pages
- » Design
- » Commerce
- » Metrics
- » Settings
- » Help

The options within each of these menu items will change somewhat based on the template you've chosen for your Squarespace blog.

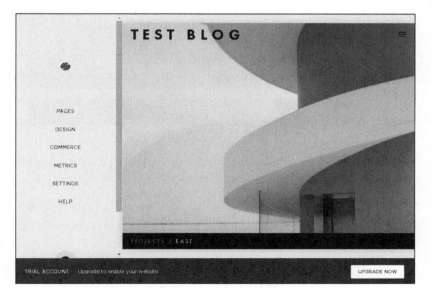

FIGURE 7-4:
Get started with your new Squarespace blog by checking out the home menu options.

Adding Blog Content

There are nearly countless customizations that you can make to your Squarespace blog — some of which are covered in the following sections — but you can feel free to dive right into content creation if you choose.

To begin adding content to your blog, select the Pages menu item in your Squarespace sidebar, as shown in Figure 7-5. In contrast to other blog platforms, Squarespace pages are comprised of blocks of content. You can change the look of your pages by adding, removing, and altering those content blocks. During the editing process, feel free to give this page any title you want, including keeping the Welcome heading.

FIGURE 7-5:
The Squarespace Pages menu item allows you to add content to your blog.

Ready to create your first original blog post? To begin blogging, select Blog from your Pages menu and click the plus symbol (see Figure 7-6).

You can now title your post and add content using a WYSIWYG (what you see is what you get) format similar to most blog platforms. From this location, you can also elect to do the following:

» Allow comments

» Add tags or categories

» Add a thumbnail image

» Change the author name

» Create a post excerpt

» Choose to make the post featured content

» Link the post title to an external location

Click the plus sign to create content.

FIGURE 7-6:
Clicking the
plus sign leads
you to content
creation on your
Squarespace
blog.

>> Add your geographical blogging location

>> Choose which social media accounts should automatically promote the blog post after it's published

Uploading images

Squarespace allows you to upload images directly to the content where you want the image to appear. For example, if you're creating a Squarespace gallery, page, or blog post, you simply add the image directly to the block or area where you want it to appear rather than having to upload the image to a special location just for media.

To add any content other than text to your blog post, such as images, select the area within the post where you would like to add the content, as shown in Figure 7-7. To add an image to your post, click the Image block icon from the content blocks button menu, as shown in Figure 7-8. You are now able to either drag and drop your image into the content block or upload an image file. When your image has been added, you can choose to do any of the following before clicking Save:

>> Add an image caption

>> Name the image file

>> Change the size of the image

>> View the image in a lightbox

>> Connect a URL to the image

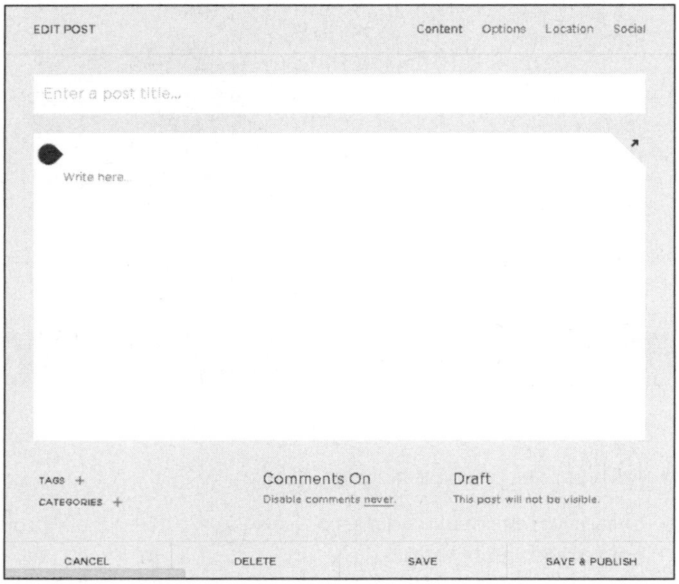

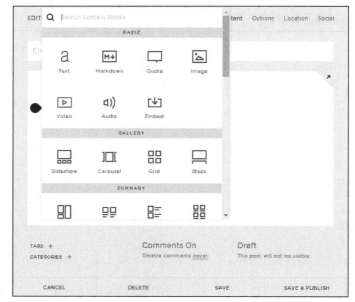

FIGURE 7-7: There are multiple options for your new blog post within the post creation area.

FIGURE 7-8: The block menus within your blog post allow you to add non-text content.

TIP

The drag-and-drop option to add images is becoming more and more popular. If you're used to uploading files to add graphics to your content, now may be a great time to give the drag-and-drop method a try!

Importing content from other platforms

One of the most exciting features of the Squarespace platform is the ability to import content from other blog platforms. For example, should you choose to move from a Blogger blog to a Squarespace site, Squarespace has methods in place to make that happen quite easily.

To import content from another platform, you need to access your settings menu in your home sidebar menu by following these steps:

1. **Under Settings click Advanced.**

2. **Click Import/Export.**

3. **Click Import.**

4. **Select the platform from which you want to import content.** The choices are as follows:

   - V5

   - WordPress

   - Tumblr

   - Blogger

   - Etsy

   - Shopify

   - Big Cartel

5. **Follow the steps specific to your particular platform and click Begin Importing.**

Should you choose to move your Squarespace blog to a different platform for any reason, you can export your content using the same menu.

REMEMBER

Squarespace offers a free, 14-day trial and the option to export your content elsewhere should you decide to move your blog to a different platform.

Customizing and Connecting

One of the best reasons to consider a Squarespace blog is the variety of customizations available to you through the Squarespace sidebar as well as the ease of connectivity to social media. Although getting your blog up and running is clearly your focus, after you've done so you'll want to take a look at both linking to your favorite social networks and utilizing the tools at your fingertips thanks to Squarespace.

Linking your social networks

Social media, covered in more depth in Chapters 17 and 18, provides bloggers with an amazing tool to promote their content and grow their online community. One of the easiest ways to utilize this tool is to connect your blog directly to the social media platforms where you are already active.

To get started linking your social media accounts to your blog, return to your home menu in the left sidebar and choose Settings followed by Connected Accounts under Website (see Figure 7-9). This area is the social media hub of the Squarespace platform and will allow you to connect your site to the most popular social media services on the web.

FIGURE 7-9:
The Connected Accounts menu allows bloggers to connect their site to social media services.

To choose which accounts to connect to your blog, click the Connect Account button on the left sidebar. A menu of social media sites appears, as shown in Figure 7-10.

FIGURE 7-10:
Use the Connect Account menu to select which social media accounts to connect to your Squarespace blog.

Linking your content to your social media channels to promote your content is a great start, but this menu area also allows you to connect beyond just social media. Squarespace allows you to connect to the following accounts among others:

- » Email
- » Dropbox
- » Flickr
- » YouTube
- » Spotify
- » iTunes Store
- » Foursquare
- » Yelp

Using the Squarespace sidebar

As you may have noticed by now, the Squarespace home sidebar is an integral part of your Squarespace blogging experience. Not only is this where you can go to change everything from your basic account information to your billing preferences, but the sidebar also allows you to customize your website from top to bottom. Some of the features of the sidebar include:

» **Blog Menu:** This area allows you to change your blog and page titles, determine how many posts are displayed per page, create a blog description, and more.

» **Settings:** The settings section is divided into general, website, and commerce. From these areas you can change your billing information, update your blog's basic information, and change security settings among other options.

» **Metrics:** The metrics area of your home menu allows you to monitor your blog's traffic, track your RSS subscribers, and even find out what search queries readers are using to locate your blog.

» **Help:** This area of the sidebar takes you to helpful articles and videos as well as an area to search common help topics.

3

Fitting In and Feeling Good

Chapter 8

Finding Your Niche

I f you're blogging only for your friends and family, you probably have a captive audience that stays interested no matter what you choose to blog about on any given day. Most bloggers, however, define blogging success as attracting, keeping, and growing an audience of interested readers who can't wait for the next pearl of wisdom or touching story.

Creating this kind of blog is no small challenge: You're in competition with every other source of news, information, and entertainment in your audience members' lives. One key to blogging success is finding a niche and exploiting it fully. This chapter provides you with ideas and suggestions for you to begin thinking about what blog niche is a fit for you. It also provides you with tips on finding others blogging in that subject area, what they're doing right, and how you can make the most of your personal niche.

Deciding What Belongs on Your Blog

You may find picking a niche and sticking with it tough to do. Fortunately, blogging gives you a lot of leeway in handling a subject, evolving your own style, and choosing what you blog about. The medium allows for a lot of experimentation, and your readers will likely welcome new approaches and ideas while you go.

To begin your blogging journey, however, you probably want to pick one broad theme and then explore within that theme. Do you like books? Why not blog about what you're reading and make recommendations? You can then take a natural leap to movies based on books, and then authors . . . and onward from there. Starting with a simple idea can give you a lot of room to grow.

Some subject areas have worked as popular and successful blog topics already. You can join existing blogging communities and start a blog about

>> **Your kids:** Blogs are a great online tool that parents can use to document their parenting experience and their children's growth. The parent blogging community is on the rise in a big way for both moms and dads. Talk about a topic that has an infinite variety of discussions, products, problems, and cute photos!

>> **Your hobby or interest:** Blogs are beautifully suited to help you make connections, so feel free to use yours to become part of a community of folks who share your passion for knitting, sport fishing, geocaching, carpentry, or whatever your interest is.

>> **Technology:** Many of the original bloggers chose technology as their focus — a great decision. People have a huge interest in technology and technology issues today. After all, everyone uses technology throughout her day, and everyone experiences problems doing so!

>> **Politics:** Because of its often polarizing and sometimes divisive nature, political commentary and criticism makes for great blog fodder. A number of popular political bloggers have even turned their online punditry into thriving careers in traditional media as commentators.

>> **Specialized news:** Offer a service for your busy readers by aggregating all the news on a particular topic, including quick tidbits and links to sources. You can create this kind of blog for both serious and comic topics — from cranial surgery techniques to coverage of the latest teen sensation.

>> **A personal diary:** If your life is full of crazy adventures, colorful figures, drama, passion, and ludicrous jokes, you can stick with the tried-and-true blog subject: You. With a unique voice and great writing, you can attract readers who can become friends.

>> **Deals and coupons:** One of the most active online communities consists of deal-seekers. If you love deal matching and coupon finding, this may be your perfect blog niche.

>> **Do-It-Yourself and lifestyle:** Do you look at trash and see treasure? Is organizing a hobby rather than a burden? The world of lifestyle, design, or DIY blogging may be a fit for you!

The following sections look at each of these topics in a little more detail.

Parent blogging

Generally speaking, parent blogging is memoir-style blogging, detailing the trials, tribulations, and general hysteria of raising children.

TIP

Quite a few parenting blogs start before much parenting is going on — before or during pregnancy — and then proceed through infancy and upward. Don't let the fact that you're not quite a parent yet deter you from starting a parenting blog.

They're often hilarious, often heartbreaking, and so easy to identify with. If you don't have children, you certainly were one once. Frankly, kids are *funny.*

You can find many great examples of parenting blogs out there, including the blog Woulda Coulda Shoulda (`www.wouldashoulda.com`). Mir, a mother of two, writes Woulda Coulda Shoulda, shown in Figure 8-1. Her blog has earned her coverage in *Parents Magazine, Redbook,* and *The Today Show;* inclusion in an anthology; and gigs speaking about blogging at the BlogHer Conference (`www.blogher.com`).

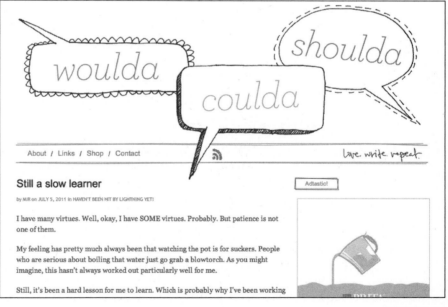

FIGURE 8-1:
Mir's Woulda Coulda Shoulda is a memoir of a mother raising two children.

© Miriam Kamin

Dads, don't think for a second that the parent blogging community is all about moms! The dad blogging community is one of the fastest growing in the blogosphere, with readers, fellow bloggers, and sponsors taking notice. Dads offer a wonderful and often unheard take on parenting, contributing to a seemingly female-dominated topic — what it means to be a parent. Check out the dads at

How to Be a Dad (www.howtobeadad.com), Life of Dad (www.lifeofdad.com), and WhitHonea.com (www.whithonea.com) to get a taste of the vibrant dad blogging community.

Turning your offline hobby into a blog

You probably already have offline hobbies that consume time and energy, and about which you have great passion. You also probably have plenty to say on the topic, but too few people are genuinely interested in hearing you expound about your hobby.

Find your compatriots online by starting a blog about your hobby and hooking into a community of people who share your passion both for the activity and for news and discussion about your hobby. You can find many terrific hobby blogs out there about everything from scrapbooking to jewelry-making to collecting airline safety cards.

One popular area of hobby blogging is the world of crafting. Bloggers who craft typically share step-by-step instructions with detailed photographs explaining their latest project. Readers love to pin their favorite ideas to Pinterest and emulate the blogger's projects in their own homes. Visit Vintage Revivals (www.vintagerevivals.com), Smile and Wave (www.smileandwave.typepad.com/blog/diy), and Homey Oh My! (www.homeyohmy.com) for just a small sample of this booming blogging community.

Talking technology

With so many devices used daily, even the most technologically savvy person needs help from time to time. How often have you brought home a new cellphone, ripped open the box with great excitement, and then failed utterly to figure out how to get your contacts imported? How many times have you uploaded your family's photographs onto your home PC only to realize that you're not sure how to get them back out? We all have the occasional technology question. Technology bloggers have figured this out, writing blogs that explain how to resolve common problems as well as blogs that whet your appetite for new gadgets.

You can find a number of highly successful technology blogs around the web, including some that have been in existence for years and years. Some of these blogs are specialized to a particular kind of tool or software; some are just about conveying the latest and greatest across the field.

If you work in technology or just have a passion for it, you can start a blog about your enthusiasm. That's what Kris McDonald did when she founded Little Tech Girl (www.littletechgirl.com).

Little Tech Girl, shown in Figure 8-2, covers anything and everything about technology. Kris converted her background as a support tech and a self-proclaimed techie into blog success.

**FIGURE 8-2:**
Little Tech Girl is a perfect example of turning a passion for technology into a successful blog.

Getting political with it

No matter where you sit on the political spectrum, you live in interesting political times. You'll never be short of topics, from the latest political scandal to the next national election.

Some of the most popular political bloggers have turned their online musings into full-fledged careers in the media, providing commentary for everything from talk shows to newspaper columns. Conversely, some traditional journalists have bowed out of newspapers and television to move to a blog.

This niche has room for many kinds of blogs, from those criticizing national policy to those covering local school board and city elections. If you have a craving to get involved in politics but don't want to run for office, a blog might be a great way to develop an effective voice. And if you're a politician, you can follow the example of Barack Obama, who used a blog as part of his campaign strategy while successfully running for the presidency of the United States. For some, the urge to sound off on politics has led to incredible blogging success while challenging the establishment. Take, for example, Truthdig (www.truthdig.com), which won four Webby Awards. (The Webbys are the web's equivalent of the Oscars.) Shown in Figure 8-3, Truthdig was started by journalist Robert Scheer and publisher Zuade Kaufman to be a source for political commentary and news that challenges the "wisdom of the day."

FIGURE 8-3:
Truthdig, winner of four Webby Awards, challenges conventional political thinking.

Reporting news

The offline world is full of general news sources — the 200-page newspaper that struggles to appeal to all its readers or the broadcast news show that does local car chases and the weather well — and not much else. Specialized news sources are hard to come by.

Online, the situation is a little different. Quite a few news outlets have opted to offer news personalization features, letting you customize the news that you consume by topics. But many folks who have specialized interests still have to look through a lot of news sources to find truly pertinent stories.

If you're doing that kind of research for yourself, you can start a blog that shares your findings with others interested in the same topic. Are you an economist collecting stories about garbage production in North America? Or a marketing expert who keeps track of the latest guerilla marketing tactics in order to keep on your toes professionally? You can turn this research into a valuable blog for others who share your interest.

You can produce this format quite easily, as well, because posts are frequently just pointers to a news story or article on another website. The value for readers in a blog of this kind is that someone else (the blogger) has already done the work of finding the news, so sending them to another site is actually an important part of the service you're providing.

Quite a few bloggers have opted to develop blogs in a specialized news area and parlayed that success into a new revenue stream or sponsorship, so creating your own news blog might even prove to be a wise business move.

Even if you don't put advertising on your specialized news blog, keeping a blog of this kind demonstrates that you're on top of your field.

Revealing it all

If nothing in this chapter appeals to you so far, perhaps you're looking for the blog classic: journal or diary blogging. Part memoir and part confessional, online journals cover every topic that life can serve up.

Personal diaries can be real snooze-fests or tearjerkers nonpareil. Much depends, of course, on the quality of the writing. But much also depends on what happens in the life being documented. *Life bloggers,* as they're sometimes called, must deal with whatever comes up next for them, from weddings to being fired or hired to being diagnosed with cancer.

These blogs are usually easy to relate to and easy to read; they're also often humorous or heart wrenching, and sometimes both. They take courage to write, whether read by millions or only five.

Sharing a deal

For some, deal-seeking is a way of life, whereas for others it is very nearly an art form. Popular couponing and deal sites are some of the most blogs on the Internet, with readers returning multiple times per day to find the latest savings or to download valuable coupons before they run out.

Andrea Deckard of Savings Lifestyle (www.savingslifestyle.com) has created a site catering to a variety of deal-seeking readers. She covers topics ranging from coupons to deals to general money-saving tips. Andrea has even capitalized on local markets by including deals specific to just the Cincinnati and Dayton areas.

To make it easier for readers to stay up to date on this frequently updating topic, Savings Lifestyle (www.savingslifestyle.com) offers a free newsletter for the savvy shopping reader who never wants to miss a deal (see Figure 8-4).

Design, lifestyle, DIY – oh my!

With the meteoric rise in popularity of Pinterest (www.pinterest.com), it's no surprise that many blogs fit into a visually appealing niche. Bloggers focused on topics such as home design and decorating, lifestyle and organization, recipe creation, and DIY projects often have huge followings, not only on their sites but across social media channels as well.

One such site is Nesting Place (www.thenester.com), written by, of course, The Nester. This work of art provides the reader with insights into the life and thoughts of the author while sharing design tips along with incredible photographs (see Figure 8-5). Readers visiting Nesting Place return again and again, knowing that they'll find not only great content but also tips, giveaways, and fun features such as blogger link-ups where other bloggers may share links to similarly themed content on their own blogs.

Examining a new niche

Have you checked out all the blog topics discussed thus far and nothing feels like a fit for you? Maybe you've given one niche a try but have discovered it's just not for you. The fact is that you can blog about absolutely anything — or nothing! There's even a popular blog comprised of nothing more than photographs of popular movie scenes re-created using cardboard boxes. If you can dream it, you can blog it!

FIGURE 8-5:
The Nester provides design inspiration and insights to her loyal audience.

If you still need a little creative inspiration to get you started, here are some additional blog niche ideas:

- Sports
- Travel
- Fashion
- Photography
- Fitness
- Life coaching
- Health and wellness
- Gaming
- Foodie
- Wedding/event planning
- Education
- Fiction
- Interior design
- Finance
- Pop culture/celebrity
- Pet

- » Automotive
- » Music
- » Religion
- » Humor
- » Homeschooling

You may even choose to combine multiple topics on your blog, creating a hybrid of sorts. After all, our lives aren't one dimensional, so there's no reason why our blogs should be! Stop by Tech Savvy Mama (www.techsavvymama.com), shown in Figure 8-6, to get an idea about how multiple genres can be combined successfully on one blog. Author Leticia Barr writes frequently about tech-related topics from social media safety to technology in education, but as her blog title states, her role as a mother is also very important. She uses her blog as a platform to also write about more parenting-focused topics including personal causes, home organization, and family travel.

FIGURE 8-6: Tech Savvy Mama breaks the niche blogging mold by covering multiple topics on one site.

Learning from the Pros

After you choose a topic, it's time to get to work on creating a highly readable blog. The following sections provide ideas for setting up a blog successfully by cultivating your own talents and observing what others are doing right.

Much of blogging success depends on the quality of your writing and your ability to make a connection with your readers. Work on developing a dialogue with your readers. Life bloggers often create this connection by revealing common, easily identifiable experiences. Businesses can choose to start a blog that gives typically silent members of a company (such as high-level executives or behind-the-scenes mechanics) a connection to customers.

Many blogs are maintained by more than one person; sometimes, contributions by several different people can enliven and enrich the conversation, as well as decrease the workload for any single blogger.

I cover creating great content in Chapter 9, and in that chapter, you can find out how to keep track of what's working for other bloggers.

Lurking on other blogs

You can best figure out what will work on your blog by seeing what's working on other blogs. If you aren't a regular blog reader, find some blogs and start reading!

The old, old Internet term *lurking* describes web users who look at blogs, mailing lists, online discussions, and forums, but don't choose to participate in them. Lurking online doesn't have any negative connotations, though the word does sound kind of sinister.

In truth, lurking can help you find out about what kinds of communication and interaction are appropriate when you're new to a web community or when you're planning to start one yourself. The vast majority of web users are actually lurkers; most people don't do more than read or look at blogs.

Start your lurking career by finding a few blogs that you like, that you regard as competition, or that you find interesting for some reason. If you want to see a blog that has a very active, vocal audience, find one that has a lot of comments and make sure that you read them all. Many of the blogs mentioned in this chapter fall smack into this category, so why not start with them?

If you want to see how a blog evolves, find one that has been around awhile, and look back through the site's archives to see how it got started. Most of all, pay attention to what you find interesting about the blog.

Here are some issues that you can figure out from lurking on a blog:

>> **Posts:** Watch what the blogger (or bloggers) posts about, how often he or she posts, and what days and times attract readers. See whether you can understand what prompts a blogger to post.

>> **Interaction:** Pay attention to the posts that get a lot of comments and responses, and try to understand what gets people talking.

>> **Resource use:** Look for instances when the blogger chooses to include a link, a quote, or other resource, and what it adds to the conversation.

>> **Design:** Keep an eye out for blog designs and styles that you might want to imitate on your own blog.

>> **Sidebar use:** Look at the blog sidebars for cool technologies and tools that the blogger uses (and that you might be able use on your own blog).

TIP

You want interaction with your blog readers, but some comments can cause problems because they're off topic or offensive. Use this opportunity to see how other bloggers handle bad comments. Pay attention to whether a blog comment policy is in place and how the blogger enforces that policy. When does the blogger choose to remove or edit comments? Do you agree with his or her choices? How do you want to handle problem comments on your own blog? I talk more about handling spam and bad comments in Chapter 10.

While you lurk, keep a list of notes and ideas for later reference, especially for items that you think are good ideas but that you aren't ready to implement quite yet. You can easily lose those first good ideas if you don't keep track of them somehow.

REMEMBER

What works for someone else might not work for you, and it doesn't have to. The blogosphere is still young, and you have plenty of room and time to try new ideas. Rules and standards that others have adopted give you a good starting point, but you don't have to use them if they don't work for you.

Participating by commenting

When you're comfortable, start participating in your favorite blogs by leaving comments. Comments can be written quickly, and they contribute to the blog by furthering conversation. After you have a blog of your own, you can use commenting on other blogs as a way to introduce new readers to your site.

Many blog comment forms give you the chance to leave a URL when you post a comment, linking to your site or most recent blog post. Commenting with a link to your blog is a bit like leaving a tiny, unobtrusive ad. When the blogger and his readers see your comment, they may click the link and visit your blog.

REMEMBER

Just as linking to your blog may bring you readers who liked your comment, it might also get you visitors who *didn't* like what you say! You invite disagreement any time you put your opinion out into the world, but don't let that stop you from doing it.

Some bloggers have made the mistake of abusing this little privilege, leaving off-topic comments simply for the purpose of getting a link back. Don't make this mistake. Be a genuine member of the blogosphere and leave comments only when you truly have something to say. You don't want to earn a reputation as a comment spammer!

TIP

Leave comments that distinguish you as a thoughtful contributor to the topic. If you can answer a question posed by the blog post or provide information that seems to be missing, you really contribute value with your comment. But you can also just leave your own opinion, even if you completely disagree with what the blogger is saying.

Reaching Out to Other Bloggers

Don't forget that other bloggers may be your primary audience. These folks are online and already familiar with blogs, and you're likely to find other bloggers with whom you have much in common. Meeting with bloggers in person and communicating with them online are terrific ways to network and market your blog. Bloggers are well known for promoting each other's content on their own blogs and via social media. You might be able to generate additional readership by creating relationships with bloggers!

Meeting in person

Meeting bloggers in person is not only a great way to grow your online community but also provides you with a network of local coworkers. Most cities have an active community of bloggers that you can join:

>> Consider joining the local branch of your Social Media Club. Often, the members of social media organizations are also bloggers.

>> Be sure to include your email address on your blog, and let people know that you want to connect with fellow bloggers. Look for similar information on the blogs that you read if you're interested in getting in touch with a blogger.

>> Look for bloggers who identify their locations, and get to know them on their blogs by posting comments.

>> Visit Meetup (www.meetup.com), and search for blogger get-togethers in your area. Many bloggers network with other nearby bloggers on a regular basis. You can even look up get-togethers when you're visiting a new place.

>> Organize your own get-together and publicize it on your blog, Twitter, or on Meetup.

Using social networks

Social networking sites are designed to connect you with your current group of friends and extend those connections out to their friends. Each site that I mention in this section has a different mechanism for making that happen, and different types of community interaction occur. LinkedIn (www.linkedin.com), for example, is a professional networking site designed to showcase your work background and interests so that you can make connections to others in your field.

You can make friends in social-networking online communities, such as Twitter, LinkedIn, Google+, and Facebook. Social networking sites usually give bloggers a way to link to blogs or even to notify others about new blog posts via profile pages. If you're looking for online connections in the blogging community, these communities are a great place to start.

REMEMBER

In fact, a lot of bloggers regard their blogs as a form of networking, and they're already looking to make these kinds of connections via social networking websites.

Facebook (www.facebook.com) is a wonderful tool for bloggers hoping to connect with other members of the blogging communities. Many bloggers participate in several Facebook groups based on various blogging-related topics from blog niche to blog promotion. After you've connected with a couple members of your blog community, ask them to invite you to join a couple of their favorite Facebook groups in order to meet additional bloggers and learn more about the craft.

Twitter (www.twitter.com) is another fabulous place to find and grow your blogging relationships. Search for hashtags related to your blog niche or even your home city to find the bloggers who are tweeting about the topics that matter to you. Because of the casual nature of this platform, you should feel free to tweet to people and introduce yourself, joining conversations when appropriate.

Google+ (https://plus.google.com) provides bloggers with another opportunity to connect with and grow their blogger communities. Check out your friends' circles to see whom you might want to add to your own. And don't forget to join the occasional Google Hang Out that fits with your blog niche!

Regardless of whether the connections in your social networks have blogs, you can use the site to let them know about your blog. With luck, you'll build up your audience and the participation on your blog by leveraging the goodwill of people you know and the people they know!

Chapter 9

Creating Great Content

Many elements work together to make a blog successful, from a well-designed layout to fancy technical widgets, but none of those elements can substitute for good content aimed at the right audience. In fact, if you write (or podcast or take photos or produce video) incredibly well and you're reaching readers who are engaged by your style and content, you can actually be successful without spending much time at all on your blog's appearance. Amazing content can even make your readers forgive an awkward interface or missing bells and whistles, such as RSS feeds or categories.

So, if you do nothing else to make your blog succeed, focus on producing great writing, photos, audio, or videos. Know what your audience wants and deliver it.

Most blogs include a written component, or are predominantly word based, so this chapter offers pointers on writing well for the web and understanding what your audience expects from your blog.

REMEMBER

In this chapter, I use the word *competitors* when I am describing other bloggers who are covering the same subject area as your blog or trying to reach the same audience you want to attract. Remember that in the blogosphere the atmosphere is very collaborative, which means that competitors can also be friends, contacts, occasional contributors to your blog, participants in your comments area, and good resources for information. So when I talk about competitors, I do so in the friendliest sense of the word!

Knowing Your Audience

First things first: How well do you know your audience? Are you hitting the right notes to attract the readers you want in the quantity you want them?

REMEMBER

Not all bloggers care about the number of readers they get, but they do care about getting the right eyes on their words. Regardless of whether you're number-obsessed or just focused on your niche, you need to understand your audience and what your readers are looking for.

You can get an idea about your audience by

>> Using statistics software to track the number of visitors to your blog and what links those visitors click

>> Noting the content that elicits the biggest and best response from your readers (or the response that you want, even if it isn't the biggest)

>> Looking at the blogs of others in your subject area to see what you can find out from their comment activity, search engine rankings, and other data

You might have to wait awhile for statistics and comments, but you can easily look at others' blogs, even if you're still developing your own blog. I talk in detail about measuring site traffic and statistics in Chapter 19, so jump there if you want to find out more about the readers you already have.

Finding your competitors

To find your competitors, you must first define your own niche. Your niche consists of what you're blogging about, the topics you cover, and what words you use most frequently in your posts. You use these keywords to describe yourself, and visitors use them to find you when they conduct a search on Google, Yahoo!, Bing, or another search engine.

Use these descriptive words (plus the word *blog*) to locate blogs that have similar content to yours. You can also use one of the blog search engines and catalogs, such as Blog Catalog (www.blogcatalog.com), Blogging Fusion (www.blogging fusion.com), Best of the Web (www.botw.org), Twingly (http://www.twingly.com) or Icerocket (www.icerocket.com). Figure 9-1 shows the results of a search on Twingly that used the terms *diy*, *wedding*, *dress*, and *flowers*. These results show posts from blogs that talk about these topics.

BLOG DATA
WITH PASSION

Twingly covers the global blogosphere

We index more than 1.2 million blog posts per day, from all over the world. We add 13,000 new active blogs every day and if that is not enough, you can easily add more yourself and we will cover them for you. Through our easy integrated APIs you get access to all of them at your fingertips!

API SERVICES

FIGURE 9-1: Use Twingly to find your competitors' blogs.

Discovering the secrets of success

While you watch your competitors' blogs, you have a chance to figure out what topics they blog about, of course, but also how they reach out to their audience.

TIP

Your competitors might not be blogging in the most effective way. While you look at these blogs, decide whether your competitors are actually reaching their audiences successfully or whether they're falling short. For example, do their blog posts receive a lot of comments? Has their content been shared often on social media sites?

While you visit these blogs, keep a journal of your impressions. Watch the following to investigate how these bloggers handle publishing and outreach:

>> **How frequently the blogger puts new posts on the blog:** Frequency of blog posts is a big deal. Any blogger can tell you to post "frequently," but almost none can tell you what that really means. I talk more about how often you should post in the section "Writing Well and Frequently," later in this chapter,

but you can explore this idea by noting how often your competitors choose to post to their blogs. Do they create new posts daily, or even multiple times a day? Or do they post a few times a week, or even once a week? When you become a reader of that blog, do you find yourself wanting more content or less?

>> **When the blogger publishes blog posts:** Time of day can have a surprising impact on how readers receive a blog post. You need to reach your audience members when they're likely to be sitting at their computers. If your audience consists of stockbrokers, time your posts so that new content becomes available just before business hours start on the East Coast, not during dinnertime on the West Coast. If you're targeting teens, try to publish before or after school hours, not while they're sitting in homeroom. (Theoretically, they are doing schoolwork at that point and not surfing the Internet!)

REMEMBER

>> Sure, your readers can visit your blog anytime and pick up content that you posted in the middle of the night, but you can impress them with a blog that always seems to have fresh content just when they want it.

>> **The length of posts on the blog:** You might be surprised to know that the ideal length of a blog post is a hotly debated topic among experienced bloggers. Some bloggers swear by the short-and-sweet recipe that guides most web writing: Blog posts should get to the point quickly and allow readers to get back to their busy days with the information that they need. Others find that longer posts — even essays — do the job, keeping readers on the site longer and providing more thoughtful commentary. The topic of your blog and your audience's appetite and available time combine to dictate the natural length of your blog posts. Looking at your competitors' blogs can tell you the number of words that they find optimal in a blog post, which you can use as a starting point for your blog.

>> **When the blogger links to outside websites:** Linking to other blogs and websites is a great way to serve the reader. By pointing out other sources of information or even other blogs, you help them become more knowledgeable about your topic and keep them engaged with it. So, when do your competitors choose to link to other sites, and what sites do they link to? Are the links designed to entertain, educate, or inform? Are links included in the text of the post or broken out at the end? What makes you click a link yourself?

I talk a lot more about linking to other sites as a strategy for reaching your audience in the section "Linking to Serve the Reader," later in this chapter.

>> **When the blogger addresses his or her audience directly:** Many bloggers use a very personal writing style that directly acknowledges the reader, the way this book does. You might enjoy being addressed directly by a blogger

because the conversation feels more personal. Or, depending on the topic of the blog, perhaps a more formal, almost academic approach is more appropriate. Either way, check out how your competition is handling this issue. When do they ask readers for input or feedback, and how do they phrase those requests? Do readers actually respond, and if so, to what kinds of approaches?

>> **Use of multimedia, such as photos, audio, and videos:** Although a whole lot of words comprise most blogs today, photos, graphics, and videos are becoming equally important in the world of blogging. Take a look at how your competitors include multimedia in their blogs. Do they use photos to illustrate the ideas in the posts or just to attract the eye? What about animation or video? Do posts that have these extras get more comments or fewer? Do you like getting information in these other formats or do you find them distracting?

>> **Posts that get a lot of comments and posts that get very few:** A blog that gets a lot of comments signals that the blogger is resonating with his or her audience — even if just to make audience members mad. A blog that has no or few comments probably just leaves people flat (or maybe isn't even read). Not all bloggers get hundreds of comments every time they post. Some blog posts just get better responses than others, and part of what makes bloggers successful is being able to know what makes those posts really work so that they can repeat the success. Watch your competitors' blogs to see when a post gets a big response and look at what kind of response it gets.

REMEMBER

>> Also, watch for the posts that don't get any responses. Try to figure out why those posts didn't work so that you don't make the same mistake!

>> **The writing style of the blogger:** Bloggers need to have good content, and for most bloggers, that comes down to having an accessible and readable writing style. For those blogs in your niche that attract participation and good press, what style does the blogger use? Personal? Professional? Humorous? What tone appeals to readers and makes them come back to the blog again and again? What approach do you find more readable and engaging?

Use these same points of analysis on your own blog. After you have your blog up and running for awhile, take a look at your content with the same critical eye that you use on your competitors. What are you doing right? What are you doing incorrectly?

You may find this exercise hard to do. I'm sure you think that everything on your blog is great; after all, no one sets out to write a bad blog post! Still, some of your posts are likely more popular with readers than others, and if you can figure out why certain posts work better than others, you can repeat that success again and again. In fact, developing a critical eye for your own content can really help you make your blog succeed: This medium doesn't hold still, and you need to adapt your style and content while your audience grows and changes. Consider conducting this kind of survey of your content a couple times a year to make sure that you stay on track and topical to the folks you want to attract, even if you're aiming for just your immediate family.

If you find it tough to view your own content through that kind of lens, but you have a friend or two who get what you are doing and can look at it critically, ask them to do a site review. Just remember, they are giving you opinions and advice, but it's your call whether you implement any of that!

Profiling your audience

When you finish your competitive analysis (which I explain how to do in the preceding section) and after you review your own content successes and failures, picture your audience in your mind's eye.

Create a clear vision of who's in your audience. If you don't have the audience you're targeting at this point, develop a picture of whom you want in your audience.

You don't actually have to draw a picture, though. You can create this profile in words that describe the characteristics of your ideal audience member. You can include anything that you want in this profile, from shoe size to personal hang-ups — any detail that helps you really know this person better and create content for this person on your blog.

WARNING

Don't just say, "My ideal audience is anybody who is interested in [*insert your blog topic here*]." You already know that. Otherwise, this person wouldn't be on your blog in the first place. You want to capture all the details that make this person different, unique, and interesting.

Take From Hip to Housewife, as shown in Figure 9-2. From Hip to Housewife (www.fromhiptohousewife.com) is a blog written by author Nancy Friedman who describes her writing as being "on aging and momming and my twenty year quest to lose the same ten pounds." This tagline combined with categories ranging from family to travel to parenting make it clear the type of reader she anticipates visiting her site.

FIGURE 9-2:
From Hip
to Housewife
clearly shows
readers the
type of content
they'll find.

Some concepts and facts to explore for your audience profile include

>> Age

>> Gender

>> The nature of their interest in your topic (for example, familial, personal, emotional, or professional)

>> Geographic location and proximity to you or to the topic of your blog

>> Lifestyle (for example, workaholic, homebody, retired, world traveler, and so on)

>> Occupation

>> Education level

>> Marital status

>> Interests and hobbies

>> Income range

>> Political leanings

When you have a reader profile in hand, you can be more targeted about what you choose to write about and how you address that audience.

Writing Well and Frequently

Two of the many ingredients for a successful blog are good and frequently updated content. But what does it really mean to provide good and frequent content?

Good content compels, satisfying the readers' immediate interests but leaving them hungry for more. Think of a blog post as being like an appetizer: It should whet the appetite, pique the palette, and sustain the diner until the next course arrives. You don't want to give your readers "annual Thanksgiving dinner" — you want them to come back, come back soon, and come back often.

Blogging is quite a personal, conversational medium, and textual blogs have a strong feel of the author and his or her personality. The first blogs were actually online diaries, and even today, most bloggers choose to use words such as *I* or *my* in their blog posts, creating an intimate and open feel — even on corporate blogs. This *first-person* writing differs dramatically from most corporate communication, which at best refers to the company as *our* and at worst only refers to the company by its full and official name.

Take, for example, one of the McDonald's blogs, Open for Discussion, which was written by McDonald's Vice President Bob Langert. In a post on August 20, 2007, Bob wrote:

RESPECTING COPYRIGHT

As a general rule, anything and everything you see on the Internet is protected by copyright. Copyright is just what it sounds like: It focuses on "the right to copy" an original creation. Copyright law protects an author by giving that right solely to him or her.

Unless the creator of an image or photo specifically licenses his or her copyright to you, you can't reuse it, *even if you give the author credit or link back to the original story*. (This rule applies to text, photos, and videos, too.) But this rule has a few exceptions: You can quote a news story or a blog post on your blog if you use only part of it, and as long as you don't take credit for the work. Commentary and critique also allow you to excerpt a piece of text or other work. But don't think that just because you're the subject of a story or blog post that you have the right to repost the entire article on your blog or website. You don't. When in doubt, ask and get permission.

At www.copyright.gov, get the goods on what you can use on your blog without running afoul of the law that protects other authors' content. You might particularly want to read the areas around fair use, especially if you plan to write reviews.

"We all have one — a pet peeve that we just can't ditch. I was recently reminded of my #1 pet peeve while reading the latest account of McDonald's Moms' Quality Correspondents. They reported that McDonald's beef is 100% pure USDA-inspected beef. Frankly, I don't think this should be any kind of big 'Aha', and I am amazed that so many people question this established fact."

Figure 9-3 shows this post.

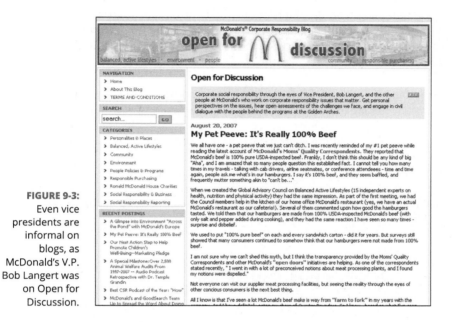

FIGURE 9-3: Even vice presidents are informal on blogs, as McDonald's V.P. Bob Langert was on Open for Discussion.

Writing in the first person isn't as easy as it looks (or reads); after all, most people spend years training to write more formally, and commonly produce all kinds of documents in which first-person writing is emphatically *not* suitable: memos, reports, news stories, invoices, and so on. You may have trouble finding an authentic, genuine voice that really feels comfortable. My best advice is to just practice, practice, practice.

If you'd like your blog to have a casual tone, think of your blog posts as being like letters or emails. Speak directly and simply, as you would in a personal note or letter. Try not to overthink your words, but don't go right into stream of consciousness (fun to write, hard to read).

TIP

One of my favorite techniques for making my blog posts readable is to read my post out loud. If it sounds close to something I might actually say in conversation, it hits the right tone for a blog post — on my blog, at least.

REMEMBER

If you make your blog informal and conversational, you still shouldn't ignore spelling, grammar, and sentence structure. Some bloggers do opt for an unedited approach, but keep in mind that people have more trouble, not less, reading poorly formulated writing. If you have a professional blog, or ever hope to make money from your blog, you definitely need to pay attention to spelling and grammar because these little details influence your credibility. Do your readers a favor — use the grammar and spell-check functions of your word processor — and proof-read, too.

WARNING

Many bloggers like to quote news articles and blog posts, and then expand on them. If you take this approach, make sure that you understand the rules of copyright law when you use someone else's words — it's always best to ask permission! For more, read the sidebar "Respecting copyright."

TIP

Although it's important to update your content frequently enough that your readers don't assume you've abandoned your blog, you also don't want to inundate them with new content — or worse, force yourself to write mediocre content just to post something.

Linking to Serve the Reader

Links — you need 'em. You may worry that by providing a link to a news story or online article, you're sending your readers away from your site into the black hole of the Internet, never to return. Your readers might, in fact, click the link and go read the article. But they probably won't forget where they found the link.

TIP

When adding a hyperlink to your blog content, be sure to change the outgoing link settings to "open in a new window." This keeps your blog post open on the screen rather than sends the reader away.

On a blog, links are just as much a resource as any other information that you provide. In fact, many blogs actually consist of collections of links around a topic or theme, pulled together to inform or entertain the blog's readers.

REMEMBER

If you're providing good content and expanding on that content by using links, you're doing your readers a service that they won't forget — one they likely come back to you for.

Kelly Whalen doesn't shy away from adding links to her blog posts on The Centsible Life (www.thecentsiblelife.com), as shown in Figure 9-4.

FIGURE 9-4:
Kelly Whalen adds links to her blog posts, helping her readers get more information.

In a December 21, 2015, post guiding readers to meal-plan, Kelly included links to everything from menu-planning printables to recipes used.

Links are the currency of the blogosphere. A lot of bloggers point their readers to blog posts that they find especially interesting, even going so far as to quote the other blogger. In general, bloggers are generous about linking to other blogs and websites because the favor is frequently returned. As the saying goes, "You have to spend a little to make a little."

WARNING

Adding links to your posts is a good thing . . . unless you're irresponsible about what you link to. Take your responsibility as a publisher seriously, and don't send people to suspect resources or throw them into an adult-oriented site without warning.

TIP

When you link to a blog post, be sure you link to the permalink URL, not the blog's home page. A *permalink* is the unique web address for an individual blog post — the permanent link to that page. You should use the permalink because the blogger might update the blog any time after you create the link, pushing the post that you mention down or even off the blog's home page.

The Web Style Guide (`www.webstyleguide.com`) covers everything from good web design standards to graphics production, but you can probably benefit most from Chapter 9 of the guide, which covers links, titles, and common online styles.

Breaking Through a Blank Screen

At times, even outstanding bloggers hit dry spells and can't think of a word to write. You can safely anticipate a day sometime in the life span of your blog when you literally have nothing to say to your readers, no matter how much enthusiasm you have for your topic.

This phase will pass, but sometimes, you need a little help pushing back to a productive spot. Here are a few tips for making it through your dry spell:

>> **Stockpile a few evergreen posts.** In newsrooms around the world, journalists regularly create *evergreen stories* (stories that can be printed or televised at any time and still be interesting). You can also put together a few evergreen blog posts that you can keep on hand for use on a day when your creative juices temporarily dry up. You can also use these kinds of posts for days when you're sick or on vacation but still want to have something publish on your blog. A lot of blog software allows you to schedule a publication date for a blog post in the future, so you can even set these posts to go up automatically while you take a well-deserved break.

>> **Ask a friend to guest blog for a few days.** Bring some new perspective to your blog when you have none left yourself by asking a friend, colleague, fellow blogger, or even critic to write some blog posts for you. Your readers might enjoy the change of style and tone (and if they don't, you make them that much happier when you come back!). Be sure to return the favor when your guest blogger has a dry spell of his or her own.

>> **Recycle an oldie but goodie.** When you can't think of exciting new content, bring out a great post from your archives. New readers appreciate seeing something they missed, and old readers might find new information in a second read. Professional blogger Darren Rowse points his readers to a list of best-of posts on ProBlogger (`www.problogger.net`). In fact, Darren pulls out

the best posts of all time, for the month, for new readers, and just some of his favorites (see Figure 9-5).

>> **Post a photo.** Rather than 1,000 words, put up a single photo. Take a picture of where you usually blog, show off your new laptop, or just take a walk in your neighborhood. You can dig out a photo of yourself as a kid or show that embarrassing haircut you had in the '90s.

>> **Post about the books, movies, or television that you're consuming.** Tell folks about the other media you're enjoying. You can even hook up an Amazon Associates account and earn a little money from your recommendations. (You can find out how to set up this kind of account in Chapter 20.)

>> **Give out your favorite recipe.** Dig out the cookbook and find your grandmother's fudge recipe or your mom's apple pie recipe and share it with your readers. Better yet, take a break from the computer and make the recipe yourself so that you can put up a photo with your post.

>> **Blog from a new location.** Sometimes, breaking the routine can shake loose those recalcitrant brain cells. Try blogging from another room in your house, or head to the local Internet cafe or coffee shop.

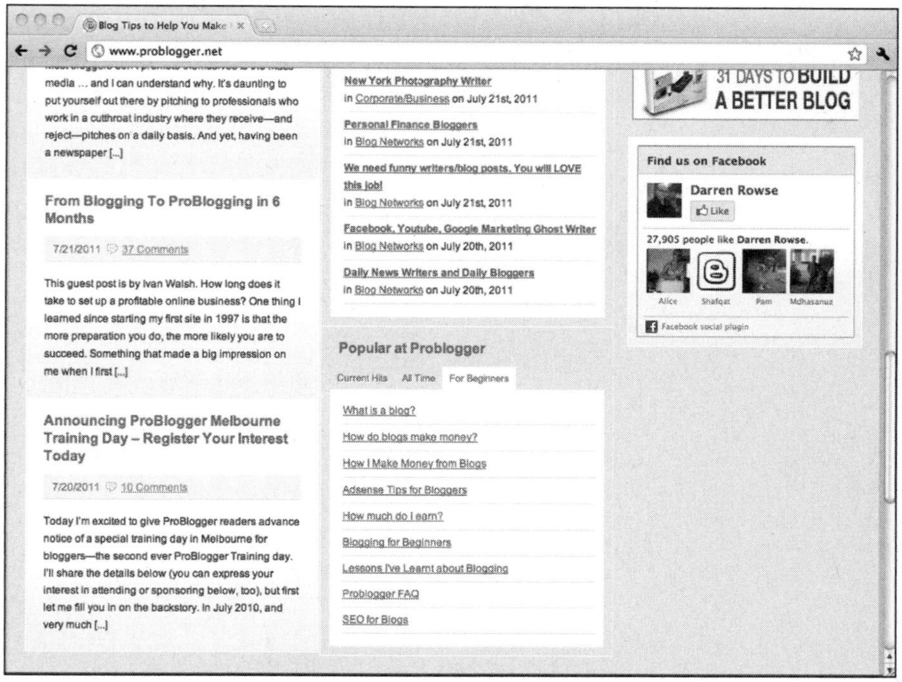

FIGURE 9-5: Darren Rowse points people to favorite posts from the past.

>> **Record an audio podcast or video blog (vlog).** If you can't write, talk! You might be pleasantly surprised and make this a regular feature of your blog. Chapters 13 and 14 cover podcasting and vlogging extensively.

>> **Do an interview.** Ask a friend, colleague, neighbor, child, parent, boss, or public figure whether you can interview him or her for your blog. Type up a few questions, email them off, and when the answers arrive in your inbox, a little copying and pasting should do the trick.

>> **Take a quiz.** Let your readers know what superhero you are or what color your personality is by playing with some of the fun quizzes and polls online. The Superhero Quiz is at www.thesuperheroquiz.com (I'm Spider-Man), and you can find loads of others on blogthings (www.blogthings.com) and Quiz Meme (www.quizmeme.com).

>> **Ask for suggestions from your readers.** Appeal to your readers for help with finding new topics to post about. Also, look through your old posts and see whether you can expand on a post that worked well; check out comments and emails from readers, too!

Chapter 10

Building Community with Comments

I n my opinion, every blog should have comments. Love them or hate them, they're an integral part of blogging. In the days before the explosive popularity of social media, comments provided the main source of interaction between bloggers and their readers. Comments allow visitors to your blog to ask you questions, share their opinion of your post, suggest your next blog topic, or even just leave a note to say hello.

Unfortunately, as interesting and thought-provoking as comment conversations can be, they're not without their challenges. Comment spam and negative commentary can take the joy out of blogging and make managing comments on your blog feel like a hassle.

How you handle your blog community determines your level of stress and success. In this chapter, I talk about how you can set your own comment rules and monitor your community. I also give you tips about how to make your blog a positive place for conversation, as well as provide strategies for dealing with spammers and negativity.

Getting Interaction Going with Comments

Comments are an important part of a blog. When a blogger opts, through choice or necessity, to turn off commenting, the blogger inhibits some of what makes blogging such a dynamic, exciting medium: the interaction between blogger and readers. But it's not only the blogger who loses out when he or she removes comments: Many blog readers enjoy the comments left by others and often form a strong community feeling for fellow visitors, even interacting with each other within the comments.

TIP

Writing a particularly sensitive post or simply experiencing an influx of negative comments on one blog post? Most blog software allows you to turn off the discussion or comments section by post. Feel secure keeping comments open on the rest of your blog while taking a chance with your writing, without the worry of negative feedback, on just one post.

For some bloggers, the main issue with comments is often related to time. A popular blogger can get hundreds of comments on a single blog post, and it takes time to read and respond to those comments, much less remove any inappropriate comments. Spam can also lead a blogger to restrict comments. Just as with email, spammers have discovered that they can throw their unwanted commercial messages (anyone need a refinance?) into blog comments, using the user profile forms to drop spamming links. Even with the best blog software, some spam messages may still end up on the blog, needing to be caught and removed by the blogger.

Still, the vast majority of blogs allows comments, and those blogs benefit hugely from the interaction and fun that comments can generate. On a blog such as The Bloggess (www.thebloggess.com), readers enjoy interacting with author Jenny Lawson and each other. Jenny even used the comments section of one post to host a "give a book, get a book" event she called Booksgiving. Now that's a great use of comments!

Getting involved

REMEMBER

If you want to have a dialogue with your readers, you need to allow comments on your blog, whether you're reaching out to your parents or to your customers.

Just because your blog posts have a comment form, though, doesn't necessarily mean that people just jump in and start commenting. You need to tailor your posts to elicit dialogue and feedback, perhaps even by going so far as to ask specifically for responses.

BLOGS THAT HAVE ACTIVE COMMENT COMMUNITIES

While you experiment with comments, see how sites that have vibrant, active communities handle the onslaught of opinion and discussion. The following popular blogs have developed an involved and vocal audience that you can explore:

- **Scary Mommy** (www.scarymommy.com): This blog that began as the personal online journal of mom Jill Smokler transformed into a community confessional for other moms who are sometimes shockingly open about their less than perfect parenting. Jill often takes a hands-off approach to comment moderation, allowing community members to keep each other in line and foster an environment in which readers feel safe to share.

- **Nuts About Southwest** (www.blogsouthwest.com): Folks from all levels of the Southwest Airlines organization post to this blog, which covers topics such as new boarding procedures, dress codes, and food offerings. Judging from the hundreds of comments on some posts, Southwest is getting plenty of feedback from its customers on experiences with the airline.

- **Truthdig** (www.truthdig.com): This news website has won multiple Webby Awards for Best Political Blog in both the Juried and People's Choice categories. The site combines commentary on current political issues with book reviews, podcasts, and interviews, and it gets loads of feedback from fans and critics.

TIP

If the comment areas of your blog look a little bare, ask some friends to help by reading and commenting for a few weeks. Comments tend to generate more comments, if you can get the ball rolling.

Of course, the problem might lie with your content or approach, so don't be afraid to experiment with your topic or style to try to get better results from your comment forms.

Clearly building a community of readers on your blog is important to you if you plan to include a comment function on your posts. Here's a quick checklist of tips for cultivating comments on your blog:

>> **Make it easy for your readers to comment.** Sometimes readers find locating the comments area of a blog difficult. Make sure that your blog design not only provides a highly visible area for existing comments but also clearly leads readers to the area to submit new comments. Consider choosing a format that asks for new comments at the top of the Comments section rather than requiring readers to scroll through all existing comments before being allowed to respond.

>> **Ask questions of your readers.** Get your readers to start participating by requesting advice, seeking information, asking them to suggest a related item (such as a recipe), or responding to a question you pose at the end of a post. The simple act of asking can do wonders for comments. Ask your visitors to tell you stories, answer inquiries, or give advice. For instance, if you're blogging about a frustrating travel experience, you might ask your readers for tips for the future. Or, if you're looking for a new laptop bag, ask your readers to recommend bags that they like.

TIP

>> Specific, rather than general, questions work best to start a conversation.

>> **Request topics or ideas.** Requesting ideas about your blog topics can generate an amazing response. You may also invite readers to send in blog posts they write that could benefit the community of your site. (If you make this invitation, make sure that you're clear about who owns the copyright! As the publisher of the content, you probably want to have the guest bloggers assign copyright to you.)

WARNING

>> A word of caution about allowing guest posts: Post a clear guest post policy on your site, and be prepared for advertisers to try to take advantage of your generosity by asking you to post their promotional content for free. Allowing guest posts can create a slippery blogging slope.

>> **Communicate with your readers.** Make sure you're actively talking to your readers by responding to the comments that they leave on your blog. If you use comment moderation features, try not to leave comments pending for too many days.

>> **Blog about timely or controversial topics.** Readers tend to have opinions about current events or polarizing topics. Blogging about these themes cashes in on the likelihood that your readers will have something to say.

Also, get involved with your blogging community. Visit other blogs and use their comment systems to get involved with their readers. In return, if you're active enough with your comments, those readers visit you, as well.

WARNING

Be sure to always comment sincerely when visiting other blogs with the hopes of building readership. Hopping from blog to blog leaving comments with links back to your site is considered spamming and may get your comments tossed in the trash!

Enabling comments

Most modern blog software, regardless of whether it's hosted or installed on your own web server (see Chapter 3), has tools that allow your visitors to comment and tools that allow you to handle the comments you receive. Check your documentation to figure out what functionality the software you're using offers — and don't forget that you may be able to customize the way in which your comment tools are configured to better suit your preferences and audience.

If you use blog software that doesn't allow comments and you don't want to change software, third-party comment solutions may be available. In fact, many bloggers who use top-of-the-line blog software opt to use another tool for comments because they want specific functionality or design.

One such tool is DISQUS (www.disqus.com), which offers a truly impressive range of functionality options — plus, it's free! You can use it to

>> Allow visitors to sign in via social media.

>> Allow visitors to rank comments on the site or reply to a comment directly.

>> Allow visitors to flag comments as inappropriate or spam.

>> Sort how the comments appear, either by date or popularity.

>> Moderate comments to remove, edit, and screen out unwanted content.

Another popular and free comment plug-in is Livefyre (www.livefyre.com). Livefyre includes a variety of unique and helpful functions, including

>> Automatically import comments about your post left on Facebook and Twitter.

>> Allow readers to add photos and videos to their comments.

>> Allow readers to like comments left by other readers.

>> Allow users to flag questionable comments.

Two other popular comment plug-ins are Commentluv and Facebook Comments. Both plug-ins are available in a free version. Commentluv is popular with readers because it allows them to link to their most recent blog post, encouraging them to leave a comment in order to build traffic to their own blogs. Facebook Comments requires readers to connect with their Facebook accounts in order to leave a comment, and each comment will appear not only on your blog but also on the commenter's Facebook Timeline. Although this plug-in exposes your blog to new readership via readers' Facebook profiles, it can be bothersome and even prohibitive to some readers who don't want to share their blog reading habits with their Facebook community. If you choose to use Facebook Comments, consider offering readers an alternative commenting method.

Managing Comments

If all goes well and readers begin to leave comments on your posts (success!), you will need to budget time to manage and respond to these comments. Although I believe the resulting community dialogue makes that effort worthwhile, I can't deny that managing comments involves real work and time. In the following sections, I talk about ways you can set up your blog for comments, prevent possible problems, and deal with problems if they do crop up.

Establishing community guidelines

You want comments, but you want the *right* comments for your site. Ideally, your visitors provide on-topic and interesting feedback that encourages conversation with other readers. Of course, we don't live in an ideal world, so setting some community guidelines for participation on your site can help clarify your expectations to your readers. Make those guidelines straightforward and clear. Your rules may exclude anything you want. Common blog rules outlaw comments that include

>> Racist or bigoted speech

>> Sexually explicit content

>> Discussions or descriptions of violent or criminal acts

>> Unlicensed copyrighted material

>> Threats, harassment, or personal privacy violations

You have to enforce these rules, but simply having them in place can deter troublemakers from posting at all, particularly if you're scrupulous in enforcing your guidelines quickly.

TIP

Although some bloggers attack writing with a no-holds-barred attitude, others prefer to keep the space PG rated. It's okay to ask your readers to follow your personal guidelines when adding to your posts with their comments!

The blogging software solution that you use might also have a set of standards in place with which both you and your visitors must comply. For example, Wordpress.com (`https://wordpress.com/`), a hosted blogging solution, places responsibility for content found within comments on the blogger (see Figure 10-1). Every hosted blogging service has its own set of rules that you should be aware of. Don't get caught breaking the rules!

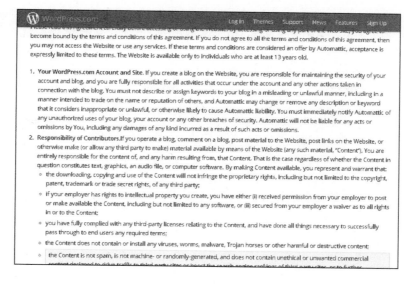

FIGURE 10-1: Wordpress.com includes comment content guidelines in the blogger Terms of Service.

REMEMBER

Over time, you may need to adapt any guidelines that you create, especially while your blog grows in popularity or changes its focus. Be sure to set a time every so often to review your own guidelines and make changes. You might include your visitors in the development of the community guidelines, checking with your readers about what you do to protect them. They'll love you for it.

Figure 10-2 shows the blog comment policy on Pistol Packin' Dad (`www.pistolpackindad.com`), a site about one man's passion for gun ownership. The site's author makes it very clear to his readers that although debate is welcome, respect is required. He also expresses his right to delete comments at any time. Remember, your blog is yours! If a comment makes you uncomfortable, you do not need to allow it to remain on your site.

Like Jason from Pistol Packin' Dad, Amy from Selfish Mom (`www.selfishmom.com`) makes it clear to her readers that their comments are welcome but she maintains the final say regarding what remains posted on her site. As she states in her policy, "Play nice, or else." You can read her entire comment policy at `http://selfishmom.com/full-disclosure/`.

TIP

If you're thinking about writing a blog comment policy, take a look at what other bloggers have done. A quick search on Google for **blog comment policy** turns up some well-done policies that might give you ideas. And remember, you can add a blog comment policy at any time and amend your policy as needed.

FIGURE 10-2:
Pistol Packin' Dad displays a very clear blog comment policy for its readers to follow when responding to blog posts.

The figure shows a web page for "PISTOL PACKIN' DAD — From Sport to Self-Defense, Sharing my Passion as an American Gun Owner" with navigation links: GUNS & GEAR, DEFENSE, FAITH, NEWS, SAFETY, SECOND AMENDMENT, LAW, STORIES, CONCEALED CARRY, and Home, About, Contact.

My Comments Policy

The World Wide Web is all about conversation. But a few simple guidelines can keep the conversation from becoming a shouting match that discourages others from participating.

Here is my comments policy. By posting on my blog, you are agreeing to the following:

1. **You may post anonymously.** I don't recommend this, but you may do so if you wish. However, you must provide a valid email address in order to make comments. Your email address will not be publically visible. I may change this rule if it abused.

The Latest from Pistol Packin' Dad
- Carrying at Home
- Long Trigger Pull
- My New Nightstand Gun Safe: Barska Biometric Safe
- Happy Independence Day
- The Assault Weapons Controversy

Editing comments

Sometimes, a reader posts a legitimate comment that you need to alter in some way. For example, you might prefer to remove profanity from otherwise legitimate comments or edit a long web link that's breaking a page layout. Whatever the situation, edit a reader's comments delicately.

Some of your readers might react poorly to having their words edited, and of course, the last thing you intend is to insult a reader by pointing out spelling or grammar issues. Use a sensitive hand, but remember that a comment on your blog is as much a part of the conversational give-and-take as your original blog posts. Not only that, but you're also responsible for the words on your blog and may feel that you have a duty to remove hateful or offensive language, especially if young audiences read your blog.

REMEMBER

Your blog is your domain, your kingdom, and your place in the world, so your word is final.

Of course, when you choose to edit a comment, you might want to alert readers that you have done so and why, as has been done in comment #7 on Buzz Marketing with Blogs (www.buzzmarketingwithblogs.com), shown in Figure 10-3. You may also want to lay out in your blog comment policy circumstances in which you'll edit comments. Both these techniques can head off accusations of censorship.

An edited comment

FIGURE 10-3:
If you need to edit comments, let people know that you've done so and why.

Deleting comments

Unfortunately, not all the comments on your blog are fun to read or even should stay on your blog. When it comes right down to it, you control which comments appear on your blog, whether you moderate them ahead of time or afterward. You need to moderate comments because quite a few of your blog's comments probably come from spammers and add nothing to the conversation. But sometimes you may need to delete comments from real people that are even on topic. Despite potential criticism from readers, every blogger has to make a choice about what kinds of comments to delete.

Bloggers choose to delete comments for several reasons:

>> Comments are off-topic for the post to which they're attached (a common issue with spam comments).

>> Comments make personal attacks on the blogger or other readers. For example, many bloggers draw the line at comments that contain racial slurs, name-calling, hate language, or speculation about things such as sexual orientation. People who leave these types of comments are often called *trolls.*

>> Comments left anonymously or by using a fake name and email address.

>> Comments feature a URL apparently included for marketing purposes.

>> Comments are libelous.

>> Comments are obscene.

>> Comments contain private information (which you don't want to make public).

>> Comments contain plagiarized material.

TIP

In blogging terms, a *troll* is an individual who posts irrelevant and often inflammatory things in blog comments. Trolls try to get an emotional response out of people and can be quite disruptive. Most blogs won't see any troll activity, but if you become popular, they will make an appearance from time to time.

REMEMBER

Deleting comments is quite a personal decision, one that any good blogger runs into. After all, you want to get people talking, so you need to have opinions that can start dialogue.

Moderating comments

The single best solution for keeping spam off your blog is to read each and every comment left on your blog individually, removing the comments that are spam or inappropriate. Sifting through your blog's comments is called *moderating*. Moderating your blog comments can add overhead to your blogging time, but if you're dedicated to making your blog successful and useful to your readers, it's time well spent.

You have several options for how you manage the time that you spend looking through comment lists, but the method you choose as your primary line of defense depends on how your community grows.

You, your community, your software, or a combination of all three can moderate your blog. Table 10-1 covers the pros and cons of three approaches that you can try. Some bloggers have strong preferences at the outset, but you can experiment with the best setup for your blog and readers.

TIP

You can choose to keep new comments in a pending folder without creating a permanent backlog of harmless comments from trusted readers. Many bloggers elect to require comment approval the first time or two that a reader comments, later allowing all future comments from that email address to appear immediately.

You can most easily maintain your sanity by using a combination of the methods in Table 10-1 to control spam. If your site becomes a popular location for online discussion, experiment with these methods to find one that suits you and your readers while letting you keep enough time in your schedule for actually writing new blog posts!

TABLE 10-1   **Comment Moderation Options**

Approach	Pro	Con
Review all comments *before* they're posted on your blog.	No spam ever appears on your blog unless you choose to allow it.	Comments are delayed before they're posted, making your blog not very spontaneous and rather slow-paced.
Review all comments *after* they're posted on your blog.	Comments appear on your blog more quickly, making conversation quick-paced.	You must review and remove unwanted comments frequently, probably daily.
Ask your readers to notify you of inappropriate comments.	Cuts down on your comment moderation hours by pointing you to problem comments quickly.	Turns your readers into police, a role that they might enjoy too much or not at all, changing the conversational tenor.
Let software weed out the bad stuff.	Using a combination of blacklists and whitelists (see more on these technologies in the section "Blacklists and whitelists," later in this chapter) means that you don't have to read through a lot of spam yourself.	You need to keep the software up to date because spammers always work out new ways to cheat the system, so budget time for behind-the-scenes technical work; software is ineffective against personal attacks or flames.

TIP   Some blogs have communities that build quickly, whereas others take more time. You might need to change your spam-prevention methods from time to time to take advantage of the community desire to help.

Recognizing Spam Comments

Spam! It's everywhere, lurking in your email inbox, waiting to pounce on an unsuspecting click. It also hangs out on your blog, hiding in the comments — you might never escape it! Fortunately, you can slow the stream of spam messages and even block most of them from appearing on your blog.

The first time you see a spam comment on your blog, you might not recognize it. Long ago, you could easily pick out the spam posts on blogs: They consisted of incomprehensible text, inappropriate images, and links to pornographic websites. But while the blogs evolved, so did the spammers, and today's spam comments might look like anything from a sincere compliment to a request for more information. Figure 10-4 shows a spam comment that was left on a blog.

REMEMBER   You — your brain and eyes — protect your blog from the outside world. If something looks suspicious to you, check it out so that you can protect yourself, your readers, and your search engine ranking.

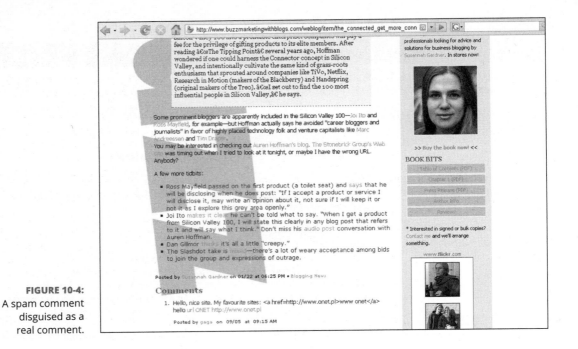

FIGURE 10-4:
A spam comment disguised as a real comment.

Because you're the first line of defense, you need to get a feel for the comments that are legitimately posted on your site. Take some time to see what your community is like. If your blog community needs time to grow, venture out onto other blogs and see what people are saying:

» Look at real comments and see how they're written.

» Get involved and add your own commentary to other blogs. The more experience you have at posting comments, the better you can identify the spam on your site.

When you take the time to read real comments, you can more easily spot the spam.

TIP

Spammers often find your blog through search engines. Rather than leave comments on your newest content, they are more likely to land on a popular post from the past. See a new comment on an old post? That's your first clue that it may be from a spammer!

Spam has certain styles. Spammers attempt to weasel into your site by looking as though they have personal or generally harmless content. Sometimes you can't tell a legitimate comment that has poor grammar and spelling from a spam comment that has similar attributes. Spammers count on this confusion. You may find sorting the wheat from the chaff a tricky bit of business, but by following a few tips, you can get through the spam onslaught with as little frustration as possible. Examine the following types of comments with skepticism:

>> **Personalized and customized messages:** A real human being creates this type of spam, as opposed to an automated bit of programming. Usually a human being, paid by a spam company, visits your blog, reads a few posts and a few comments, and then customizes messages that fit in with the tone and style of the site. Often, the spammers even direct these messages to you by name. You can easily miss these messages when you're watching for spam comments.

If the link that's included with a comment isn't related to the subject of the comment or the topics on your blog, the comment is suspect no matter how on-topic it might seem.

>> **Generic commentary or questions:** The generic message spam either requests that you do something or makes a very nonspecific remark. You often see comments such as You've got the same name as I do, Have you seen the new video?, Check out my blog?, Need you to do something for me, or Your blog is broken you need to see this.

>> **Flattery:** Finally, spammers use flattery. Spammers may send comments such as "Your blog is awesome" or "I like your blog, click to read mine." As a general rule, regard these kinds of brief praise with suspicion (well, unless your blog really is awesome, of course!). Real fans usually elaborate more about what they like about your writing.

TIP

In general, a spam comment includes a link, usually to an advertising website or a site designed to look like a blog. The spammers hope that you or your blog visitors click the link, giving those spammers a traffic boost and potentially allowing them to collect a fee based on the number of times users visit the site or click a link. Look closely at comments that include links.

Many comment spammers are annoyingly ingenious about finding ways to disguise their messages. (Some aren't — you can easily recognize as spam the comments about Viagra or the ones that contain gibberish.) But the generic nature of comments gives them away. Keep your wits about you so that you can identify new trends and formats in comment spam techniques when they appear. The techniques described in this chapter can help you prevent or remove spam, but the human brain is endlessly inventive, which keeps the spammers a step ahead of any software solution to the problem.

WARNING

Don't just leave comment spam on your blog and let your readers sort through the mess. Spam attracts spam: If you don't remove these kinds of comments, you actually end up with more spam on your site. And when your readers click the spam links, spammers realize that you're not tending your blog, so they flock to it. Delete your spam. Your readers will thank you.

Unfortunately, spam isn't the only unwanted comment material you might deal with. Some of your legitimate commenters may use language that you don't want on your blog or post personal, offensive *flames* (or attacks) aimed at you or other readers. You're just as entitled to remove this kind of comment as you are to remove spam. In most cases, you can use the techniques described in the following section to handle flames and spam comments alike.

UNDERSTANDING WHY SPAM EXISTS

Junk snail mail, email spam, and blog spam all exist for the same reason: because someone, somewhere, makes money on them. You may find this fact hard to believe if you just look at spam comments — a lot of them don't really make much sense, much less look like something you might click.

But spam comments aren't necessarily designed to make you or your readers click them. Blog spammers usually just want to raise the search engine profile of a site that they link to in their comments. Search engines use secret formulas to determine the result listings that you see when you do a search. The formula works to determine and display the most relevant results — the ones that best match your search terms — at the top of the list. One of the ingredients in this secret formula is the number of websites that link to a site, and another ingredient is the words used for that link.

So, when you write a blog post about a company that has a product you love and link to the company, you're really doing it two favors: You've praised it publicly and you've given it a little boost in the search engine rankings, which helps it come up a little higher the next time someone searches for the product you reviewed. Aren't you nice? Now imagine that ten more customers do the same thing on their blogs. The company gets a lot of search engine love for all those different links.

Spammers are trying to scam this process by creating dozens, even hundreds, of links from many different web pages to the website that they're attempting to boost in the search engine rankings. When a site appears high in the search engine rankings, you know what happens: More people visit it more often.

Ultimately, comment spam might simply want to get people to visit a particular website, but it takes a fairly indirect path to that result. After someone opens the website, the unfortunate visitor might get a chance to buy a product, click a link, provide information that he or she shouldn't about bank accounts, or view a page that has ads on it. And that's where the spammers make profit.

REMEMBER Don't avoid blogging just because of the amount of spam you're bound to get. After all, junk messages aren't anything new. You see spam in your email all the time; heck, you even see it in your snail mail box, and you probably aren't about to stop getting mail delivered, right?

Fighting Spam with Software

Spam is a pain. But consider how much spam you really have to deal with: Do you get three spam messages every few weeks, or are you getting 500 an hour? If you're receiving only a few every month, you might not need to install any software because you can moderate the few problem comments yourself pretty easily. If your blog gets dozens of comments every day, however, spam fighting can take up a lot of your time. The following sections explore some of the many blog software solutions available to make this task a little faster and easier.

Protecting your comment form

The tools described in the following sections are designed to give spammers trouble filling out the comment form on your blog. These tools try to prevent the spam from ever reaching your blog so that you don't need to deal with reading and deleting it.

REMEMBER These tools do that job fairly well, but they also present something of a barrier to people who want to leave a legitimate comment; remember, you want to cut down on spam, not real comments! Keep your audience's needs and abilities in mind when you implement any spam-fighting tools.

CAPTCHAs

A *CAPTCHA* (an acronym for something really long and boring) is a challenge-response test, meaning it's a question that your reader must answer correctly in order to post a comment. On a blog, CAPTCHAs are most commonly implemented in such a way that humans can complete them but computers can't. A CAPTCHA on my Resourceful Mommy contact form (www.resourcefulmommy.com) requires the would-be commenter to duplicate the letters and numbers shown in an image in order to submit a comment, as shown in Figure 10-5.

CAPTCHAs were created to stop spammers from adding comments to blogs by using automated scripts that try to fill out any web form that they find, especially blog comment forms. But spammers are inventive: Some blog comment scripts can now recognize letters and numbers in an image, so many sites that use CAPTCHAs distort the text by stretching it, or layering it with graphic random graphic elements.

WARNING

Many readers (and fellow bloggers!) find CAPTCHA gateways to comments to be annoying and aggravating. Although this is a great line of defense against spam, you may not want it to be your first one.

Other sites use CAPTCHA questions that are simple for humans to answer, such as trivia or mathematical questions. For example, "What color is a red balloon?" These kinds of CAPTCHAs are an updated version of the original CAPTCHAs and have become a fairly popular tool for bloggers.

Your blog software may have CAPTCHA technology built in, or you might be able to add one by using a plug-in. Check your blog software's documentation and support tools for suggestions on installing and configuring a CAPTCHA system.

User registration

Registration is a popular option with larger communities, especially online forums. The community requests or even requires that users who want to leave comments sign up for a user account. These accounts are typically free, but to complete the registration process, you must provide a name and valid email address, thereby cutting down on the number of spam scripts that can create an account and therefore post comments. Sites that require registration actually prevent anyone who isn't registered from leaving a comment; sites that simply request registration reward registering by recognizing members or by marking a registered user's comments in some highlighted way.

This setup lets you keep a record of everything that a particular poster adds to the system, easily identifying your most frequent contributors and visitors. Also, if a poster gets out of hand, or an automated spam system acquires an account and posts by using that username, you can simply close the account and stop the poster from posting again by using that account.

Blog software is increasingly offering registration, so be sure to check your documentation. If your software doesn't offer registration, look for a plug-in that does.

Screening for spam

Software that filters the incoming comments in various ways can provide a defense against spammers by identifying and removing comments that look like spam. These filters give a blogger great tools: They run all hours of the day and they don't require any effort on your part. But an automated process is never as smart as a human, so you might occasionally lose a valid comment if you use a filtering system.

A third-party software solution called Automattic Akismet (see the sidebar "Akismet," later in this chapter) is the clear leader when it comes to spam filtering, though many blogging software applications have added their own internal tools, as well. Check to see whether your blog software has any of these technologies in place for you to use; you can probably find some of them available. If you don't, check www.akismet.com to see whether you can add Akismet to your blog.

Keyword filtering

Keyword filters can help you identify incoming comment spam. This kind of filtering is probably the oldest type of protection for blog comments. It might not work all the time because spammers have become much smarter since this technology was first used. Spam filtering usually works by comparing incoming comments against lists of words and/or phrases associated with spam. Matches indicate spam, and the filter yanks those comments.

Keyword filters are typically updated frequently to keep up with the ploys that spammers use. Some of these lists contain web addresses and other computer identification information as well as keywords. Users also can submit and maintain their own lists in case custom spelling or other methods of tricking the anti-spam system come into use (for example, using V1agra rather than Viagra).

Several services over the years have allowed different blog tools and platforms to take advantage of a central keyword listing. These lists are maintained and updated by a third-party company. Today's most popular antispam system, Akismet (see the sidebar "Akismet," later in this chapter) falls into this category.

One problem with this kind of filter system is that some spammers leave nice messages that include bad links. These messages get past the filter because they aren't offensive and don't violate any rule that you have.

Blacklists and whitelists

A blog *blacklist* is a method of keeping spam off your website by preventing certain known spam systems from accessing your comment system or your website as a whole. By specifically identifying spammers from certain addresses, countries, or computers, or by using certain URLs, you can block those individual spammers, keeping your blog much safer.

Most blogging software comes with a blacklist system built in or a system that you can easily add by using a plug-in or third-party solution. Consult your blog software documentation to be sure that you understand how to keep your blacklist up to date and how you can contribute to the blacklist.

Whitelists perform the opposite action of a blacklist by specifically permitting certain visitors or types of visitors. A *whitelist* is a preselected list of visitors whom you know won't post spam on your blog. Bloggers use a whitelist in conjunction with a blacklist. Whitelists can allow you to accept comments from visitors who have been misidentified as spammers in the past. Essentially, you're making your blog accessible to certain people or computer networks. If you want to guarantee that your mother, for instance, can always post to your blog — or even if you want to set it up so that she doesn't have to comply with a CAPTCHA or other antispam techniques — add her to the whitelist so that she can post with impunity. Whitelists are uncommon, so if your blogging software doesn't offer this functionality, you probably can't find a good third-party solution.

IP banning

Similarly to blacklists, IP banning prevents certain IP addresses or a range of IP networks from accessing your website. IP banning is probably the oldest method of protecting blogs.

An IP (Internet Protocol) address is a series of numbers that identifies a network, a computer, or any networked electronic device within a computer network. Devices such as printers, fax machines, desktop and laptop computers, and some telephones can have their own IP addresses.

Many blog software solutions offer lists of banned IP addresses that they collect from other users of the same software who have identified spammers, and you can automatically update your own list to prevent those spammers from posting to your site.

A potential problem with banning networks or certain IP addresses is that the offending poster may connect via a different IP address the next time that he or she posts something. Banning by IP address can work for known spam companies, but it's highly fallible because so many computers regularly obtain new IP addresses through their Internet Service Providers (ISPs). IP banning can also affect people whom you don't actually want to block. For instance, if you block a computer on a particular network, others who use the same network but are blameless might end up using the offending IP address at some point and be blocked. Many bloggers discount IP banning, saying that it has no real usefulness in today's mobile world.

Dealing with Coverage on Other Blogs

You can't do much about negative blog posts or comments about you on other blogs, although many a blogger has stayed awake all night worrying. (It doesn't seem to help.) You can easily post a comment that responds, but you may not want to respond when you're feeling angry and emotional because you may post something you would regret.

REMEMBER

You're taking part in a public conversation, and free speech means that people can openly express their opinions about you, your blog, your opinions, your business — you name it. You can find negative criticism hard to take, especially when you feel it's unjustified. Before you send off an angry email or post a vicious comment, sit back and take a little time to consider your options. If you can be objective, try to understand exactly what the other person is criticizing and whether the critic has a point.

Here are four ways that you can handle a case in which another blogger posts a negative statement about you or your blog:

>> Point to the negative coverage on your own blog and get some other opinions on the issue without taking a position yourself.

>> Ignore the post and comment about it only when someone specifically requests your opinion.

>> Post respectful comments on the blog in question and constructively add to the conversation there.

>> Counter the criticism, in a respectful manner, on your own blog.

Whichever path you choose, make sure that you deal with the comment in a respectful manner. You can easily escalate a conflict online because you don't have to deal with people face to face. The anonymous feeling people get when they're on the Internet can lead them to behave in ways that they wouldn't in person. Try to take the high road as much as possible, if only because an uninvolved reader is more likely to see you as right if you handle things more courteously than your critic.

In some cases, criticism of an individual or business on a blog has led to legal ramifications, from copyright violation to libel. If you feel that the negative comments about you online might fall into the legal realm, consult with a lawyer about the best course of action.

REMEMBER

You might not be the only target of criticism: Some bloggers use their blogs as a way to publish attacks on everyone, from public figures to private individuals. Some other bloggers might even attack your readers and ignore you. Deal with these kinds of situations quickly and with as much care as you can provide. Think of yourself as the referee in a situation that involves personal attacks from one member of your audience to another, and look for ways to defuse the situation and prevent future occurrences.

Chapter 11

Blogging Anonymously

E ver been on a blog and had difficulty figuring out who is writing it? That might be intentional, especially if the topic of the blog is sensitive. Many bloggers who want to be heard in a public forum prefer to do so without using their real names.

Perhaps you are thinking about blogging about politics but hold a position where your political views shouldn't be common knowledge. Maybe you're a survivor of childhood abuse who wants to contribute to current discussion and help other adults, but without having your identity become common knowledge. You might work for an employer that you believe is engaging in unsafe business practices and feel ethically obligated to share that information; getting fired would mean you don't have access to office information any longer. Or perhaps you have a personal journal that details your essentially mundane life, but would just prefer for others not to know who you are.

Many bloggers rely on (perceived) anonymity to keep one aspect of their lives from becoming attached to the others. However, the nature of the Internet and digital identity means that it can be surprisingly easy to connect the dots from one Internet service to another. As potential employers, family members, potential relationship partners, and others research you, they may find information you want them to have, mixed right in with information that isn't appropriate. An Internet search on your name might return your over-the-top Instagram pics in the same list of results as your professional resume. Anonymity seems like the answer.

REMEMBER

Before you start down the path of anonymous blogging, it's worth really asking yourself the question of whether it's worthwhile to put something online if it would cause a problem if it was linked to you. The single best way to prevent others from finding out information you want kept private, or information you don't want your name on, is to keep it out of the public eye. And let's be clear: The Internet is as public as it gets.

WARNING

Please regard this chapter as a resource, guideline, and starting point, and not a recipe for guaranteed anonymity. Technology and laws change, and although what I say here may help protect your identity, it should not take the place of you doing your own research and of making your own decisions about what to publish. This is especially true if you are using this book some time after its publication or are outside of North America. Basically, I make no guarantees that following this advice means your identity will remain unknown.

Also, this is not meant to protect you from being caught for doing anything illegal. Don't break any laws, and if you do, don't post anything about it on the Internet. Seriously.

Deciding How Much Anonymity You Need

The reasons for a decision to blog anonymously may be widely varied, and so are the potential consequences of being found out. What this means is that not every blogger needs the same level of identity protection. A teenager dishing on his friends might not want to get caught, but if he is, he's unlikely to face the risk of criminal prosecution (or worse) as would, say, a political activist in a country where free speech is not protected.

Give some thought to the level of protection you need as well as to what might happen if your identity is exposed. If speaking your mind on your blog puts you at risk for jail time, physical harm, or prosecution, you clearly need to take the utmost levels of precautions as you go about setting up and publishing to your blog. You may even want to seriously rethink joining the blogging world.

TIP

Don't need to blog anonymously, but don't want readers to have easy access to identifying information such as your mailing address, phone number, and even just your last name? Register your domain using private registration so that your contact information will not appear in a WHOIS domain ownership database search. For just a couple dollars more at the time you purchase your URL, you can also buy a little peace of mind. See Chapter 3 for more information about domain registration.

Those who choose to blog about topics their employers might object to, or even to blog about their employers, clearly also need to be very careful, although the consequences of being identified here are likely to involve finances rather than physical safety.

The next question is whether anyone is going to pursue discovering your identity. There are also those who might simply prefer to keep some facets of their lives separate from others. A soccer mom might prefer that her kids don't stumble across her personal musings on sexuality, for example, or rather that their friends' parents don't stumble upon such a blog and connect the dots.

Having said that, keep in mind that anytime you reveal yourself as the author of an anonymous blog, even to a trusted friend, you crack the door open a little wider to that information becoming public. Many anonymous bloggers have been exposed not through complicated technical detective work but because someone chose to leak a secret.

TIP

Do you plan to blog anonymously yet still interact with the blogging community at events and conferences? Create social media accounts matching your pseudonym so that your blogging friends don't accidentally tag your personal account when posting pictures of you together.

While you're thinking about risks, consequences, and who might put two and two together, pause and give some thought to others who might be harmed if your identity was revealed. If you can be identified, and you've blogged about friends, family, former relationships, employers, and others in unflattering ways, or revealed sensitive information about them, you're creating the possibility of consequences affecting their lives, too. Risks that might be acceptable for you may not be so for others, particularly if they are put in harm's way unknowingly.

TIP

I recommend that you read through this whole chapter before taking any of these steps, because I move from low- to high-level precautions; if you decide you need to set yourself up at the highest level, some steps described later need to be done first.

Going Anonymous

Clearly, you shouldn't use your own name or photo on your anonymous blog. Beyond that, there are still other basic precautions you should take while setting up protections for your identity. Most of them are based on good common sense.

Although this chapter outlines steps to take to blog anonymously, I cannot stress enough that there is no way to guarantee anonymity. If you are not willing to risk having your identity discovered, do not pursue blogging anonymously.

Establishing a pseudonym

It's obvious, but I'll say it anyway: No matter who you are, what your blog is about, or what might happen, every single anonymous blogger needs a *pseudonym*. A *pseudonym* is a fake name, preferably one that doesn't cleverly suggest your real name or provide any clues to who you really are. For example, "CEOsecretary" isn't a good pseudonym for that blog you write about how much your employer irritates you, but "Fed Up Worker" will do just fine.

If you have created an account on a social networking service, or really any sort of membership website, you may have been asked to create a username to use on that site. It might be tempting to use that nickname on your anonymous blog, but don't do so. You're much better off to choose a new pseudonym, one you've never used before.

Setting up a new email address

The next step in anonymity is to set up a new email address using your pseudonym. Regardless of the blogging service you decide to use, they all require you to have an email address to get started, and you can't use an email address that is associated with any of your real identifying information.

Create an entirely new email account (and don't use any identifying information in the account settings). As well, don't import your contacts.

You can find many free webmail services out there. Ideally, you want to choose a service that offers a secure connection, such as Gmail (www.gmail.com) or RiseUp (www.riseup.net). A secure connection means that your visit to the email website can't be spied on by technical snoopers. You have a secure connection if you can get to the email website prefaced by https:// instead of http://.

Choosing passwords

How many times have you used the same password when signing up for a new web service? If you're like me, it's a bunch! Most people I talk to admit that they have one or two passwords they use in rotation, one that might be a little more secure than the other, or one that they use whenever there is a credit card involved.

Let me tell you a little story: Ravelry is a very popular knitting social network (www.ravelry.com). Now, Ravelry is a great site for knitters — hardly a high-value target. The site also doesn't ask for much personal information and doesn't store financial data or other important records. But in June 2011, the site was targeted by hackers who managed to break into a server and capture many of the Ravelry community usernames and passwords. Although the passwords were encrypted, Ravelry was concerned that the hackers might be able to crack them. Ravelry recommended that all Ravelry members change their passwords on the site and stepped up security precautions.

But there are larger implications for any Ravelry community member who might have used the same username and password on another site. If a hacker tried those usernames and passwords on another, more sensitive site, such as a bank site or a photo sharing site, some of those usernames and passwords would probably work. Long story short, choose unique usernames and passwords for any service that you really want to protect — like an anonymous blog.

TIP

Ideally, you should choose passwords that contain a variety of lower- and upper-case characters, as well as numbers. You can even use some punctuation characters. Don't choose a password that spells out a word, even if you replace some of the letters with characters or numbers, and definitely don't use a password that is the name or birth date of a family member or pet.

It's a good idea to change your passwords frequently. It's also a good idea not to write down your passwords or record them anywhere (especially on your computer). Of course, none of this does you any good if you can't remember your passwords as a result, so experiment with some set of good password practices that still lets you log into your services.

I'm a fan of the Norton Identity Safe Password Generator (https://identitysafe.norton.com/password-generator) which lets you generate a random set of characters to create a truly strong password.

Starting your anonymous blog

Your safest bet to maintain your anonymity is to choose hosted blogging software (I talk more about this in Chapter 3) that doesn't require you to have a domain, web hosting, or to buy a license.

Two options are

>> WordPress.com (www.wordpress.com)

>> Blogger (www.blogger.com)

REMEMBER

Be sure to sign up using your anonymous email address and to leave out any identifying information in the account information, name of the blog, and so on.

WARNING

Be cautious about what sites you include in a link to; linking to any of your friends or linking to your own nonanonymous blog is a quick trip to outing yourself.

Being time and location aware

One way you might inadvertently give clues about who you are is to suggest what time zone you are in based on when you post to your blog. Consider changing the times and dates of your posts so that they go live at times when you might be asleep or otherwise occupied, but don't go so far as to never post at a time that would be appropriate for your time zone.

Changing the time and date also divorces when you're online and posting from when the post is published, which makes it a little harder to correlate Internet access to a specific person. This can help if someone is trying to track down your identity by accessing log files of when your computer is on the Internet, or when your blog software was accessed.

Approaching Content Cautiously

You are far more likely to be identified because of *what you are writing or posting* than anything else. Be extremely careful about details that provide clues to who you are, where you are, what you do, and so on.

Be very cautious about giving specifics. Here are six examples:

>> The number of employees in your workplace

>> Your geographic location

>> Your profession

>> The stores you commonly shop at

>> The names, numbers, breeds, and descriptions of your pets

>> The names of friends and colleagues

Any single detail likely won't be enough to identify you, but cumulatively they may paint the picture for a savvy reader. This becomes a bigger issue over time: The longer you blog, the more information about yourself you have provided.

Remember that photos are records of a particular time and location, so if you put one on your blog that you took, you're telling the world that you were at that location at that time. It's a good idea to remove that photo from your computer and your camera card, and certainly you shouldn't post it anywhere else on the Internet. You also want to scrub any meta information out of the image itself.

TIP

When it comes to your subject material, you should be especially careful to understand whether you are violating any laws in what you say. For bloggers, the main concern is libel. *Libel* is any seemingly factual statement that is both false and damaging to a person's reputation.

Publishing harmful information about another individual is a good way to get him interested in figuring out who you are so that he can stop you or pursue legal action.

Stepping Up Security

Now let's talk about the big guns. You have a blog and you *really* need to make sure you aren't identified as the author. For starters, don't do anything that involves making a credit card payment, such as register a domain name, buy a blog software license, or sign up for web hosting. Your credit card information isn't on your blog, but a financial transaction that ties you to the domain of your anonymous blog is a quick route to identification.

REMEMBER

Many of the other precautions involve a fair amount of technical know-how. Remember that I am giving you the basics, and use this as a jumping-off point to do more research!

Understanding IP addresses

The primary technical consideration for maintaining anonymity online has to do with your IP address. An *IP address*, or Internet Protocol address, is a numeric identifying number assigned to every single device that connects to the Internet, from your computer to your smartphone. An IP address identifies the device uniquely and works like a mailing address to tell other computers how to find that device.

Every time you go online, you leave a history that includes this IP address, whether all you do is send an email or post a comment on a blog. This means that if you set up an anonymous blog and the IP address of the device you use to post to the blog can be traced to you, the blog can be attributed to you as well. In fact, some web-mail services even include the IP address as part of the header in email messages you send.

An IP address can be permanent — a web server is typically always located at the same IP address — or it can be dynamic, which is the case for most home comput-ers on the Internet. If you access the Internet via an Internet Service Provider, sometimes the IP address is assigned at the time you actually connect to the ser-vice. That means your IP address changes, but it can still be traced to the ISP and the right legal pressure can force an ISP to give up the records of which customers used what IP addresses when.

TIP

Curious to know what your IP address is? Visit www.whatismyip.com and you see the number at the top of the page.

Clearly, hiding your IP address is necessary for the highest level of identity pro-tection. This is not a simple process, but there are ways to do this. The resources at the end of this chapter can help, and you can also look into:

>> Anonymizer (www.anonymizer.com)

>> Tor (www.torproject.org)

Using software safely

Even after you implement a good IP address strategy, there are some other impor-tant technical ways of protecting yourself. You may not need to do all of these, but remember that every additional precaution lessens your chances of being identi-fied. Here are seven recommendations:

>> Use a web browser that is up to date and known to be conscientious about security holes. Mozilla Firefox is a good choice; Internet Explorer is not.

>> Run your browser in Privacy Mode (Private Browsing in Safari).

>> Install and regularly run antivirus software on your computer.

>> If you write your posts on your computer, delete them from your computer and use software intended to permanently remove files from your computer. The Mac makes this easy — simply choose Secure Empty Trash from the Finder menu. On the PC, look into installing software such as Ccleaner (www.piriform.com/CCLEANER).

>> After you go online to post to your blog, make sure to clear your cookies, passwords, and browser history. The technique for doing this will vary depending on which browser you are using, so be sure to read through the documentation provided to make sure you know how to accomplish these tasks. Clearing your history means that your computer is clean if others use it or it is lost. You should also do this if you use a public computer.

>> Be cautious in how you participate in commenting on blogs, using forums, or signing up for services using your anonymous identity. Many of these services collect IP addresses when you post to them, or when you sign up.

>> Blogging in public is a double-edged sword. On the one hand, using a publicly available computer — in a library or Internet cafe — means muddying the waters in terms of who posted to a blog from that computer. On the other hand, if you're in public, others can likely view your screen, you yourself can be seen, and you don't know what software might be on the computer you are using.

Keeping up

Keep up to date on the technical issues involved. Don't assume that you've set things up that will protect you permanently. The Internet is a very fluid place: Technology and tools change constantly, and having all your bases covered today is no guarantee that you will be safe tomorrow. For instance, simply upgrading your browser to the latest version has implications for security!

This goes for legal issues around anonymity as well. Know the laws in your country, or those that apply to you, so that you can be deliberate about what laws you violate (if any) or what the consequences might be if you are identified.

Resources

Above all, don't take my word for any of this! You should do your own research so that you can blog anonymously with confidence. Here are four resources you may want to read:

>> How to Blog Safely (About Work or Anything Else), Electronic Freedom Foundation (www.eff.org/wp/blog-safely)

>> 5 Reasons to Blog Anonymously (and 5 Reasons Not To) (www.problogger. net/archives/2011/06/28/5-reasons-to-blog-anonymously- and-5-reasons-not-to/)

>> Anonymous Blogging 101: a Quick and Dirty Primer (www.problogger.net/ archives/2010/07/04/anonymous-blogging-101-a-quick-and- dirty-primer/)

>> Hints and Tips for Whistleblowers (http://ht4w.co.uk)

4
Going Beyond Words

IN THIS PART . . .

Making your content pinnable with images

Creating podcasts and drawing an audience for them

Discovering vlogging (video blogging) and why and how to do it

Managing diversity and a large following by creating a forum for your blog readers

Chapter 12

Working with Photos

I t's a fact: People love photos! In this image-driven online world, including photos and graphics within your written content is quite nearly a requirement. You can increase your readership and decrease your writing time by including photos in your blog posts or putting photo badges (code you can place on your blog that shows off your photos) into your sidebar. Many bloggers have discovered that including a photo in a blog post, even if the photo is only tangentially related to the post, ensures that more people read the post than read entries without photos. Most importantly, including images and graphics within your posts makes them more shareable on social media, especially platforms such as Instagram and Pinterest where photos are king!

If you own a smartphone, then you already own a decent digital camera. If you have access to the Internet, then you're set with photo-editing software! Chances are that without ever picking up a traditional camera or purchasing a single editing program, you already have the tools at hand to start putting photos into your blog quickly. But in case you're new to photography, this chapter also includes information about choosing a digital camera or software.

Putting graphics on your site is incredibly easy, and today's wonderful photo-sharing websites and photo-enabled blogging platforms make posting photos online quick and easy. In fact, if you already have a Flickr account that you use to share your digital photos, you can jump right to the section "Inserting Photos into Blog Posts with Flickr," later in this chapter (though this is not at all necessary). You'll be pleased as punch to find out how easily you can do it.

Getting Equipped

Most people today own a digital camera or, at the very least, a phone or tablet that allows them to take digital images. Most digital cameras can take photographs in file formats that you can use on the web with no further processing, but you can also pick up software that helps you convert your photos to the right format quite quickly. Some cameras shoot photos in particular formats, some of which are not web compatible, so you have to convert them into web-friendly formats like JPG and GIF. (I cover the more nitty-gritty details of web-compatible file formats and photo editing in the section "Editing Photos," later in this chapter; if you're in the market for a camera, make sure that you know in what format or formats the camera captures pictures.)

The ingredients to getting photos onto your website are

>> A digital camera, smartphone, or tablet

>> A way to get your photos from your camera onto your computer, such as a USB cable or storage card

>> Image-editing software that can help you crop, resize, and touch up your photos (included on some blog platforms)

>> A photo-sharing service or blog software that has file-upload tools

The following sections cover these items in detail.

Picking a digital camera

Digital cameras come in all kinds of price ranges and with tons of different features. When you take a photograph, the image is saved on a storage card or small hard drive, and most cameras have a nice preview screen that lets you see the results of your photography right away.

When you need your photos, you can remove the storage card from your camera and then insert it into the card reader hooked to your computer, or even into a printer. Some cameras may allow you to transfer photos to your computer via Wi-Fi or even email images to yourself. You may want to have a removable storage card if you plan to take a lot of pictures because you can easily carry several cards with you, switching them out when you fill one. Some cameras can also connect directly to your computer.

REMEMBER

Digital cameras usually come with several quality settings that determine the resolution of your image and the sizes that look good when you print your photograph. If you choose higher-quality settings, the resolution is higher, and the file sizes are also larger. This means fewer images fit on your storage card, but the resulting photos look better, print more sharply, and can be resized more easily than lower-quality images. Web images are usually compressed so that the file sizes are reasonable for visitors to download, but taking images at higher-quality settings (which usually means that the resolution is also higher than is needed for the web) gives you more options down the line and better looking photos even after compression.

Today, even relatively inexpensive digital cameras and even most smartphones take high-quality images suitable for use in almost any medium, so the real challenge is to pick a camera that suits your picture-taking style.

Be realistic about how you plan to use the camera and how comfortable you are with it when you look at the options:

>> **Digital SLRs:** If you're a professional photographer or a dedicated amateur, you likely want a high-end dSLR camera. But these cameras are quite large, which makes them awkward to carry and use unobtrusively on a day-to-day basis. They can be expensive, too.

>> **Low-end point-and-shoots:** If you're a photography amateur, super lightweight cameras can get a lot of admiring glances. But they might lack important features, and their tiny size might also make them hard to use and hold steady.

>> **Midrange:** If you're not a professional photographer but want more than just the basics that low-end cameras provide, look for a camera in the midprice range. These cameras come in a range of styles and sizes and with a wide range of features designed for use by completely inexperienced to professional photographers.

>> **Mobile cameras (phone and tablet cameras):** Almost all smartphones come with cameras built in — convenient, but the photos may not look as wonderful as those taken with higher-end cameras. If you plan to use your phone to take pictures for your blog, keep that in mind when selecting your phone. Some phone cameras rival point-and-shoot cameras!

After you have an idea about what kind of camera you'd like to purchase, visit a site such as CNET (www.cnet.com) or Digital Photography Review (www.dpreview.com) to read reviews of specific cameras in your preferred category. Even if you find the best price online, I recommend visiting a store first to make sure that you feel comfortable handling that particular camera.

Choosing photo-editing software

Many computers and digital cameras come with the software that you need to upload, organize, and sometimes even edit your photos. You may still choose to find additional software or online tools to edit and organize your images. You have loads of options, at all pricing levels including free. When you're looking for image-editing software with the ultimate goal of getting your images online, consider these criteria:

>> **File formats:** You need to be able to create images in the right format for display on the web. These formats are JPG, GIF, and PNG. These formats also allow you to compress the file size of your images for the web.

>> **Standard editing tools:** At a minimum, you need image-editing software that allows you to resize, crop, rotate, and adjust brightness and contrast in your photos. These tools should be quick and easy to use.

>> **Organizing tools:** Look for software that helps you keep track of your images by using thumbnail previews, naming schemes, and search, especially if you take a lot of photos.

>> **Photo sharing:** You don't need a program that integrates with the blogging tool that you use or with a photo-sharing service such as Flickr, but it can reduce the time it takes to post a photo online. I discuss inserting photos with Flickr in the section "Inserting Photos into Blog Posts with Flickr," later in this chapter.

REMEMBER

With these ideas in mind, don't forget to think about whether you want an image editor that can do more than just get photos into shape for online publication. If you plan to print photographs, be sure to look for photo-editing software that has good tools for printing.

I cover two software programs (Google Photos and iPhoto) in the following sections. Other image-editing programs also work well for touching up and formatting photographs:

>> **Adobe Photoshop Elements:** Under $100; version 9 and higher support Windows and Mac (previous versions support only Windows); www.adobe. com/products/photoshop-elements.html. This program is suitable for users who have the patience to figure out how to use a full-featured program but don't need professional features, such as the capability to produce color separations for high-end professional printers. Photoshop Elements is a great compromise between basic and high-end software.

>> **Adobe Photoshop Lightroom:** $9.99 per month; Mac and Windows; www. adobe.com/products/photoshoplightroom. This software is intended specifically for photography. Serious amateur photographers and professionals find this program valuable for managing large collections of photographs.

>> **Adobe Photoshop:** $19.99 per month; Mac and Windows; www.adobe.com/ products/photoshop. For anyone who isn't a designer or very serious photographer, Adobe Photoshop can be overkill. But this program can make your photos look especially great if you are willing to pay the premium price.

Advanced editing tools and more control over the quality of the images you are using for your blog put this package heads and shoulders above the more basic toolset of Adobe Elements.

Google Photos

`http://photos.google.com`

Google Photos, shown in Figure 12-1, is free and works especially well for photographers who want to put photos online. It has highly developed organizational tools, allowing you to do everything from automatically importing and naming photos from your camera when you hook it up to your computer, to quickly labeling and tagging your photos, to rating good photos, to creating photo albums. You can automatically upload images from all your devices and even save edited photos on those devices after editing online.

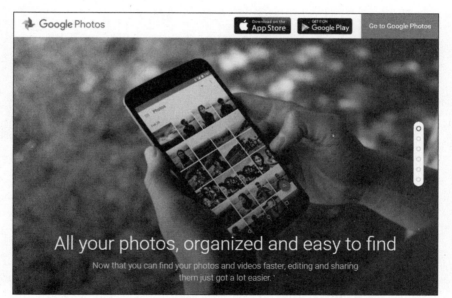

FIGURE 12-1:
Use Google Photos to quickly import, edit, and share photos.

Google Photo includes both incredible photo-editing tools as well as sharing tools, even for friends and family not using the app. You can use tools to email photos, get them onto the web, create online slideshows, and put photo collections onto other devices. You can also print photos quite easily and create slideshows with music and captions.

iPhoto

`www.apple.com/ilife/iphoto`

If you're a Mac user, you have a great image-editing program in Apple's iPhoto (see Figure 12-2). It gives you all the basic tools for cropping, straightening, adjusting color and brightness, and resizing. Plus, you can dabble with fun effects, and increase or decrease highlights and shadows in your photos.

FIGURE 12-2: iPhoto is Apple's solution to image-editing and organization tools.

iPhoto also comes with excellent organizing tools: You can categorize, tag, caption, and title your photos quickly and easily, and the simple search interface helps you find old photos.

You can use iPhoto for more than publishing your photos on your own blog. Share your photos via email directly from iPhoto, or post your pictures via Facebook, Twitter, Flickr, Messages, or using the iCloud Photo Sharing system.

You can also use iPhoto to print a real photo album, calendar, cards, and individual prints. iPhoto frequently comes packaged on new Macintosh computers, but if you don't have it, head to the Apple Store (http://store.apple.com) and buy a copy of iLife. It includes iPhoto and other digital applications.

Choosing a photo-sharing tool

When you're ready to put your photos online, regardless of whether you ultimately want to include images on your blog, you have plenty of options.

Photo-sharing websites have become full-fledged members of the Web 2.0 movement, offering friends lists, tagging, and other sophisticated tools.

The media darling of photo-sharing sites is definitely Flickr (www.flickr.com). For avid photographers, Flickr has nearly replaced the need to have a blog at all because many of the best blogging tools are integrated into the Flickr service.

On Flickr, you can

>> Create a list of friends whose photos you want to follow.

>> Upload and organize photos by using *tags* (keywords), sets, and collections.

>> Start groups around a visual theme and add your photos to other groups.

>> Set privacy controls to dictate who can see your photos.

>> Use your photos to create books, prints, calendars, business cards, DVDs, and stamps.

>> Post photos in your account and receive comments (see Figure 12-3).

>> Create slideshows of your photos.

>> Upload, tag, and share video.

>> Browse other members' photos and leave comments.

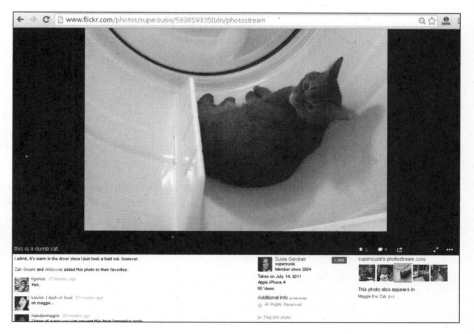

FIGURE 12-3:
When you post photos on Flickr, your friends and other Flickr members can leave comments for you.

Basic Flickr accounts are free for 1 Terabyte worth of photos and two videos each month. You can display only your most recent 200 photos, though. Ad-free accounts cost $49.99 a year and receive unlimited uploading and image display.

WARNING

If you elect to use an online tool to organize and store your photographs, you are at the mercy of that website. Note that you are taking a risk that your images could disappear if the site is taken down. Additionally, if you upload images to your blog directly from such a tool and that service eventually ceases to exist, those images will likely disappear from past blog posts.

In the section "Inserting Photos into Blog Posts with Flickr," later in this chapter, I show you how to put Flickr to work for you when you want to add images to blog posts.

TIP

Whatever service you choose, look for tools that can make your life easier when it comes to putting your photos on your blog. For example, look for services that

>> Integrate well with the camera you own, your mobile phone if you use it for photography, or both devices.

>> Let you post a photo to your blog or give you code to put the photo in your blog post.

Other online photo-sharing tools to consider include

>> **Photobucket (www.photobucket.com):** This site includes the basic photo-editing tools that you'll need before uploading images to your site. It also includes some creative tools such as the ability to add filters and text. One cool feature of the Photobucket app for both iPhone and Android is the ability to create animated GIFs. 2GB of storage is included in your free account with additional storage options beginning at $2.99 per month.

>> **Shutterfly (www.shutterfly.com):** Shutterfly is the undisputed king of the photo product with an unrivaled collection of photo gifts available to users. What many people don't realize, however, is that Shutterfly is a great photo storage and sharing option. Users have access to free, unlimited photo storage, and friends don't need to create an account in order to view photos.

>> **ThisLife (www.thislife.com):** ThisLife is a photo aggregating tool owned by Shutterfly. Its purpose is for users to import and organize photos from a variety of services including Flickr, Facebook, and Instagram. Once inside ThisLife, users can organize the photos by categories such as date and place as well as create slideshows and galleries for sharing. Storage is free and photos are unlimited.

>> **Amazon Prime Photo Storage (www.amazon.com):** Amazon Prime members have access to free, unlimited photo storage, which allows you to add photos via a mobile app, upload pictures from your desktop through the Cloud Drive app, or upload images via your Amazon account online.

» **Instagram (www.instagram.com):** I would be remiss if I didn't include the social media giant in a list of photo sharing options. Instagram is a fantastic option for photographers interested in sharing their images with the world. Users can edit photos for everything from brightness to contrast as well as add a large assortment of filters. The platform is free and allows for unlimited photo storage.

Choosing Visuals for Your Blog

Far be it from me to tell you how to take photographs — I'm a rank amateur when it comes to photography. But I can give you tips on taking photos that you can use for a new blog post, which I do in the following sections.

Taking photos

Bloggers often add pictures to posts that all but require them, such as the recipe posts on Home Ec 101 (www.home-ec101.com) shown in Figure 12-4. Blog posts about cooking and restaurants are seriously enlivened by the addition of beautiful food photos. Who doesn't salivate at the sight of a beautifully prepared dessert?

FIGURE 12-4: Photos are an invaluable addition to a food blog.

THE POWER OF PINTEREST

Launched in beta in March of 2010, Pinterest (www.pinterest.com) is a pin-board style photo-sharing site that allows users to create thematic collections of images, with each image linking back to the photo source. Bloggers have found that including "pinnable" images within blog posts encourages readers to share that blog post with their friends and followers on Pinterest. In fact, many bloggers now receive more traffic from Pinterest than from any other source. That's great motivation to include some fantastic images in your posts!

If you want to take photographs to put on your blog, keep your eyes open all the time for visuals that inspire or interest you. You don't have to be a rocket scientist to find good picture subjects, but you do need to be thinking about your blog and your camera more often than you might normally. In fact, some bloggers find that carrying a camera with them actually helps them find things to blog about and illustrate regular blog posts.

TIP

Here are four tips for taking photos for your blog:

>> Is your mobile phone camera inadequate? Consider carrying your camera with you when you leave the house, even if you're just running down to the grocery store.

>> Keep fresh batteries in your camera so that when you need to use it, it isn't dead. If possible, keep a second set of batteries in your camera pouch.

>> Don't worry too much about taking the perfect picture. Just take the picture! Photo editing and good cropping can salvage many a bad shot, but they can't help you if you never even pushed the shutter button.

>> Take photos of the people you meet and talk to, and your friends. Be sure to ask them whether you can use their photos on your blog. Then, when you blog about going to a movie with Bill, you have a photo of Bill to include.

Using art from other sources

One nice thing about the web: You can find tons and tons of photos and other images, graphics, and visuals out there to inspire you. Some bloggers have taken advantage of this vast offering by including some of those great visuals in their blog posts. Photos attract readers' attention better than a few paragraphs of text. You may decide to use photos on your blog, as long as you have the rights to republish those images.

Here are three tips when you need images other than your own:

>> **Check the public domain:** Some materials are designated *public domain* works, which means anyone can use them for any purpose, although you must still give the author credit. If you're interested in featuring public-domain and licensed images on your blog, do a search for **public domain photos** on your favorite search engine. You can investigate a number of good resources.

In the United States, anything published before 1923 is considered public domain, but other countries don't necessarily have the same policy.

>> **Search through Creative Commons:** By using the Creative Commons licensing tool, you can look for works that authors have licensed for republication. To find additional works that you can use, visit `http://search.creativecommons.org` and search by using keywords that describe the material you're looking for. (Creative Commons licenses allow blog authors to make known their copyright wishes for the copying to their blog content.)

>> **Ask for permission:** If you see something that you like and want to use, but it's protected by full copyright, consider simply asking whether you can use it. Many photographers, especially those who don't make a living selling their work, willingly let you use their work, especially if you give them credit!

REMEMBER

Many of the photos on the Flickr photo-sharing site (`www.flickr.com`) have been licensed for use on other websites and blogs. When you're looking at a photo on Flickr, check the copyright information on the right side of the page.

Editing Photos

As long as you have the rights to do so, you can edit any photo. In general, you can do what you like to photos that you acquire from a public domain website or a picture that you take yourself. Photos that you obtain permission to use, or use under a special license, may have restrictions when it comes to making edits. Be sure you understand what you're allowed to do.

One very popular photo editing website is Picmonkey (`www.picmonkey.com`). Users can edit photos, add fun features like text and graphics, and share their images through social sharing tools all at no cost (see Figure 12-5). For a nominal fee, users receive access to additional tools. Many bloggers prefer this platform over others because it allows them to create collages and other highly "pinnable" (see "The power of Pinterest" earlier in the chapter) images.

As mentioned previously, another popular editing platform is Google Photos (`http://photos.google.com/`). In the following sections, I show you how to do some of the most common photo-editing tasks using Google Photos.

FIGURE 12-5:
Picmonkey allows
users to add
creative features
beyond standing
photo editing.

The most common photo-editing tasks are resizing, cropping, adjusting lighting and contrast, and adjusting the color of a photo. For each of the following tasks, you should have Google Photos open and have a photo available to edit.

Getting photos into Google Photos

Before you can edit a photo, you need to get it into Google Photos. Follow these steps:

1. **With Google Photos open in your web browser, select the cloud image to upload photos.**

2. **Select the image you'd like to upload from your computer's photo storage.**

3. **Click Open to upload that image to Google Photos.**

   Google Photos connects to the device, and displays the available photos.

Cropping a photo

Cropping a photo allows you to remove unneeded or unattractive parts of an image. For example, if you take a picture of a group of friends and then want to include a photo of just one of the individuals in your blog post, you can crop out the other people in the image.

To crop a photo that you've imported into Google Photos, follow these steps:

1. **Open Google Photos and, in the Photo Library, double-click the photo that you want to edit.**

   The Editing screen opens.

2. **Click the pencil-shaped Edit button.**

3. **Select the cropping icon.**

4. **Use your mouse to click and drag over the area that you want to retain in your photo.**

   While you click and drag, the area that will be cropped out of your photo appears slightly grayed out, leaving the portion that will be retained at the original brightness.

   If you want to start over, click Reset to remove the cropping box that you created. If you don't want to crop after all, click the Cancel button to exit the Crop tool.

5. **Click the Done button to crop your photo.**

   Google Photos displays the cropped photo.

Adjusting brightness and contrast

Sometimes, despite your best efforts, photos end up looking too dark or too light. By using photo–editing software such as Google Photos, you get a second chance because you can adjust brightness and contrast.

To adjust the brightness and contrast, follow these steps:

1. **Open Google Photos and double-click the photo that you want to edit.**

2. **Click the pencil-shaped Edit tab in the upper-right corner of the screen.**

3. **A slider menu appears. Drag the slider bar below Light to adjust the brightness of the image.**

   Google Photos adjusts the displayed image while you move the bar.

   If you're lightening the photo, watch the brightest parts of your photo to make sure that they don't get too bright, losing information you want in the photo. If you're bringing down lightness, watch the darker areas of your photo so that you don't end up with too much black in your photo. Let your eyes be the judge of a well-adjusted image.

Adjusting color

Color in photos frequently needs a little adjusting. We've taken too many greenish photos in fluorescent lights! With a little help from photo-editing software such as Google Photos, I can turn my friends' skin back to normal colors.

To adjust the color of a photo, follow these steps:

1. **Open Google Photos and double-click the photo that you want to edit.**

2. **Click the pencil-shaped Edit tab on the upper-right side of the screen.**

3. **A slider menu appears. Drag the slider bar below Color to adjust the color tone of the picture.**

   Color can be tricky to adjust. As a good rule, look for an element in the photograph that you know should be a particular color, and then adjust the overall color to make that element look right. Then, look at the overall picture and adjust, if necessary. Elements that you can use for the purpose include eye color, skin color, sky, and other consistent elements.

Optimizing a photo for the web

Digital cameras commonly store photos as high-resolution files suitable for print, but that high-resolution is more than you need for display on a blog or website. And you probably don't want to make your blog visitors download a great big image when they don't need to. Usually, you compress the file size of your image when you plan to put it on your blog.

TIP

If you plan to upload your image to Flickr, don't worry about compressing the image when you export. Flickr can handle large files and can resize the photo for you.

You may also need to change the image's dimensions in order to fit it into your blog layout, or even create a thumbnail version.

Inserting Photos into Blog Posts with Flickr

If you have a photo prepared for use on your blog, you're ready to upload it to the web. You can take two approaches to get your image online:

>> **Uploading directly to your blog:** All blog platforms and software allow you to upload images directly into your blog. One good thing about a direct upload is that the image will remain in that post even if a site like Flickr should suddenly

no longer exist. Unfortunately, uploading images directly to your blog may become an issue because of file storage restrictions.

>> **Other online sharing sites:** If your blog software doesn't include an image-uploading tool, you can upload your photos to an online sharing site, such as Flickr. You can then add your photo to your post from that site.

Follow these steps to add photos to Flickr:

1. **Log into your Flickr account and select the uploading cloud icon on the home page.**

   The Upload to Flickr page appears.

2. **Click the Choose Photos and Videos button.**

   A Select File dialog box opens, showing files on your computer.

3. **Navigate to the location of the photo that you want to upload, select the photo, and click Open.**

   Your photo goes into an upload queue on the Flickr page. You can add a description at this time.

TIP

   If you want to upload more photos, click the Add More link and add those photos to the queue, as well.

4. **Make sure that your Privacy setting is Visible to Everyone so that readers can view your photo when you put it on your blog.**

5. **Click the Upload Photos and Videos button.**

   Flickr displays a progress bar and notifies you when it has fully uploaded your photo.

6. **Give your photo a title, description, and tags that describe it in the text boxes provided.**

7. **Click the Done button.**

   Flickr adds your new photo(s) to your photo page. After you've completed your upload, you are sent back to your main photostream.

8. **On your photo page, click the photo that you just uploaded.**

9. **Select the Share arrow from the toolbar beneath the photo.**

TIP

   To post your photos directly from Flickr onto Facebook, Twitter, Tumblr, or Blogger, select the appropriate icon and skip the remaining steps. Flickr shows you the starting point for configuring the connection between Flickr and your blog. Have the web address for your blog's publishing interface, your username, and password ready.

10. Select the appropriate share format from the options as shown in Figure 12-6.

Flickr opens the code screen, as shown in Figure 12-6.

11. Click in the code box and copy that code into your Clipboard by pressing Ctrl+C (⌘+C on a Mac) or choosing Edit ⇨ Copy.

12. Go to your blogging software and start a new post.

13. Paste the code from Flickr into your post entry field.

After the Flickr code, type your post as you normally would.

14. Publish your post.

Be sure to check how it looks on the blog.

FIGURE 12-6: Clicking the Grab the HTML link in the Sharing menu gives you access to the HTML code for your photo.

FLICKR UPLOADING TOOLS

You have four ways to upload your photos to Flickr: You can use the method described in this chapter, download the Flickr Uploadr tool and install it on your computer, use a plug-in for iPhoto, or upload via email. If you upload via email, don't forget that you can use your mobile phone to email pictures directly onto your Flickr photostream.

To find out more about the Flickr uploading tools, go to www.flickr.com/tools.

Chapter 13

Starting a Podcast

B y adding *podcasts* — either audio or video files that you publish on the Internet for people to download and listen to or view — to your blog, you reach a wider audience and reach your audience in different locations: People might listen to you while they drive or commute, or they might watch your videos on their televisions, iPods, smartphones, or other devices.

The production process for a podcast is (in theory) simple: You go out into the world, record a video or some audio, edit it on your computer, and then upload the files to your blog for release onto the Internet. Your blog's readers then download the files, and they can still leave comments and interact with your blog in the usual way.

Intrigued? Podcasts are attracting a whole new audience to the blogosphere. With the creation of improved software and mobile devices that can consume these kinds of media, you might want to seriously consider adding podcasting to your blog.

TIP

If you want to become the coolest podcaster in your neck of the woods, check out *Podcasting For Dummies,* 2nd Edition, by Tee Morris, Chuck Tomasi, Evo Terra, and Kreg Steppe (John Wiley & Sons, Inc.).

Deciding to Podcast

Podcasts come in all flavors. You can find personal podcasts, technical podcasts, sports reports, music samples, recorded social gatherings, previously recorded radio broadcasts, book reviews, and audio books. If you can think of a topic, you can probably find a podcast for it.

I Simply Am (`www.isimply.am`) is a blog about one man's journey to live life as his authentic self as well as a source of tips and tools for others hoping to do the same. The I Simply Am podcast page (`www.isimply.am/category/podcast/`) is shown in Figure 13-1.

Blogs and podcasts can look very similar; the main difference is that a podcast entry contains a media file that the consumer can download, either by directly accessing the website or by subscribing to a syndicated *blog feed* (also known as the RSS feed). See the section "Delivering your podcasts," later in this chapter, for more information about your options.

Many bloggers who want to podcast don't because of the learning curve to build and maintain a podcast. As wonderful as podcasts can be, writing, recording, uploading, hosting, and promoting one requires a higher level of technical proficiency than written blog posts do. However, you may find figuring out how to work podcasts worth it if you think they can help grow your audience, enhance your blog content, or improve and expand your blogging skills. In the following sections, you can take a closer look at the advantages of podcasting and figure out how to choose between audio and video podcasts.

PODCASTING IN ANCIENT TIMES

In 2003, a number of bloggers thought it would be interesting to record their thoughts out loud and then publish the audio, usually as MP3 files, through their blogs. Some of those bloggers started releasing audio blog entries on a regular basis. What happened next was a bit of a surprise. Because of the rising popularity of MP3 players, such as Apple's iPod, the audience for these podcasts grew extremely quickly. And thanks to RSS feeds, listeners could easily retrieve and download the latest recordings. People from all over the world started listening, recording, and publishing their own audio blogs. Several audio blogs became popular enough to gain some notice within the mainstream media. A hidden audience had been discovered.

In fact, most people believe the word *podcast* comes from the Apple iPod device, a popular MP3 player that can store and play podcasts and music. This belief comes close, but it isn't the whole truth. Podcasts arose at the same time that Apple's device came on the scene, and bloggers conceived the name *podcast* to echo the idea that people could listen to these audio files on the go by using a hand-held device. But many devices could play the files, and in fact, people listen to most podcasts on a computer, not an MP3 player. Some say the word comes from a combination of the acronym *pod* (*pod* standing for portable-on-demand) and the word *broadcast,* but this meaning evolved after the word itself, probably in response to Apple's attempts in 2005 to try to restrict the commercial use of the word *pod.*

Although some bloggers were also experimenting with video in 2003, it took until 2005 for videocasting to start to truly gain traction. Two technological shifts helped make this happen. iTunes, the program most people used to subscribe to podcasts, started supporting video; YouTube, the video-sharing site, made uploading and sharing video a much more common online activity.

Reaching a wider audience

Podcasting can help you reach a different audience. Many people like to read and enjoy taking in a well-written blog post. However, some blog readers enjoy listening to what you have to say as an audio recording. Other blog followers like to watch, rather than read, your blog post — especially if you have a compelling voice or are more photogenic than average. Also, some of the things that you want to talk about on your blog might work better as an audio recording than a text post, such as interviews, soundscapes, or special events. And video is even more powerful: You can show off much more of your personality than you can by using just a text blog, and you can demonstrate things that you might find difficult or impossible to convey with just words.

Think about when and where people might play your podcast, and use that knowledge to help focus your entries.

Choosing between audio and video

If you're ready to take the plunge into producing a podcast, you need to decide what format you want to use. Both audio and video require specialized skills to produce.

Your level of technical competence and comfort can determine what medium you choose. You need to consider what type of podcast fits with your blog's audience — don't use videocasting, for example, if your blog targets those who use low-bandwidth connections.

Here are a few tips that can help you decide what type of podcast to use:

>> **Audio:**

- Easier to produce than video because of a larger availability of open source software. Most software for professional video editing is expensive.

- Easier and generally quicker to edit than video.

- More portable than video. Fewer portable devices are designed to deal with video than with audio.

- Less of a space hog than video, making audio files less expensive than video files to store on a web host.

>> **Video:**

- More compelling. The visual and auditory components combined are more likely to keep a viewer from becoming distracted.

- You can make video shorter than audio. Audiences likely feel satisfied with a 2–4-minute video podcast, whereas they might want a much longer audio podcast.

- Gives you more visual elements to work with — both when you're designing your blog and in individual entries.

- Has more related sites online where you can upload and share files.

- Requires the viewer's sole attention, whereas people can listen to audio podcasts while completing other tasks. You can listen to an audio podcast while driving to work, for example.

WARNING

Video and audio files can get very large. When you upload them to your web server, you fill up your available disk space more quickly than you do if you upload only text and photos. Also, distributing audio and video requires more bandwidth. Keep an eye on your disk space and bandwidth usage so that you aren't hit with unexpected overage charges. Ask your web host how to keep tabs on those elements, any fees that you may accrue, and whether you need more space and bandwidth.

If video is the medium of your choice, be sure to read Chapter 14 for tips and tools specific to video production.

Planning Your Podcast

To create a podcast, you first need the desire to make it the best experience for the listeners that you can. If you aren't having fun, it shows in the final result. Remember, even if you find your very first podcast a little frustrating, it gets easier.

Here are a few key ingredients that you need for a good podcast:

» **Planning what you'll say:** You can make a single podcast about anything, so have a clearly defined topic before you start. Some podcasters write a script for every podcast they record. Although you may find that a script is overkill for you, jotting down a few notes or creating an outline to follow can help you streamline the creation process. You can find a list to help you brainstorm topics and the flow of your podcast later in this section.

» **Finding your voice:** You need to establish the tone of the piece before you go forward. How will the format of your overall podcast determine how you shoot or record it? Do you want to use some kind of traditional show format, or do you want to improvise the entire program each time? Taking these kinds of questions into account when you're planning your first podcast can help you make your program a success.

» **Timing:** Technically speaking, you can use as much or as little time as you want in your podcast. You may find, however, that you get a better end product when you give yourself limits, rather than chattering on about your favorite color or a funny thing your cat did when you really should be getting to the point of your recording session. Think about how much time you can reasonably expect your audience to give you, and target that length for your podcasts. In general, podcasts range from a few minutes to an hour. Also, make sure that you have enough time to record the entire podcast in the same location so that you don't have awkward changes in the background noise, which can distract your listener or viewer.

>> **Recording conditions:** When you want to record anything, you need to take into account environmental considerations before you hit the Record button. Is the environment you're in quiet enough? Background noise from fans or computers may annoy the listeners! For video, do you have sufficient lighting to produce watchable video? Try to eliminate distractions, such as phones ringing or people walking by. And if you can, do some test recording that you can listen to or watch so that you know what the quality of the final product will be before you record your entire podcast.

REMEMBER

Blogging in writing is relatively easy in comparison to recording a podcast, and you can also more easily hide your inexperience in a text blog because you can rewrite and edit before posting. Although you can edit audio and video, removing stuttered speech or inappropriate facial expressions is harder than revising text in a blog post. The good news is that practice can help eliminate awkward moments.

TIP

If you get stuck thinking about a podcast topic or format, ask your readers for suggestions. Even if only five or ten readers respond, you can get some good ideas and direction.

Here's a short list of podcast ideas that have been successful for other podcasters. Use this list to spark your creativity to find other topics that interest you:

>> **One-on-one interviews:** Fascinating people in your neighborhood are just waiting to get on your podcast — especially people involved in a cause, an organization, or a business. Discover more about your family's background or the adventures of your friends. See who in your acquaintance might fit the theme and direction of your podcast.

>> **Show your expertise:** Show off what you know and share your knowledge with others — maybe even show your audience how to do something.

>> **Soundscapes:** You can find fascinating sounds all around you that you can document. Record yourself walking through a forest or park. Make some observations about your surroundings, describe each sound, and explain why it's important to you. Remember, what's ordinary for you (waves at the beach, a passing train, construction noise, or a barn owl) might fascinate someone living on the other side of the country or the world.

>> **Events:** A performance at your local coffeehouse, a city hall meeting, or a surprise party all might make for an interesting podcast. Make sure to get permission before recording or publishing a podcast of an event.

>> **Discussions:** General discussions in social settings can reveal some great conversations. Take your recorder along to your next BBQ or evening social, and direct the conversation along a theme or idea.

If you take the time to plan what you want to share with your subscribers, you can make your podcast happen. With a recording device, a plan, and maybe even someone else to talk to, you can have a complete podcast episode in no time.

Assessing the Tools

Making your podcast requires a bit more than your fingers and a computer keyboard. Podcasts require recording equipment for audio and video. Here's what you're looking at:

>> **Computer:** You need a computer of some kind. You can use a desktop or a laptop, although laptops allow more flexibility and allow you to edit on-the-go. The computer must be able to handle editing audio files and, more important, video files. Video is a computer-intensive medium and requires a computer with a lot of power and disk space to process the large files that you record. Audio files can also be fairly large.

>> **Microphone:** Microphones these days are built into almost every laptop, and you can easily buy external microphones. Consider purchasing a good microphone from a professional audio store because the microphones that you get from the average computer store or on the typical laptop are poor quality. Ask a podcaster or the staff of a good audio store for advice about the best microphone for the kind of recording situation that you expect to be in. Expect to spend at least $40 for your microphone: It isn't the item to economize on.

>> **Collaboration tools:** Many successful podcasts involve more than one podcaster or, at the very least, the occasional special guest. Online tools aimed at making collaborating a breeze are a podcasting team's dream. Check out WriterDuet (www.writerduet.com) for script writing and Doodle (www.doodle.com) for scheduling. Want to record video with multiple people in multiple places? Check out Skype (www.skype.com), another incredibly useful and free tool, or Google Voice (www.google.com/voice/), a simple and straightforward way to record conversations.

>> **Sound-recording and sound-editing software**: Unless you're the sort of person who never deviates from a script or says "um," you need software to edit your audio or video. Solutions range from free to the price of a small automobile. Let your budget be your guide. You may want to start small and upgrade when you know more about podcasting and your own needs. A good starting point for audio software is the free program Audacity (http://audacity.sourceforge.net). Audacity (as shown in Figure 13-2) is available for Windows, Mac OS X, and Linux/Unix. It's the program of choice for many

podcasters, largely because it's free and open source. Audacity is a *multi-track recording* program, which means you can have two pieces of audio, such as a voice and a piece of music, and you can mix the two at different volumes or even fade from one to the other. A high-end solution is Sony's Sound Forge (www.sonycreativesoftware.com/soundforgesoftware).

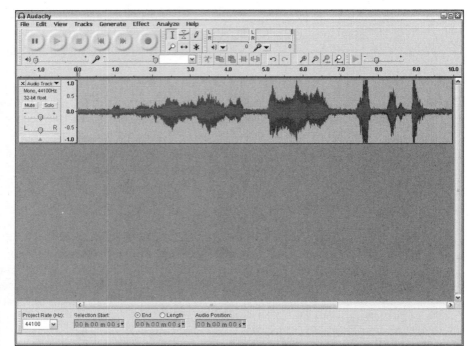

Dressing Up Your Podcast with Music and Sound Effects

Nothing spices up a podcast like a little intro or background music. But podcasts — even if they're produced and released at no cost to the listener — aren't exempt from copyright restrictions. You need to find music or images that are in the public domain or licensed for republication.

WARNING

Let me be clear: Even if you use only a little bit of a copyrighted song or give the performer credit, you're still violating copyright if you don't have a license or other permission to use the music. The same goes for using copyrighted images and video clips in videocasts.

But plenty of this material is available for you to use. The term *podsafe* has appeared to describe music, sounds, and other clips that are available for free, unlimited use in podcasting, but no specific license exists to identify that a clip is podsafe. Read the terms and conditions before you integrate sound or audio into your productions.

Creative Commons Search

`http://search.creativecommons.org`

Creative Commons is an organization that has evolved a set of licenses that you can use on your own content to permit or disallow use by others. If a publisher applies a Creative Commons license that allows republication, you can search for and find that content in the Creative Commons search area, specifically requesting content that you can use for commercial purposes or modify (see Figure 13-3).

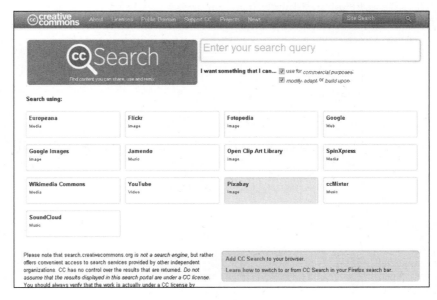

FIGURE 13-3: Search Creative Commons for licensed content to use in your podcast.

Some of the types of licenses are

>> **Commercial Use:** Permits use of the content for business and revenue-generating purposes.

>> **Noncommercial Use:** You may use this media only for noncommercial podcasts.

>> **Attribution:** You can use the work only when you give credit to the creator.

>> **Derivatives Allowed:** You can cut, chop, and excerpt this media to create new works.

>> **No Derivatives Allowed:** You must leave the media intact and unchanged.

Magnatune

www.magnatune.com

Magnatune is a record label that helps artists promote and share their music, and make money doing it. The label and artists sell their albums on CD and via download, and they split the money evenly. The music on Magnatune (shown in Figure 13-4) is available for download and purchase, as well as to noncommercial podcasters. To help promote artists, podcasters are granted a waiver to use Magnatune music without paying a royalty fee.

FIGURE 13-4: Magnatune is one of the only record labels that specifically allow noncommercial podcasters to use music for free.

Freesound

www.freesound.org

This online database is the result of a collaborative effort, bringing Creative Commons–licensed sound effects to the Internet for use in podcasts.

Free Music Archive

www.freemusicarchive.org

The Free Music Archive is another online database that allows podcasters to search for music to use in their recordings. It is free to access and use the database, but be sure to check out artist bios and information regarding the use of their art.

Publishing Your Podcast

You can put your podcast into the blogosphere fairly simply: Write a blog post about your podcast, upload your podcast media file, and then publish it by using your blog software.

But before you do that, you have a couple of tasks: You need to add metadata to and choose a file format for your podcast.

Assigning metadata

Metadata, simply put, is data about data. In the case of podcasts, metadata is data that describes your video or audio podcast. When you publish a podcast, whether audio or video, you need to provide descriptive metadata that podcast systems such as Apple's iTunes and the RSS feed can read. After all, the computer can't listen to or watch your podcast and figure out what it contains!

Common metadata types include

>> Title

>> Author name

>> Publication information

>> Topics covered

>> Type of file

>> Descriptions

>> Keywords

Your editing software (both video and audio software packages) asks you to enter metadata when you create your audio or video files, and software such as iTunes, which is designed to support podcasts, also offers you a chance to provide metadata.

Choosing a format

Creating video and audio for general release means that you need to choose a file format that your audience can consume.

Most audio bloggers release audio files in the MP3 format. MP3 files are easy to create and play on a variety of devices. Most computer users are familiar with the format, and both browsers and preinstalled audio players have good built-in support for MP3s.

Other options are available, such as OOG, an open format, and AAC, a format popular on Apple computers. Windows users can play AAC files, too, if they install QuickTime. The Apple iPod can't play OOG files, which is a significant issue for most audiences. AAC has some nice features, such as audio bookmarks.

Storing your podcasts

When you have a podcast ready for primetime, you need to figure out where to put it online. Posting your podcast poses two problems:

>> **Storage:** You need a place to put the actual file. Audio and video files are larger than text files, so you may run into an issue with disk space when you store them.

>> **Bandwidth (the amount of data your audiences downloads):** You have to account for the additional bandwidth required for your audience to download those files. It takes more bandwidth to deliver audio or video to your audience than it does text or images.

You have two options for getting the storage and bandwidth you need: your web-hosting server (the one that hosts your blog) or a free storage website.

Putting your files on your own web-hosting server

Check with your web host to find out how much disk space you have available and what it costs to increase your allotment. Be aware that if you keep podcasting, you'll eventually run out of disk space, even if you start off with quite a bit. If you're a video podcaster, you want a hosting package that has several gigabytes of storage space. If you stick with only audio, you need a few gigabytes to start. When your podcasts grow in number, you'll require more and more space, so keep that in mind. I talk about choosing a web host in Chapter 3.

You also need to consider bandwidth when you choose your hosting service. Most web-hosting packages offer a standard amount of bandwidth, and you're charged if you and your audience use more than that. Most web hosts have pretty reasonable fees, unless your podcast becomes the hottest thing on the web and your traffic becomes astronomical.

To give you a better idea about how file sizes can affect your web-hosting costs, I show you some reasonable working numbers. You can compare these to your hosting package bandwidth:

>> **1MB (megabyte) audio file:** If you have 100 subscribers and you post one audio file a week, your estimated bandwidth for that file is about 100MB.

>> **10MB (megabyte) video file:** If you have 100 subscribers and you post one video file a week, your estimated bandwidth for that file is 1000MB or 1GB.

From these numbers, you can see how your bandwidth needs may skyrocket. Thinking about these almost hidden costs is important because you can get stuck with a hosting bill you weren't expecting.

TIP

Bandwidth can be a confusing concept, especially when dealing with a podcast. Websites like Podtopia (`http://podtopia.net`) have tools that let you generate estimates on how much it can cost you to host your own files.

REMEMBER

Most hosting packages come with a finite amount of disk space and bandwidth. You most likely can post only a certain number of podcasts before your hosting package runs out of space. Unless you have the dollars to spend, you probably need to find an alternative for storing your files.

Using a free storage and sharing website

Luckily for podcasters, a great service called Archive.org (`www.archive.org`) is the home of the Internet Archive, a nonprofit organization founded in 1996 to build an Internet library in which researchers, historians, and the general public can store and access text, audio, moving images, software, and a vast collection of archived web pages.

TIP

You can upload your podcasts to the Internet Archive for free, as long as you comply with its guidelines and describe your content. The system also provides and converts your video or audio format into other formats for increased accessibility.

You can find other podcast storage options, too, such as YouTube (`www.youtube.com`). When you upload a video to YouTube, your video is listed on the site, where visitors can view and comment on it. But you can also grab the code for the file and embed it directly into your website or blog post. Files that you upload to YouTube are reformatted into Flash video. They must be shorter than 15 minutes and less than 2GB in size.

If you think 15 minutes isn't long enough for your blog, YouTube offers a YouTube Partner Program (www.youtube.com/yt/creators/get-started.html). Members of the program are granted permission to upload larger video files, have videos longer than 15 minutes, and share advertisement revenue. If you think video blogging is for you, check it out! You should also stop by Chapter 14 to learn more about video blogging, also called vlogging.

Delivering your podcasts

After you have your audio and video online and your blog post created, you need to make sure that your blog has an RSS web feed. Podcasts are typically delivered to playback software (such as Apple iTunes) through a subscription to your blog's RSS feed. I talk extensively about setting up and using RSS in Chapter 16.

Suffice it to say that you need an RSS feed so that your viewers and listeners can subscribe to it themselves, but also so that you can promote your podcast by using some of the handy podcast promotional directories and software out there. (See the following section for the promotion details.)

If you already subscribe to a number of blogs, you know that a syndicated blog feed contains information such as the title of the post, the main content, and maybe some author information. A podcast feed, in addition to the typical entry information, contains a link to a media file. If a consumer subscribes to a podcast feed by using an RSS reader, most modern readers automatically download the files so that the user can listen or watch at his or her convenience.

Promoting Your Podcast

Publishing your podcast on your website can help you promote it, but you can get the word out in more effective ways. If you already have a good promotional system built into your site and a decent-sized audience, you can get users to subscribe to your podcast without too much additional marketing. If you need a little more promotion, however, you also can use a number of other strategies.

Adding your podcast to FeedBurner

FeedBurner (http://feedburner.google.com) provides custom tracking and customization of podcast feeds. If you submit your podcast to FeedBurner's service, you can implement good promotion tools to help your podcast get more play.

Now a Google company, FeedBurner has a lot to offer bloggers and podcasters. You can use FeedBurner to do the following:

>> Add metadata to your files.

>> Make your feeds compatible with every RSS reader available.

>> Add your podcast to the major podcast directories, making sure that people can find your podcast.

>> Track the number of subscribers to your feed.

>> Keep track of which podcasts visitors actually download.

To use FeedBurner, you must already have an RSS feed. If you're using blog software, it probably offers you a feed. Check your documentation for more information and jump to Chapter 16 for more about RSS feeds.

Follow these steps to create a feed with FeedBurner:

1. **Go to** `http://feedburner.com`.

2. **Create an account on FeedBurner if you don't already have one.**

3. **On the FeedBurner main page (shown in Figure 13-5), paste the web address (URL) of your RSS feed into the Burn a Feed Right This Instant field.**

FIGURE 13-5:
Get a podcast feed going with Google's FeedBurner.

4. **Select the I Am a Podcaster check box.**

5. **Click the Next button.**

   FeedBurner verifies that the feed is working and loads the Welcome screen.

6. **Give your feed a title, if it doesn't already have one, by entering it in the Field Title text box.**

   You can also customize the feed address in the Feed Address text box, if desired.

7. **Click the Next button.**

   FeedBurner creates your new feed and loads a screen that displays the web address of your feed.

8. **Click the Next button.**

   FeedBurner loads the podcast configuration screen.

9. **Fill out the configuration screen.**

   FeedBurner offers these configuration options:

   - *Create Podcast Enclosures from Links To:* Select the kinds of files that you want to include in your podcast — any, audio, video, or images.

   - *Include iTunes Podcasting Elements:* Deselect this check box if you don't want your podcast listed in Apple's iTunes Store.

   - *Category:* Select a category from the drop-down list. You can also select a subcategory in the text field that appears.

   - *Podcast Image Location:* If you created a graphic for your audio or video podcast, paste the web address of the graphic into this field. This graphic is like an album cover for your podcast. iTunes uses it to fill in the album artwork.

   - *Podcast Subtitle:* Expand on your title in this field.

   - *Podcast Summary:* Provide a short description of your podcast.

   - *Podcast Search Keywords:* Provide descriptive keywords for your podcast.

   - *Podcast Author E-Mail Address:* Enter your email address.

   - *Include "Media RSS" Information and Add Podcast to Yahoo! Search:* Deselect this check box if you don't want to be included in Yahoo! Search.

   - *Contains Explicit Content:* Select the Yes, No, or Yes (Cleaned) option button. Click the Information icon if you want help understanding how FeedBurner defines explicit content.

   - *Copyright Message:* Provide a short copyright message.

   - *Podcast Author:* Fill in your name.

10. **Click the Next button.**

FeedBurner loads the traffic statistics screen.

11. **Fill out the Feed Traffic Statistics screen.**

These options appear on this screen:

- *Click-throughs:* Select this check box if you want to know when subscribers use your feed to come to your website.

- *Item Enclosure Downloads:* Select this check box if you want to know which podcast entries your subscribers actually download.

12. **Click the Next button.**

FeedBurner finishes burning your feed. You can begin monitoring subscriptions and activity on your feed by using FeedBurner.

After you create a feed by using FeedBurner, head to your site, put the link to your new feed on your blog, and urge your blog visitors to subscribe. Want to verify that your feed is working? Stop by Feed Validator (`www.feedvalidator.org`) just to be safe.

By using FeedBurner, you can actually keep track of how many subscribers your feed has and how they're using your podcast, which is useful information if you plan to pursue funding or sponsorship. After you have set up a podcast with Feed-Burner, log in and select it to view traffic information in the Analyze section of the site.

Adding your podcast to iTunes

Because of the overwhelming popularity of Apple's iTunes software as the main podcast viewer, you absolutely must submit your podcast to its service.

Before you submit your podcast to iTunes, you need to do the following:

» **Sign up for an Apple ID.** Each submission is associated with a user account. If you have iTunes installed on your computer and have purchased songs or other media from the iTunes store, you already have an Apple ID. To get an ID, download iTunes, which you find at `www.itunes.com`; after you install the software, select the iTunes Store option on the left of the main screen to begin setting up your ID.

» **Set up an RSS feed.** If you're using blog software, you likely already have a feed. Check your documentation for more information, and jump to Chapter 16 for more about RSS feeds.

TIP

» **Have a few entries in your feed and make sure that the feed is working.** You can test your feed by making sure that your own feed reader can subscribe to your feed. If you see your posts in your reader, the feed should be working fine.

» If you have a FeedBurner feed set up, you've already taken care of some of the optimization to make your feed work well in iTunes. Be sure to use the FeedBurner feed address when you sign up in iTunes.

Before iTunes adds podcasts to the Store, Apple iTunes staff reviews podcast submissions. The staff can refuse podcasts for even very small reasons. You may have problems getting a podcast added if you've been turned down before.

If you have the iTunes software installed on your computer, you can submit your podcast by using the iTunes interface. In order to get your podcast into the iTunes Store, follow these steps:

1. **Start your iTunes software.**

2. **Click the iTunes Store navigation item in the left column (its location depends on the version of iTunes that you have, though).**

   The iTunes store interface opens.

3. **Select the Podcasts link from the iTunes Store menu on the top of the screen.**

   The Podcasts page appears.

4. **Click the Submit a Podcast menu item located in the top-right of the page.**

   iTunes loads the Submit Podcasts page.

5. **Enter the RSS feed of your podcast in the Podcast Feed URL field and click the Continue button.**

   If you're not logged in to the iTunes Store, you're prompted to log in at this point.

   iTunes submits your feed for review by Apple staff.

After you submit your podcast, it might take several days or even weeks until your feed shows up in the iTunes library of podcasts. If your podcast is rejected for any reason, you receive an email from Apple. (Unfortunately, it doesn't provide reasons for rejections.)

Getting listed in podcast directories

Podcast directories help would-be listeners and viewers find known podcasts. Getting listed in these directories is an easy way to let people know about your podcast. Most directories are organized by topic, and many of them offer subscription features that allow people to quickly sign up for your podcast. Listing your podcast in these directories can most certainly provide you with new traffic to your blog and podcast.

Here's where you should get your podcast listed:

>> **Castroller** (www.castroller.com): One of the newer websites for subscribing, organizing, and listening to podcasts. You can sort podcasts you listen to into "channels," and it is easy to recommend podcasts (including your own!) to others. It is easy to use and has a lot of social media functionality built in. This makes it easy for your listeners to promote you.

>> **PodNova** (www.podnova.com): More than just a directory. You can subscribe, listen, view, read, and maintain your feeds online by using PodNova.

>> **PodBean** (www.podbean.com): Another directory where you can publish and host your podcast. You and your audience can listen and view your podcasts and share them on other websites like Facebook.

And if you don't want to put your podcast on any of the sites in the preceding list, check out the extensive list of podcasting resources at ProPodder (www.propodder.com).

Chapter 14

Diving into Vlogging

Mentioned briefly in Chapter 13, vlogging has grown from just an occasional enhancement to a blog post to become a type of blogging all its own. Vlogging, or video blogging, allows bloggers to communicate with readers beyond the written word. Interested in monetizing your blog? Vlogging also provides you with new opportunities to turn your hobby into a money-making proposition. (Stop by Chapter 20 for more about making money with your blog.)

In this chapter, you find out the reasons to consider adding vlogging to your blogging repertoire as well as how to get started, from selecting the right vlogging platform for you to choosing the best equipment. This chapter also walks you through ways to promote your content and find viewers.

Defining Vlogging

Although vlogging is a strange word to type and an even stranger word to pronounce, when you understand its source, it makes sense. Just as *blog* grew out of the word weblog (pronounced web-log), *vlogging* is the shortened word for video blogging or video logging, and is pronounced just like blogging, but with a *v*. With vlogging, rather than share your content with the world through words on a page, you share the same types of content through uploaded videos.

TIP

In Chapter 11, I cover the topic of blogging anonymously. If this sounds like something you'd like to consider, you probably shouldn't consider vlogging. It's tough to hide your identity when you're on camera for the world to see, especially in light of facial recognition tools found throughout the web.

Understanding why you should vlog

Even with the presence of online communities, meet-ups, and blogging conferences, the fact is that blogging remains a medium that allows participants to hide behind the computer screen, sharing only what they're willing to share in carefully chosen words. Some bloggers, in fact, enjoy blogging for that reason alone — the ability to hide behind their blogging mask.

So why vlog and expose yourself by coming through the screen and into your readers' homes and phones through the power of video? The answer lies not in the readers that you have but the viewers that you don't. Although fewer new readers are exploring blog content than were in the initial blogging boom, video continues to bring more viewers to their content. In fact, according to Cisco's Visual Networking Index (`http://www.cisco.com/c/en/us/solutions/collateral/service-provider/ip-ngn-ip-next-generation-network/white_paper_c11-481360.pdf`), nearly 70 percent of all Internet traffic will be tied to online video viewing by 2018. Video is booming, and now may be the time for you to get a piece of the action.

Beyond following the turning tide of Internet use, you can realize other benefits of adding vlogs to your blogging repertoire:

>> Providing your readers with an opportunity to connect with you on a more personal level, connecting a voice and face with a blog

>> Increasing traffic to your existing blog

>> Enhancing already highly visual content such as demonstrations or product reviews

>> Helping you get through a period of writer's block

>> Connecting with additional bloggers through a shared interest — vlogging!

>> Potentially saving time

Unless you're blogging professionally or hoping to do so, your blog is all about *you*. This means that if vlogging sounds like an absolutely horrifying pursuit to you, it's perfectly fine to ignore the research and never upload a moment of video ever!

Discovering available vlogging platforms

By now, you've likely at least paged through the chapters in Part 2 and have become familiar with available blogging platforms. The great news is that blog platforms recognize the importance of video in today's blogging landscape. Everything from a basic, free Blogger site to a self-hosted WordPress blog offers the ability to upload video. However, you may find yourself highly restricted in terms of file size. For that reason as well as vlog promotion, which I discuss later in the chapter, it's worth taking a look at some of the available vlogging platforms.

YouTube

By far and away, the most popular video platform is YouTube (www.YouTube.com), shown in Figure 14-1. In fact, YouTube claims to have 1 billion+ active users each month, with 300 hours of video uploaded every minute. Creating your own YouTube vlogging channel — which is free and relatively simple — allows you to tap into an existing audience that is simply mindblowing. Unfortunately, with the vast amount of content uploaded every second of the day, it may be tough for your content to grab the attention of that audience.

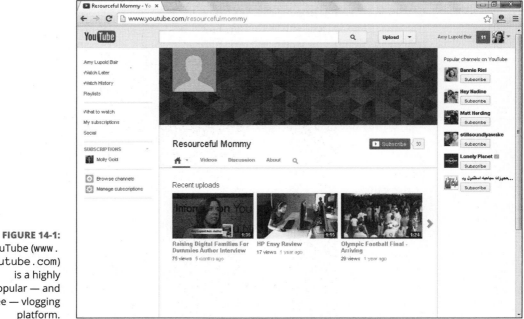

FIGURE 14-1:
YouTube (www.youtube.com) is a highly popular — and free — vlogging platform.

Even if you don't choose to create and promote a vlogging channel on YouTube, you may want to upload your content to that platform for a couple of reasons:

>> **File size:** Uploading your content to YouTube rather than to your blog directly helps you clear the file size hurdle on most blog platforms.

>> **Ease:** Most blog platforms provide you with an option to upload video content directly from YouTube.

>> **Organization:** Perhaps you'd like to just occasionally upload a vlog post to your current site. By uploading them to YouTube first, you've also created a place that holds all your video content in one easy-to-find location.

Maker.tv

Another online video-creation platform worth a look is Maker.tv (`www.maker.tv`). This is an especially good option if you're planning to create a series of webisodes or want to make your vlog into a regular content series.

Vimeo

Vimeo (`www.vimeo.com`) is another highly popular video platform that has less of the junk content than you'll find on YouTube. Ideally, this means that your content has a higher probability of being viewed and a smaller chance of receiving the kind of inappropriate feedback that users sometimes experience on YouTube.

Facebook Video

A great way to find a viewing audience is to create your content on one of the most popular online platforms — Facebook! Facebook videos autoplay in newsfeeds, grabbing the attention of viewers. Platform options include playlist creation, designation of featured videos, and the option to include a call-to-action at the end of the video.

Vine

Created in 2012, Vine (`vine.co`) has exploded in the social media world, with some Vine content creators achieving the kind of online celebrity previously reserved for YouTube stars. Each Vine video, also called simply a *vine* for short, consists of 6-second-long looping video content. Vines are easily shared across other social media platforms including Twitter and Facebook.

Setting the Stage

One of the great things about vlogging is how quickly you can hit the ground running. Most cameras include a video function, computers typically include a webcam that records video, and free vlogging platforms provide anyone in the world with a location to upload content. However, you shouldn't necessarily just grab your old digital camera and begin recording and uploading content willy-nilly. As with any other form of blogging, putting in a bit of time and care provides you with incredible benefits. Want to present a polished, finished product? You need to begin by setting your vlogging stage.

Choosing the right equipment

Any vlogger will tell you that your final product is only as good as your video equipment. If your audience can't see or hear you, it doesn't make much difference what content you're sharing. The good news is that you may already have the equipment you need, and if not, it's now less expensive than ever to obtain quality video equipment.

If you plan to film all your vlogging content within reach of your computer, you may want to get started by using your computer's internal webcam. For better quality, consider investing in an external webcam that provides you with more flexibility.

You may want to film on the go, on-site at events, or in locations that prevent filming with a webcam from being a viable option. Investing in the following can take your video quality to the next level:

>> External lighting

>> External microphone

>> Tripod

TIP

Does one room in your home have incredible natural light? Consider making this your vlogging location. Natural light provides for high-quality videos. Indoor natural light cuts down on the background noises that you may encounter if you film outdoors.

Creating a vlogging space

You know those moments in reality television shows when the stars answer questions or provide additional commentary? The background is always the same: the furniture comfy but perfect; the decorations trendy yet not distracting. The secret is that those areas aren't just a quiet corner in the homes of the reality TV stars. They are actually staged sets created specifically for the purpose of shooting that footage.

Now, I'm not suggesting that you do away with your children's playroom so that you have space to create a vlogging set, but I do suggest that it's a good idea to designate one area of your home or office where you typically film your videos. Take the time to look at the following before you decide to film:

>> **Lighting:** Are you in good, natural light? If not, can you bring in additional light without too much hassle?

>> **Sound:** Life doesn't stop while you vlog. Be sure not to choose a location too close to noisemakers such as the dishwasher or laundry room.

>> **Decor:** Before clicking Record, look behind you and to the sides to see what your viewers will also see. Although it's nice to think that they'll be looking only at you as they hang on your every word, the truth is that they may be zooming in to figure out where you are in that family vacation photo over your right shoulder.

Editing Your Vlog

By now you've thought about your video equipment, the vlogging platform you'd like to use, and where you're likely to film your vlogs. You're ready to go! But wait. What about editing that raw footage before sharing it with the world?

Certainly, many vlogs are filmed on the go and posted to the Internet with no editing whatsoever — and that is absolutely okay! But should you wish to polish your content before putting it out there, tons of tools are available to you to do so.

Start by checking out the computer you already own. Your computer might have come with a program such as Windows Movie Maker (shown in Figure 14-2) or iMovie. These types of video editing programs are typically incredibly user friendly, with drag-and-drop features and even the ability to upload directly to YouTube. These standard editing programs also feature some nonstandard tools, such as ones that give you the ability to share directly to social media and add an underlying soundtrack. With just a bit of time and practice, your vlogs can feature captions, credits, and more!

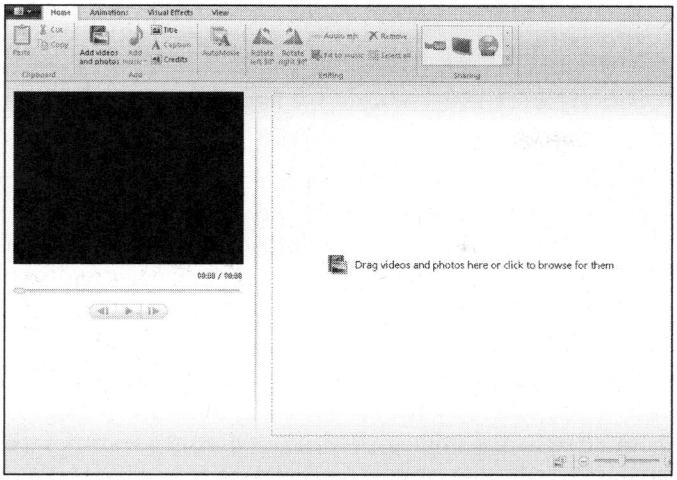

FIGURE 14-2:
Windows Movie
Maker is one
example of a
video editing
program that you
may already have
installed on your
computer.

As you begin to play around with video editing for your blog, keep these things in mind:

>> Focus on audio over video if forced to choose.

>> Don't go overboard with special features such as transitions.

>> Keep your video length to an easily consumable period of time.

>> Know how you want your video to look and sound before you begin the editing process.

Promoting Your Vlog

After you've created your video content, it is time to promote that content and, with luck, bring a new audience to your blog or vlog channel. If you've already begun blogging, the first place to start is your own blog. Even if you choose to host your vlog on an additional platform such as YouTube, your blog still creates a prime opportunity to promote your new vlog content:

>> **Use sidebar promotion:** Let anyone stopping by your site know that additional video content is available by featuring that content in your sidebar. Post an image letting readers know about your vlog and asking them to click through to your vlogging platform. Better yet, install a video viewer so that readers can view your vlogging content right there on your site.

>> **Write an announcement post:** Do you have an established readership who may have no idea that you've also begun vlogging? Let them know by writing a post announcing your new venture into the world of video. They'll likely be excited to check out the new offerings from one of their favorite bloggers.

>> **Write a round-up post:** One of the best ways for bloggers to promote any additional content they're posting elsewhere on the Internet is through a weekly, bi-weekly, or even monthly round-up post. Rather than let your readers know every time you post new video content, tell them periodically with short summaries and links to that content.

Social media is likely to become your best friend when it's time to promote your video content. Most vlog platforms — and certainly all blogs — provide you with ways to directly and immediately share your new video content with the world through some of the most popular social media platforms. Consider taking all the steps to promote your vlog that you would with a written blog, such as creating a unique Twitter account or Facebook page for your vlog channel or webisode series.

As with all content promotion, community is key. Check out a bit more about building your own community with forums, RSS feeds, and social media in the upcoming chapters. One of the best ways to get your community to promote your content is to spend more time promoting theirs than promoting your own. It may seem counterintuitive, but the truth is that if you're a good steward of the relationships you're building online rather than taking advantage of your connections, those community members will step up to promote you when the time comes — such as the launch of your fantastic new vlog!

Chapter 15

Leveraging Community with Forums

I magine your blogging career five years in the future. Your blog has thousands of visitors every single day. Comments are being left on your blog posts by the hundreds every hour. A blogging career couldn't get any better, could it? You've reached the big time! People love you!

But wait! You also have a problem: You can't keep up with the conversation, and now that you think about it, a lot of your contributors are talking to each other. Although you love reading what they have to say, these conversations aren't really directed at you anymore. One possible solution to this awesome dilemma is to add a *forum* to your blog. On the Internet, a forum — which might also be called a message board or bulletin board — is software that permits date-sorted conversations between members, generally organized around topics. Members can reply to messages posted by others, or start their own topics. Unlike blog posts, forums are typically not maintained by an author. Members are all on an equal playing field when it comes to the conversation.

Sounds good, right? But should you do it? Is it a good idea? What if members talk about things unrelated to the topics you normally discuss on your blog?

In this chapter, I discuss the benefits of setting up a forum, what types of forum software are available, and how forums differ from your blog's comment system. I also tell you about common features of a typical forum package and how you can add a forum to your blog without disturbing the natural flow of the blog itself.

Deciding Whether Forums Will Work for You

The neuroscientist and author Sam Harris has a blog combined with a forum on his website at www.samharris.org. Sam is sometimes known as "America's leading atheist," and his writings cover the intersection of religion and science. As you can imagine, this is a set of topics that generates a huge amount of discussion, and Sam has responded by housing some of this conversation on the forums of his website (www.samharris.org/forum), shown in Figure 15-1. This neatly solves one of Sam's biggest problems — as a single individual, he simply can't respond to the sheer volume of conversation that his chosen field generates, but discussion of which he encourages.

FIGURE 15-1:
Sam Harris's website offers visitors both a blog and a forum.

There are many reasons to add a forum to your blog. The first and most common reason is that your frequent visitors may ask you to add one, but you may also see the need for it yourself.

The second most common reason is that discussions have simply outgrown the blog commenting system. This isn't a bad thing; it just means your blog is incredibly popular. You should be pleased that visitors enjoy what you are doing so much!

Some bloggers find that comments are great ways for dialogue to start, and that forums allow that discussion to expand. But how does a forum benefit your blog itself? How can you use a forum to grow your community? Here are a few examples of what a forum can do besides give your readers a way to chat:

>> **Increase traffic to and page views on your blog:** By offering a place where people can exchange ideas and chat directly with one another, you can reap the rewards of additional content. Each posting on your blog is an individual page that people can find by searching the Internet. The same thing applies to forum posts. The more discussions you facilitate, the more pages and locations search engines can index. This means that you can use your forum as a place for friendly conversation and to generate more traffic and page views.

>> **Find a new type of audience:** A forum may attract a whole new type of readership. People who like to leave comments on blog posts may not be invested enough to carry on longer chats with other commenting visitors. Providing them with a platform where they can expand on their comments and offer additional opinions can, however, help build a new audience by tapping into a larger audience that enjoys participating in wider discussions that are not specific to individual blog posts. People may be attracted to your forum and then start participating in the comments.

>> **Keep tabs on your audience's interests:** Even though you write your blog to put your ideas out into the blogosphere, you may run dry from time to time. You can look through the comments on your blog to find new ideas or expand on existing posts, but a forum can generate a whole new set of ideas. This is a great tool for taking the pulse of what your community finds compelling or interesting and what its members have questions about, all of which can feed directly back into what you choose to discuss on your blog.

>> **Build additional credibility:** If you are already blogging and attracting readers, you are likely developing some visible expertise with your community. Forums can help build that reputation with a larger audience, and on a broader set of topics. (You may even learn a thing or two from your community members while you're at it!)

>> **Have more "you" time:** Comments on blogs tend to be directed toward you, the blogger. This means that people who leave comments want to hear your reaction to their thoughts. You need to spend a lot of your time not just

writing your blog but also responding to comments. Adding a forum gives your community members the chance to help each other out, taking a bit of the pressure off you to be the only source of information.

Does it sound as though adding a forum to your blog is worthwhile? Don't worry if the answer is "No," "I'm not sure," or "Not right now." Forums aren't for every blog, or every blogger, but they can naturally evolve from online discussions and commentary. No stock answer exists — the final call is up to you! If you're on the fence, you might want to write a blog post and see what your readers think.

If your answer is "Yes, let's go!" jump to the next section for answers to what I'm sure your question is now — what kind of forum software is available?

Researching Software Options

A set of "out of the box" features comes with most forum software packages, but it's worth reviewing the basics to make sure that you're meeting your audience's needs when making your selection.

TIP

A great online source where you can "kick the tires" on a bunch of different forum software can be found at `http://php.opensourcecms.com/scripts/show.php?catid=5&category=Forums`.

The website is dedicated to providing demonstrations of blog software, forum software, and general content-management systems. It's a great place to try out forum packages without installing them yourself.

Another option to consider before you start installing software is to find some online forums (whether or not they are on a blog) and spend some time using them. You can often find out what software is being used by looking near the bottom of the home page of the forum. You can then make your choice based on the user experience.

Choosing between Free and Commercial Forum Software

One of the first decisions you must make is between free forum software and commercial software. Both categories offer great options.

Budget is, of course, one of the biggest differences. There's free . . . and *not* free. If you have zero budget, well, the choice is pretty simple! But if you do have some money to spend, commercial forum software generally offers some level of customer service and technical support that free software lacks. If something goes wrong or the forum does not perform correctly, answers can be a little easier to come by. If you aren't terribly technical yourself, having reliable technical support may be cheap, whatever the cost.

Selecting the software that will benefit both you and your audience is paramount to the success of your forum, so be sure to thoroughly kick the tires before you make your final choice.

In addition to forum software you install on a web server, you can also use hosted software that runs elsewhere. See the "Hosted forum solutions" sidebar, later in this chapter, for information about these lighter-weight options.

Browsing commercial forum software

Here are four of the most popular packages with commercial support:

- » **vBulletin** (www.vbulletin.com): This feature-rich forum software offers commercial support and a variety of licensing models. Cost starts at $14.99 per month and increases based on additional features and support levels.

- » **UBB.Threads** (www.ubbcentral.com): Available since 1997, UBB pricing starts at $139, and you can pay to have the software installed.

- » **XenForo** (www.xenforo.com): This option offers a free demo so you can really check it out and make an informed decision before purchasing the software.

- » **IP.Board** (www.invisionpower.com): Part of a suite of website tools, this forum software can be purchased on its own from $10 per month.

Perusing open source forum software

Here are a few open source alternatives:

- » **phpBB** (www.phpbb.com): This very popular open source package has been available since 2000 and you can find good user-created resources.

- » **Vanilla Forums** (www.vanillaforums.org): This tool promises a high degree of flexibility and integration with existing websites and blogs.

- » **Simple Machines Forum** (www.simplemachines.org): This free software is PHP based, uses MySQL on the backend, and promises customizable forums that are easy to use.

>> **bbPress** (`www.bbpress.org`)**:** From the creators of WordPress, this forum software works very well for bloggers already using the WordPress platform.

>> **miniBB** (`www.minibb.com`)**:** miniBB is a lightweight forum package that prides itself on being small and fast.

Getting Finicky about Features

Of course, it isn't all about the cost! Features matter when it comes to forums, particularly those that need to host a high volume of messages, users, or both. It's worth noting that although you can migrate from one forum software package to another, the process is notoriously complicated, so you can save yourself time if you think through the options up front.

>> **Availability:** Some blog software actually offers forum software, or integrates easily with a particular forum software package. Check your blog documentation. If you're lucky and the blog platform you selected has forum features built in, all you have to do is turn them on. If it doesn't, check to see whether there is a forum software package commonly used by others who blog on the same platform, or if there are compatibility recommendations. bbPress, as mentioned earlier in the chapter, was created by the makers of WordPress and can be easily implemented on WordPress blogs (`www.bbpress.org`).

>> **Threading:** One of the most important forum features is whether conversations on the forum are *flat* or *threaded. Threading* groups sets messages together, relating them. For example, if you post something on a forum and someone replies to you, a threaded conversation displays a visual cue that indicates that the forum postings are part of the same conversation. You can

track which conversations are which and who is replying to what postings. You can see an example of a threaded forum in Figure 15-2.

>> **Look and feel:** Forum software is incredibly visual, and typically a software package comes with several default themes, or design packages. Many offer additional themes, for free or for a fee. You may also be interested in creating a custom theme that matches the design of the blog you're adding the forum to.

>> **Ignore lists:** Not everyone on the same forum is the best of friends. Unlike the comment system, in which users always know who is writing the comment (unless they post anonymously, but those types of people don't really want to have real discussions), you want to give a little bit of control to your users to make sure that their experience on your forum is a good one. *Ignore lists* allow a forum member to hide other users and their posts. This is somewhat like blocking someone on a social network and is a handy feature that lets your community members aggressively dislike another member and still have a positive experience.

>> **Signatures (sigs):** Forum users are addicted to *signatures*. A signature is a lot like it sounds — a way for users to append identifying information to the posts they make on the forum. Signatures generally allow for imagery, links to external websites, famous quotes, and even some good old-fashioned silliness. As you might expect, forum members are quite attached to them.

>> **Emoticons:** Who doesn't love emoticons? Don't answer that. ☺ Emoticons are whimsical text or visual icons intended to convey emotion. Many forum users

use them to indicate the tone of their message and prevent misinterpretation. Emoticon options differ from software package to software package but are usually appreciated by the forum members.

>> **Polls:** Polls are a nice feature that allows visitors to vote on questions that other users create. Questions can be asked, and answers can be preselected by the user asking the question. The answers are then calculated and a graph is produced.

>> **Membership tools:** Most forum software offers a set of membership tools, such as registration, profiles, avatars, and so on. Membership allows the software to understand that posts come from the same user and keep track of the user's activity across the life span of the forum. Membership requirements decrease the amount of spam on a forum as well as allow moderators to remove or block problematic users.

TIP

If your blog already has registration turned on for comment posting, you may want to look for forum software that can be tied into your existing membership database so that visitors don't have to create and remember two different accounts.

>> **Spam controls:** If you thought that spammers would leave a forum alone, think again. I'm sorry to say that spam is as big a problem on a forum as it is on a blog. Membership (see the preceding bullet) can help, but a good forum software package should offer you some options for identifying, preventing, and removing spam posts and users.

>> **Images and rich media:** Some forum software allows users the capability to post images, upload files, and embed rich media from other locations on the web. This can make postings and discussions more vibrant.

At the end of the day, the features you choose help your users communicate better — more quickly, easily, and effectively. So do your homework!

Installing Forum Software

After you decide to press ahead with installing a forum for your readers, it's time to think about what you need to run it. If you already have web hosting for your blog, this process may be quite simple. In fact, check with your web host; it may have a forum software package available as an add-in or may even be able to take care of the installation for you.

If you don't have web hosting, it's time to find some. I talk about web hosting in Chapter 3.

TECHNICAL STUFF

As well as establishing web hosting, you must think about the URL for your forum. Your blog, for example, may have a URL like www.example.com. When you install your forum software, you can't use the same URL because your blog already lives at that location. The forums need their own addresses. A couple of options are:

>> www.example.com/forum

>> www.forum.example.com

Consult with your web host to see what the best options are, or if they have any guidelines for where and how software of this kind should be installed.

The installation process for your forum software will vary from package to package, but they all come with installation instructions. Refer to those in order to complete the installation of the package you've chosen.

A typical installation process, however, looks a lot like this:

1. Download the forum software from the web.

2. Decompress the file on your computer.

3. Upload the forum software files to your web hosting account.

4. When the files are in the correct location, go to the installation script page in your browser and click the Install button to be walked through the installation procedure.

5. When the forums are installed, visit them and test all the common tasks your users need to accomplish, such as registering, logging in, resetting a password, formatting a member profile, and of course, posting!

REMEMBER

If you have any problems with the installation procedure, make notes about any error messages you see and where the failure occurred in the installation process so that you can ask good questions using whatever support tools are available to you. And if you've opted not to spring for support, a search engine query on the error may help you track down the problem.

Cultivating Community Standards

As Chapter 10 mentions, building community standards is important. Establishing a good set of rules will encourage readers to get involved and add their own ideas to the conversations. Ideally, the dialogue on your forum stays civil, respectful, and on-topic. However, sometimes your community may need a little push in the right direction. Establishing your expectations regarding behavior up front can help set the tone for the kinds of conversations that occur on the forum — and give you a way to remove members who don't follow the rules without being accused of censorship.

TIP

Many forums appoint or hire a community manager to help ensure that forum rules are followed and to begin new conversations and cultivate forum threads.

Typically, forum guidelines should direct members to conform to some basic standards:

>> **Be polite:** Being rude on a forum is tempting for some people. You probably want to make sure that politeness is one of your first and foremost rules.

>> **"No flaming, no trolls."** Many forum owners explicitly indicate that flaming and trolls aren't allowed. *Flaming* someone is the act of posting hostile messages. Flames are often posted by *trolls,* people who participate in a forum with the purpose of sowing havoc with off-topic or offensive content.

>> **User accounts:** You may want to make it clear that the user accounts you provide to all of those who chat in your forums exist on your terms, and that people who violate terms lose their accounts.

>> **Links:** Some communities restrict their users and do not allow linking to other websites. Others allow users to post links, but only after members have been active for some time. Because some links can take people to unwanted material, spam, and malware websites, links can become problematic.

>> **Pictures:** If your software allows users to post photos, either as part of their member profile or within the body of posts, you need to specify whether particular types of imagery are acceptable. Nudity, for example, is typically excluded.

>> **Legal stuff:** A mention about copyright is worth including. Forum software lets users post images, audio, and text, but the users must be held to a standard that means they are not posting the work of others.

Some of this stuff sounds a little daunting, I know. But most people appreciate the additional resource of a forum and aren't actually out to post troublesome content. If you're thinking about guidelines, visit some existing forums and review their terms of use for additional ideas and considerations. Forums that have been around for some time may be especially useful for this purpose because their guidelines probably evolved as the community ran into particular kinds of problems.

When it comes to community guidelines of any sort, they are entirely up to you. As with comments, you may consider it your duty to protect everyone who posts on your blog and your forums, or you may feel that the community should police itself. You can encourage a very structured conversation, or you can let it be a written "wild west."

5

Marketing and Promoting Your Blog

IN THIS PART . . .

Understanding how to build your audience with content marketing

Using social media to enhance your blog and increase your audience

Joining the most popular social media platforms to generate traffic, network, and more

Knowing the stats: Measuring and monitoring your blog's presence

Chapter 16

Making Your Blog Easy to Find

You've chosen your blog's name, selected the hosting plan that is best for you, and gotten into a publishing rhythm that works with your life. Now, how do you go about helping your blog's audience locate that amazing content? If a blogger blogs and no one reads it, did they really blog?

Thankfully, there are a variety of methods meant to connect your potential audience with your blog as well as keep your current audience reading regularly. Although everything from your social media presence, discussed in Chapters 17 and 18, to your interaction with the blogging community, covered in Chapter 10, will help grow your audience, the methods covered in this chapter carry a big bang for your buck.

Diving into SEO

Search Engine Optimization, or *SEO* for short, is the art of maximizing your blog's potential to be found by search engines. If your site is succeeding at search engine optimization, your content is likely to appear high on the list of results that a search engine returns. In a similar manner, if your site falls short in the area of SEO, your blog will likely appear a few pages into search engine results. The goal of SEO is for your blog to be found by people conducting searches of words and topics related to your content.

Understanding SEO

SEO can feel a bit like an elusive magic formula to bloggers hoping to climb up the ladder of search engine results. For bloggers already investing time and money in other aspects of their craft, it may seem like just one more task in a growing to-do list. The main trick to maximizing your blog's search engine potential is understanding how SEO works in the first place.

Because such a large proportion of Internet traffic comes from search engines such as Google and Bing, it's important to help those search engines locate your blog. The content on your site, from the words you use to the titles you give your images, can either make your blog more visible to search engines or bury it.

Imagine search engines sending out millions of tiny, information-gathering spiders to "crawl" every site on the web. These crawlers return to the search engine and report on what they've found. They're hoping to provide one very important piece of information: How well does this website answer a search engine question?

Although the information about SEO can fill an entire book (*Search Engine Optimization For Dummies,* 5th edition, by Peter Kent, John Wiley & Sons), the important piece to know is that you have the power to decide what those search engines will find when they come crawling at your door.

Creating an SEO-friendly blog

Perhaps you've gotten to this point in the chapter and you're wondering if you're blogging for yourself, for your readers, or for some nameless, faceless search engine. Let me reassure you that you should not be creating content simply with the purpose of charming those crawling search spiders. There are some ways, however, that you can make your already awesome content more appealing to the search engine results.

For starters, search engines still prefer words over images. As mentioned in Chapter 12, carefully crafted images are a key component to blog post sharing in the age of popular sites such as Pinterest. To help those images do their job in pushing your blog to the top of search results, be sure to always utilize the "alt text" field when uploading your images (as shown in Figure 16-1). Think about what words readers might search for that would drive them to your post and use those keywords in your image description.

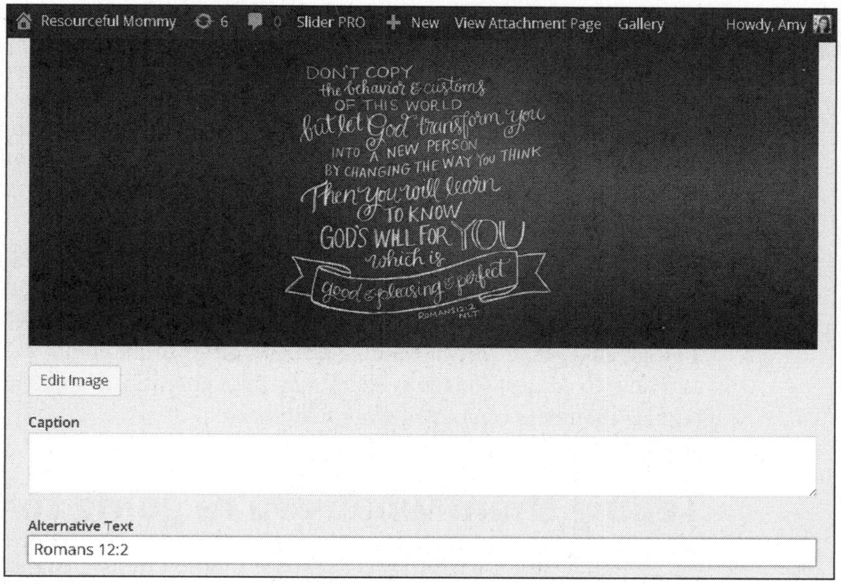

FIGURE 16-1:
Utilize the "alt text" field when uploading images to help search engines locate your blog.

Speaking of keywords, you may not be sure where to start when selecting search-friendly wording for your posts. A variety of keyword tools are available to help you select the best search engine–friendly words for your blog content, including the following:

- » **Keyword Tool** (www.keywordtool.io)
- » **Wordtracker** (www.freekeywords.wordtracker.com)
- » **SEO Book** (tools.seobook.com/keyword-tools/seobook/)
- » **Google Trends** (www.google.com/trends/)
- » **BuzzSumo** (www.buzzsumo.com)

Utilizing SEO tools

If all this sounds a bit overwhelming, don't throw in the towel just yet! Free WordPress plug-ins are available to meet your SEO needs. Search engine optimization plug-ins are some of the most downloaded on the Internet, so know that you are in good company! Here is a small selection to get you started:

- » **WordPress SEO by Yoast** (www.yoast.com/wordpress/plugins/seo/)
- » **SEOquake** (www.seoquake.com)
- » **LinkPatrol** (www.linkpatrolwp.com)

Branding Your Blog

When you see a red dot inside a red circle, what store comes to mind? How about those golden arches? Does a particular brand name come to mind when you see the swoosh symbol?

Just like popular stores, restaurants, and shoe companies, bloggers need to think about their personal brand. Your blog is far more than words on a page. Your blog is a snapshot of who you are, what you're trying to communicate to the world in a quick snippet of information. Taking time to think about your blog's branding and how to convey that to readers may take potential visitors and turn them into regular members of your reading audience.

Telling them what you're going to tell them

Once upon a time I used to teach middle school English. One of the first things I taught students was how to write an informative essay, and I always told students to begin by telling readers what you were going to tell them. You want visitors to your blog to know immediately what they'll find if they spend some time clicking around your site.

One way to make this clear is with a great tagline for your site. In Chapter 9, I introduced you to Nancy Friedman's blog, From Hip to Housewife, which uses the tagline "on aging and momming and my twenty year quest to lose the same ten pounds." Readers know immediately that they're going to find a specific kind of content if they stick around long enough to read a post.

Showing them what you're going to show them

As you may have figured out by now, blogs are a very visual medium and have as much to do with what readers see as with the words they read. Effective blog branding includes using visual elements of a blog to convey your blog's purpose to readers at a glance.

Take a look at Figure 16-2, which showcases the site The Centsible Life by author Kelly Whalen. Everything from the title, to the logo, to the quick author bio in the sidebar shows the reader quite clearly that time spent reading this particular blog is meant to bring readers financial savings. Think about what you want readers to know about your blog at first glance, and then play around with ways to convey that visually on your site.

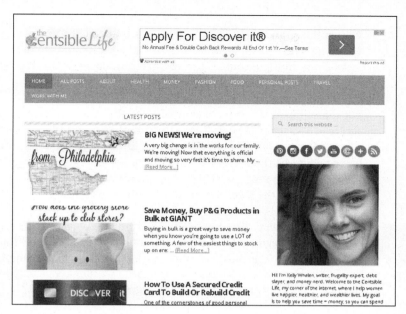

Reaching Out with RSS

No fashionable blog would be caught dead without a web feed. It's essential for both accessibility and promotion of your blog. What is RSS? *RSS* (*Really Simple Syndication*) feeds, or web feeds, give you an easy way to distribute your content, such as blog posts and podcasts, to your web audience. In this section, I explain what an RSS feed is, how to create your blog feed (it's easy), how to subscribe to feeds, and more.

Getting the goods on web feeds

Since 2003 — which is when blogs truly reached mainstream awareness — blogs and other technologies have adopted RSS at an exponential rate. Companies such as Mozilla, Microsoft, IBM, and many others have created really interesting ways to use RSS feeds to share information, both through their websites and through internal communication processes.

Put simply, when you syndicate your blog by using a web feed, feed software reads your blog posts, which it formats by using XML (eXtensible Markup Language). XML is an Internet standard and marks your prose so that software applications can understand and display it properly for readers who subscribe to your blog.

Why is RSS a good thing? Well, it means that code can be used to easily display your blog's feed on other websites, from blogs to search engines. Sites that pull in news from multiple sources use RSS feeds to do so, and being syndicated in this way can earn you traffic from those sites back to your blog.

But more important, newsreader software that any visitor to your site might use can read RSS feeds, and visitors can then access your blog quickly and easily. By subscribing to a blog via an RSS feed, visitors don't have to bookmark hundreds of blogs and check them every 20 minutes to see whether the bloggers have updated them. Instead, a user can simply log into his or her newsreader software to see in one window all the feeds to which he or she subscribes.

TECHNICAL STUFF

On the web, several different terms describe the subject of this section: *RSS, Atom, web feed,* and *news feed* are a few. Website developers use all these terms interchangeably, but the most accurate one is *web feed.* RSS is simply a type of web feed. Even though web feed is the most accurate name, I usually refer to RSS feeds because that's how most blogs and bloggers refer to them.

Breaking it down further

Essentially, RSS gives your blog the capability to break down its content into a basic text file. Software creates this text file in a special XML format that makes up the feed. Blog software then distributes this plain-text version of your blog content to other websites, search engines, and blogosphere tracking services. Figure 16-3 shows the code behind an RSS feed.

A few acronyms for RSS are floating around out on the Internet. Here are the acronyms you're most likely to see, and if you want to talk about RSS with your blog readers, you can use any of them (but the first one tends to be the most popular):

>> Really Simple Syndication

>> RDF Site Summary

>> Real Simple Syndication

>> Rich Site Summary

REMEMBER

You can use RSS to syndicate content on your blog, but most mainstream news agencies also use RSS to make their news information more accessible. News services such as Reuters, CBC, CNN, and the *Washington Post* use RSS technology to spread their articles beyond their own websites.

FIGURE 16-3:
Web feeds aren't
very pretty to
look at.

Many web browsers use XML to handle displaying RSS feeds in a more attractive format. If you click an RSS feed link and find that the content that loads looks rather user friendly, you're probably using a browser that understands and formats XML nicely.

TIP

For a really excellent short video that describes just what RSS is and how it works, visit the Common Craft blog at www.commoncraft.com/video/rss. This video uses simple graphics and words to get across the concepts that make RSS so groundbreaking.

Confused? Well, don't worry, because nearly all blog software automatically builds your RSS feed and helps you advertise it to your blog visitors. So, you're most likely covered, in any case — but if you know a little bit about RSS and why it's important to your blog, you can ensure that your blog content reaches a wider audience.

Generating web traffic

Some bloggers have a tendency to limit the distribution of their content and keep it off other sites. The reasoning goes that you worked hard to create that content, so why should other sites and software get to display it for free?

Actually, because of its ease of use, RSS can help you gain more readers. Your website can travel further than ever because you can distribute RSS feeds with little to no effort on your part. Because syndication of your content includes links back to your blog, people who are exposed to your RSS feed probably click those links and come to your blog.

So, because the RSS feed is only text, it doesn't have to stay in one place. Any number of websites and blogs can pick it up and display it.

Creating a feed for your blog

Unless you really want to mess around in the code of your own RSS files, you shouldn't need to do anything special to get started with RSS. Most blog software already includes an RSS feed that pulls together and syndicates your blog. At most, you might have to turn on the option to have an RSS feed.

Then, just blog normally and ignore the feed. Your users can find it and subscribe, and your blog content flows automatically into the feed.

Chances are that your blog software already has RSS capability. Check your administrative settings and documentation. If it doesn't, you might also be able to add the functionality by using a plug-in.

If you don't have software that creates an RSS feed, you have a couple of options. If you're a programmer or coder, you can probably pick up enough XML to hand-code an RSS feed yourself. But an even better option is to use some of the third-party feed creation tools available today:

>> **Feedblitz** (www.feedblitz.com): One of the most popular feed services in existence, Feedblitz specializes in migrating blog feeds away from other feed generators and then providing special services to help market the blog's feed more effectively.

>> **Google Feedburner** (feedburner.google.com): A favorite of many bloggers, this free tool allows you to create an RSS feed for your blog as well as manage and promote that feed.

>> **Feed43** (www.feed43.com): Set up a feed for your blog quickly and for free. Increase the frequency with which your feed is updated by buying a higher level of feed, starting at $29 a year.

>> **FeedForAll** (www.feedforall.com): Use this tool to create and edit RSS feeds for your blog or podcast. You must be able to install software on your web host to use this tool. Pricing starts at $39.95.

When a feed exists, you don't need to do anything else. Search engines and software tools automatically find it when they index your blog, and your readers can subscribe to your feed when and if they choose to do so.

Making the Most of RSS

You can use RSS in all sorts of ways. Industries as diverse as financial sectors and breaking news organizations have adopted RSS because it's so flexible and generates website traffic, attracting new readers from search engines and news aggregators. But that's not all you can use RSS for. Here's more:

>> **Syndicating content:** In the blogosphere, *syndication* means that you publish your information on the web so that newsreaders and other websites can display it.

>> **Aggregating news:** Do you like other blogs that deal with similar topics as your own? You can use their RSS feeds to include their content on your website. You can link directly to it or, if your blog software has such functionality, display other blog content on your own blog.

>> **Replacing email newsletters:** Some RSS advocates make astounding claims that RSS will be the death of email. Although this dire prediction hasn't yet come to pass, RSS definitely has many advantages over email newsletters. The most important is that you can avoid spam. How? You can simply choose to read an RSS feed rather than receive more email; by not giving away your email address, you don't put it at risk for being sold to a spammer.

>> **Keeping communities updated:** RSS feeds are terrific for keeping people updated. Some feeds merely post information, such as sports scores — as fast as a goal is scored, an RSS feed can be updated. Here are five kinds of things you can share that people might want to know as soon as possible:

- Security bulletins

- Classified listings for apartments

- Emergency weather changes

- Changes to bids on eBay or Amazon

- Product availability at retail stores

Because of the simplicity of using RSS technology (yes, the actual building of RSS feeds might still be too geeky for most bloggers), you can use it in many ways to augment the communication channels of your blog or within your community that you haven't quite figured out yet. Get creative!

Chapter 17

Getting to Know Social Networking

E ver been "liked" on Facebook? Done any tweeting lately? What about endorsing someone on LinkedIn? Is this all gibberish to you? Welcome to the world of social networking, consistently the hottest topic online.

At first glance, social networking can look overwhelming and difficult to understand because it uses a lot of jargon and so many players are in the field. Never fear, however. Social networking is a simple concept: You can connect with others online by using a website or online service. At the very heart of it, social networking is the simple process of finding people you want to hang out with or connecting online with people you already hang out with.

The web has opened the door to meeting people who share your interests, but whose geography or professional careers — to name just a couple of possibilities — made it unlikely you would ever meet in "real" life. Social-networking websites are designed to bring together people who share hobbies, careers, friends, geographic regions, and other interests, and then encourage communication and sharing. And believe me, social-networking sites exist for everything under the sun!

In this chapter, I introduce you to some of today's most popular social-networking tools and show you how they can tie into your blogging efforts.

Thinking Strategically

Social networks allow you to connect with current friends and make new ones while sharing photos, videos, text, and more. They've exploded in popularity in recent years, and many social networks have even added blogging tools. From Twitter to Facebook, these tools are proliferating and their quality is improving. Social networking can build

>> **Friendships:** You can form long-lasting bonds with people you meet online. By building your social network, you inevitably find others who share your interests.

>> **Communities:** Connecting with other people is one of the greatest ways to improve your blogging experience. Other bloggers are using social networks to connect with those who share their interests and passions.

>> **Audience:** Bring more eyeballs to your blog. The fact that these eyeballs belong to folks you already have things in common with — well, that's a bonus!

TIP

In general, social networks are incredibly valuable tools for bloggers. It is now all but a requirement that bloggers use social media tools to promote themselves and connect with readers.

Most blogs include a tool on each post that allows readers to share the post title and a link to it across a variety of social networks. You can include this tool in your own blog by activating a built-in feature if available or by installing a social sharing tool.

Because this book talks about blogging, I focus mainly on how social networks can benefit your blog. However, you may want to dive into social networking by selecting the platforms that work not only for your blog but for your life in general. The following sections give you some tips on choosing a network or networks. In Chapter 18, I take a closer look at a few of the most popular social networking sites.

Connecting with your audience

The key is to know your audience and to choose what information to share. The more information you share among the social networks you use, the more attention you can bring to your blog. Take the time to not only identify your current audience and choose networks in which that audience is active, but also to grow your social media following with the purpose of building your blog audience. Be sure that the social networks where you spend time are those that likely can repay that effort.

Most bloggers tie their blogs and their social networks together, letting blog readers know about their actions on social networks and vice versa. The payoff is not only an increase in readership but also a deeper connection to the audience you already have!

Social media sites attract huge audiences, and by connecting with your readers on these platforms, you make it more likely that they'll share your blog with their online friends and affinity groups. The friends and contacts you make through your own social networks and groups may also very well be hungry for good blogs to read . . . like yours!

Selecting networks

Integrating social networks into your online activities and your blog does require some planning. With so many options, how do you determine which networks to spend time on? You could just dive in and sign up for a bunch of social networks and then see where the chips fall, but if you want your time spent using social networks to pay off, consider the following questions:

>> What do you want to accomplish with your online efforts?

>> Which networks are most popular in general and therefore frequented by your future readers?

>> What networks does your current readership use? What about your friends and family?

>> If you're unsure what networks you have to choose from, the section "Getting Familiar with Social Networks," later in this chapter, introduces you to a variety of popular networks.

TIP

>> Which networks have the best functionalities, especially for bloggers?

>> How active is your audience on social networks? What does your audience seem to be getting out of that interaction?

>> Is your blog content subject-appropriate for any particular social networks? On the flip side, is your blog inappropriate for any of them?

>> Does your audience want to know about you in ways that a social-networking tool might fulfill?

>> How much time do you want to spend playing around with social networks?

You need to consider these types of questions when you're looking to fit a social network into your blogging life. Take a look at where your readers are coming from, and using the analytics information that you should be collecting for your blog (see Chapter 19), find out what attracts visitors to your site. Post a question on your blog about a social-networking website and solicit responses and advice.

Protecting your privacy online

You may worry about the security of your identity online if you're jumping head-long into the social-networking world.

REMEMBER

Be smart. Don't post information on any social-networking website that you feel is inappropriate. You want to keep certain bits of information private. If a social-networking website asks you to provide information that you aren't comfortable sharing, don't share it. If the website insists you share that information, don't use that service. It's as simple as that.

WARNING

Social networks often feel safer than the Internet at large because they require membership and logins, and of course, profiles of your new friends often include photos and other elements that look convincingly real. However, remember that these sites offer very little barrier to creating an account — the accounts are free, the services don't require identity verification, and the social networks can't prevent people from including misleading information or outright lying about who they are.

So remain vigilant. If you're aware of what information you place online, you should be able to protect yourself without much of a concern. Just like writing on your blog, consider using this guideline: If you wouldn't blog it, don't social network it.

Getting Familiar with Social Networks

Almost any interest group and almost any method of sharing have a social network. Deciding which ones to try out depends on what you want to get out of the social networking. If you're a photographer, social websites such as Flickr (which allows you to share photos) may be your cup of tea. If you like to read books and talk about them, LibraryThing and Goodreads may be the places to hang out.

In the following sections, I show you some of the most popular so that you can get familiar with social-networking sites and decide where to get started.

REMEMBER

You can find many more sites that I don't have the space to cover in this book, so make this chapter a starting rather than an end point while you explore social networks.

Friend-based networks

Some of the most popular social networks allow their users to share almost anything, from photos to friends to games. Social networks such as Facebook simply try to throw everything and the kitchen sink into the mix; others, such as Twitter, go with a more minimal approach.

Here are three all-purpose social networks:

>> **Facebook** (www.facebook.com): Facebook is the most popular social-networking platform, with an estimated 1.63 million users as of 2016. Created in 2004 by Mark Zuckerberg, Facebook was initially intended to be a communication tool for university students but quickly grew beyond that audience.

The service allows users to share photos, audio, and video; install apps, such as games and horoscopes; and "friend" others, among other constantly changing and growing services. *Friending* is the method of identifying people you want in your network. On most social networks, Facebook included, friends are entitled to see more of your shared information than other members of the network.

TIP

For more information about Facebook security settings, check out *Facebook For Dummies,* 5th Edition, by Carolyn Abram (John Wiley & Sons, Inc.).

Not surprisingly, you can also post messages and short status updates, and you can set up your profile to let others know when you post to your blog. In fact, most bloggers create a page specifically for their blog and that blog's fans (see Figure 17-1), keeping their personal and blogging Facebook audiences completely separate if they want. Numerous Facebook services are available for bloggers, including widgets that you can install on your blog that automatically post a Facebook update when you create a new post.

>> **Twitter** (www.twitter.com): Although Facebook currently wears the social media crown, Twitter is constantly nipping at its heels. Twitter is a micro-blogging tool that allows you to post small bursts of text, called *tweets,* about absolutely anything, from what you had for lunch to what you think about your boss, world affairs, or the meaning of life. Following other people's Twitter feeds means that you can stay abreast of their activities, as well. Whereas some people tweet from their computers, most Twitter users check messages from friends and update their own Twitter feeds via their mobile phones.

Though you can post up to only 140 characters of text at a time, you can use Twitter to share photographs, links, and even videos. Many businesses have jumped onto the Twitter bandwagon and use the tool to let their customers know about sales, specials, and other news. I cover Twitter in detail in Chapter 18.

>> **Google+ (**`http://plus.google.com`**):** One of the newer social networks online, and one that is still trying to build steam, may also be one of the most powerful for bloggers. Google+ allows you to gain followers, much like Twitter, and create communities and collections of friends, much like Facebook. But unlike other social networks, Google+, as the name indicates, is part of Google, the search engine powerhouse. It is a proven fact that content shared on Google+ receives more search engine attention than content not shared on Google+. If you'd like to find more sets of eyes for your blog, get thee to Google+!

Hobby-based networks

If you have a hobby that you share with a large enough group, you can probably find a social network out there designed just for you. These networks may be just the place to locate new readers for your growing blog. Here are a few examples:

>> **LibraryThing (**`www.librarything.com`**):** A great website that allows you to tell others about the books that you're reading. You can catalog your collection and find information about your books by using a variety of libraries, such as Amazon.com or the Library of Congress.

  The tie-in with your blog? Widgets let you share what you're reading and have read with your blog visitors.

>> **Goodreads** (www.goodreads.com): Goodreads is another social book-cataloging website that allows you to build virtual bookshelves of books that you've read or want to read. You can recommend books to others, compare what you're reading with others in the forums, and even run a book club. And, of course, there are widgets for your blog.

>> **Last.fm** (www.last.fm): Founded in 2002, Last.fm (shown in Figure 17-2) is a social-networking site that allows you to share your musical tastes. You can track the music you're listening to and share what types of music you enjoy with others. If you install Last.fm's *audioscrobbling* widget, it records automatically whatever music you play on your computer, phone, or MP3 player. It then posts this information on your profile on the website.

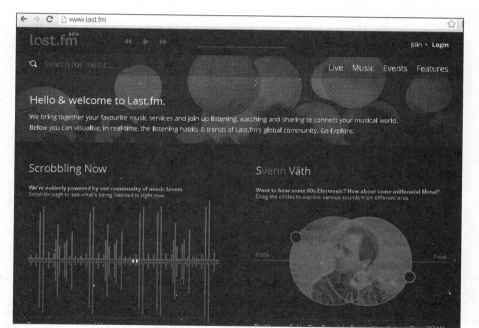

FIGURE 17-2: Last.fm shares what music you play and recommends music that you may like.

Over time, you can see what music you listen to most often, and then the website and the community can make suggestions about what other music you may want to check out. You can tie Last.fm widgets to your blog so that your readers can subscribe to your music playlist and also be your listeners.

>> **Blip.fm** (www.blip.fm): Blip.fm is another, and more recent, addition to the music social-networking realm. This tool is tied closely to Twitter, so users of the one social network get the benefit of the other.

Blip.fm allows you to sign up, identify your friends, search the web for music that you want to recommend (or just listen to), and then build a playlist based on the results. Do you have a friend who has impeccable musical taste? Get him or her signed up for Blip.fm, and then listen to his or her playlist. This site also allows you to give *props* (as in praise) to users who *blip* (post) a song you like, giving feedback about what you want more of.

You can even link your Last.fm account to Blip.fm and let your computer do all the work of blipping songs for you.

>> **Ravelry** (`www.ravelry.com`): Ravelry is a social network designed for knitters to share information about what they're making or thinking of making, how they did it, and other such conversation. You can add friends and send messages, and of course, if you have a knitting blog, you can pull your blog posts into Ravelry and get your friends from Ravelry over to your blog.

Professional networks

The business world has latched onto social networking, as well. Many businesses are using social-networking tools to find new clients, build more creative advertising, and create a conversation with the public. Many of them use the existing popular social networks, from Facebook to Twitter, but another big player in business-related social networking is LinkedIn.

LinkedIn (`www.linkedin.com`), which claims to have more than 400 million members, targets its service to your professional life. Looking to find a new employee or a new job? LinkedIn can put you in touch with others in your industry, recommend partners, help you locate contractors, and generally get the lowdown on those you work with.

One of the most useful features of LinkedIn is that your profile looks much like a résumé, so you can refer people you want to work with to your LinkedIn profile. You can also connect with past and present colleagues, and make use of their networks so that you can make connections with people they interact with. The business world can become a surprisingly small place, thanks to these connections.

Media-sharing networks

The web has allowed all of us to share more than just text — you can easily display video, audio, and photos online, and a number of social-networking sites let you do just that, regardless of whether you have a website or blog. Here are the big hitters:

>> **Instagram** (www.instagram.com): Love taking pictures on your phone and sharing them with the world? Then Instagram is the social network for you. This app-based network — available for both iOS and Android platforms — allows users to take, filter, frame, and share images with their followers and the world. Instagram is a great place to locate new blog readers through your fun and fantastic phone photos!

>> **Vine** (www.vine.co): Just as Twitter limits sharing to 140 characters, Vine limits its medium of choice — video — to only 6-second snippets. These short videos, known as vines, loop continuously. Creatives have taken to Vine to create everything from political satire to animation to micro magic shows. If you're a budding movie maker, Vine may be the place for you to connect with your peers!

>> **Pinterest** (www.Pinterest.com): Pinterest is not only one of the most popular media-sharing social networks, it is rapidly becoming one of the most popular social networks, period. In fact, many bloggers will tell you that Pinterest drives significantly more traffic to their blogs than any other source — social media site or otherwise. All bloggers should not only have and use a Pinterest account but also keep in mind that they are blogging in the age of Pinterest, making it all the more important to create and include "pinnable" images within their posts. Read more about including photos on your blog in Chapter 12.

TIP

I cannot stress the importance of Pinterest to blogging too much! Pinterest is so important, in fact, that it merited not one but two *For Dummies* books. Be sure to pick up *Pinterest For Dummies* and *Pinterest Marketing For Dummies*, both by Kelby Carr (John Wiley & Sons, Inc.).

>> **Flickr** (www.flickr.com): Flickr allows you to post and store your photographs and even videos online. You can share these photos and videos with the community at large, as well as your friends and family. Viewers can mark each photo as a favorite, as well as leave comments and feedback for you.

You can use Flickr to build albums, galleries, and even slideshows of your photos. Best of all, you can place your photos online with Flickr and then quickly and easily embed those photos into your blog posts (see Chapter 12).

>> **YouTube** (www.youtube.com): For the video bloggers out there, YouTube is probably the most popular social-networking video platform online today. Even bloggers who share video only occasionally should consider creating a YouTube channel with their blog branding. People from all over the world record, edit, and post videos, and then share them with the YouTube community. You can post these videos and also embed them into your website or blog.

Informational networks

Initially, social bookmarking was just an online service that allowed you to save all your bookmarks without worrying about whether you'd lose them. As social networking became more popular, social-bookmarking websites got into the act and began to offer all kinds of ways by which you can share your bookmarks with others or discover new and interesting websites to visit. Use these sites to organize your bookmarks, recommend websites, and surf the web:

>> **Delicious** (www.delicious.com): Early on in the life of the web, someone realized that we all spent a lot of time emailing each other links ("You *have* to see this; it's hilarious!") and that a more efficient way to share that kind of information probably existed. Enter Delicious.

Delicious (see Figure 17-3) enables you to record and tag links for later retrieval. You no longer have to be at the same computer to remember what websites you've visited or bookmarked. You can make your bookmarks private or share them with the public. This incredibly easy-to-use social-bookmarking service is also incredibly powerful. You can share your bookmarks by using the built-in RSS feeds and by sharing your bookmarks with your personal network of other users.

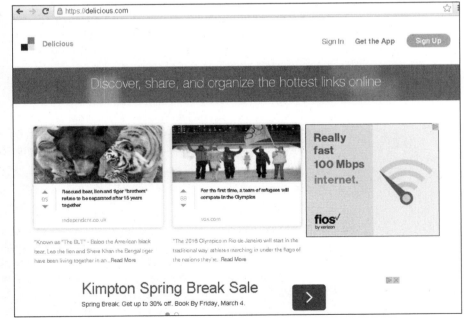

FIGURE 17-3:
Sharing your bookmarks with Delicious lets you share links with others.

Social bookmarking is a little different from creating bookmarks of sites that you go to often, which you probably already do with your browser. I use Delicious to keep track of research around a particular topic — for example, looking up activities to do on my next trip to Asia.

>> **StumbleUpon** (www.stumbleupon.com): Many people have called StumbleUpon one of the biggest time wasters online today. But that isn't actually a bad thing. Web surfing is a time-honored way of negotiating the World Wide Web, and StumbleUpon simply acknowledges that fact and then gives you some outstanding tools for more efficiently and intelligently surfing.

With StumbleUpon, users post and recommend interesting things that they find on the web, and others view those recommendations and add their own endorsements, effectively creating a snapshot of the most interesting and compelling links on the web. You can imagine how useful sharing becomes when you create a community on StumbleUpon of your friends and colleagues; if you combine their recommendations with the personalization options that StumbleUpon provides, it's like reading a personalized (albeit somewhat eccentric) newspaper.

Location-based networks

A bunch of networks allow you to post your location on a map or track your (and your friends') geographic whereabouts. Typically, these kinds of social-networking applications need a little forethought before you use them. Do you really want your colleagues to know where you are at all times? I didn't think so. But these kinds of programs can help you create impromptu coffee meetings or figure out whether someone you want to see is "checked in" nearby. Many location-based networks also give you information based on your current location for nearby great places to eat, shop, or visit.

REMEMBER

These services are really designed for mobile phone users who have signed up for data plans.

One network to try is Swarm by Foursquare (www.swarmapp.com), which allows you to use your phone's GPS tracking device to check in to locations you're visiting. The app tracks your location, checks you in at the places you visit, and awards points for everywhere you go. If you're the most frequent visitor to a location in a 30-day period, Swarm by Foursquare declares you the mayor of that location, and you can even earn badges. Swarm by Foursquare has some handy apps for different types of phones as well as a mobile phone website version.

Some businesses are rewarding users with freebies and recognition. You can link your Swarm as well as your traditional Foursquare accounts with your Twitter and Facebook updates.

Sharing It All

Clearly, you can choose among many social networks, widgets, and bits of code to include on your blog. You can spend a lot of time customizing, but I have good news. If you would like to make the pages of your blog easy for your visitors to share with others via social networks, you have an easy way to get the job done. ShareThis (www.sharethis.com), Shareaholic (www.shareaholic.com), Add This (www.addthis.com), and Add to Any (www.addtoany.com) offer solutions. Sign up with one or more of these free services and add the code, plug-in, or widget to your site so that you can quickly and easily add these tools to your site in a single step.

Each of the services mentioned offers similar services with the ability to do everything from enabling readers to share your content via social networks to tracking sharing metrics. Some even allow you to merge your social sharing metrics with your blog analytics. See Chapter 19 for more about tracking your blog's traffic.

Figure 17-4 shows the use of Shareaholic sharing tools on my blog, Resourceful Mommy (www.resourcefulmommy.com).

FIGURE 17-4: Use Shareaholic as a shortcut to getting more traffic to your blog.

TIP

Don't just make it easy for your readers to share your content on their social media accounts. Be sure to also invite them to follow you on *your* social media accounts by including links to your blog's Facebook fan page and Twitter account, for example, somewhere prominently displayed on your blog.

Chapter 18

Joining the Big Four Social Networks

I f you're part of the 65 percent of American adults who use at least one social media platform (www.pewinternet.org/2015/10/08/social-networking-usage-2005-2015/), then this chapter is right up your ally. If you're in the non-social media using minority, then this chapter may guide you to finally dip your toe into the social media waters! No matter where you stand when it comes to personal social media usage, participating in platforms such as Facebook and Twitter is a must for bloggers in this day and age.

In this chapter we'll take a look at what I'm calling the big four social networks: Facebook, Twitter, LinkedIn, and Pinterest. All four platforms are popular with the non-blogging world, which means, of course, that they're the perfect location to meet your future reading audience. The connections are ripe for the picking. You just need to dive in and get started!

Joining Facebook

Facebook remains the world's top social media platform with nearly 1.5 billion monthly active users worldwide (source: Facebook). Although search engine results drive tons of blog traffic — see Chapter 17 for ideas about how to increase your search engine traffic — bloggers will tell you that Facebook is a huge contributor to their site traffic.

So what's the big deal with Facebook and blogging? The big deal is that the same people who wake up, grab their smartphone, and share the latest funny meme with their Facebook friends are likely to click on your blog post link, like it, and share it with those same friends. Facebook users love to share great content, and if you play your cards right, that content could be yours.

Creating a Facebook Page

Chances are that you've already got a personal Facebook account, but if you're one of the last remaining holdouts, let me preface this section by telling you that you need a personal Facebook account in order to proceed. Facebook requires Facebook Page creators — including the Page you're going to make for your blog — to begin with a personal account.

No need to fret! Signing up for a Facebook account, shown in Figure 18-1, is quick and easy. To join Facebook perform the following steps:

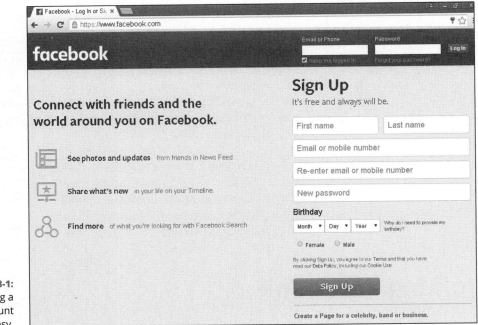

FIGURE 18-1:
Creating a
Facebook account
is free and easy.

1. **Point your web browser to** www.facebook.com.

2. **Enter the following information:**

   - First and last name

   - Email or mobile number

   - Password

   - Birthday

   - Gender

3. **Click Sign Up.**

Welcome to Facebook! Now it's time to create a Page for your blog. Put simply, a Facebook Page is a Facebook profile for businesses, brands, and organizations. Instead of creating a personal profile on Facebook for your blog, you need to create a Page in order to connect with your audience on Facebook.

Just like creating a personal profile, creating a Facebook Page for your blog is free, quick, and easy:

1. **Sign in to your Facebook account.**

2. **Point your web browser to** www.facebook.com/pages/create/ **(shown in Figure 18-2).**

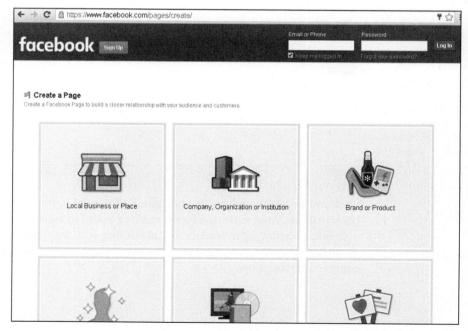

FIGURE 18-2:
Use the Create a Page section of Facebook to connect your blog with the Facebook audience.

3. Select Brand or Product.

4. From the drop-down list, select Website.

5. Type your blog name in the Brand or Product Name field.

6. Click Get Started.

Utilizing your Facebook Page

Now that you've got a Facebook Page for your blog, it's time to dive in and utilize your new social media tool. The first thing you're going to want is for your current readers to "like" your blog's Page. Head over to your blog and make sure that you're making it easy for readers to find your new Facebook Page via a social media icon (see Figure 18-3) prominently displayed on your site.

FIGURE 18-3:
Social media icons lead readers to your social media pages and accounts.

Once you've had your Page up and running for awhile, you should use your Facebook Insights Page to learn a bit more about your fan base. Facebook Insights not only tells you how often readers are interacting with your Facebook content, but it also shares reader demographic information ranging from age and gender to country and language.

Take your new Facebook Page for a drive, kick the tires, and see if it could use a little tune-up. Have you created a cover photo that fits with your blog branding (learn more about blog branding from Chapter 17)? Are you consistently posting links to your content on your Page? Have you included images, links, and videos that your fans will want to like and share? As with anything, the more time you put into your blog's Facebook Page, the more you'll get out of it.

REMEMBER

The connection between Facebook and blogging goes far beyond having a Facebook Page for your website! Make it as easy as possible for your readers to share your blog content on Facebook and other social media sites by including sharing buttons on your site. Sometimes the path for new readers to get to your blog via Facebook begins with current readers going to Facebook via your blog!

Understanding Twitter

Although I like to think of Twitter as the pesky little sibling of big brother Facebook, over the last several years, Twitter has progressed from a confusing niche platform to a mainstream tool. Even so, that doesn't mean that you don't have questions, so this section gets down to brass tacks.

Twitter (www.twitter.com) is a free social network used for *micro blogging,* which is essentially blogging, but in very short form. How short? Well, on Twitter, your posts are limited to 140 characters — barely enough for a couple of sentences. If you use Facebook, you may be surprised to know that you're already familiar with micro blogging.

Although you can post only up to 140 characters of text at a time on Twitter, you can use it to share photographs and links, even videos. Many businesses have jumped onto the Twitter bandwagon and use the tool to tell their customers about sales, specials, and other news.

TIP

If this chapter whets your appetite for even more Twitter tidbits, be sure to check out *Twitter For Dummies,* by Laura Fitton, Michael Gruen, and Leslie Poston (John Wiley & Sons, Inc.).

Twitter started in 2006 and grew slowly into the phenomenon it is today. It's fundamentally difficult to explain both its popularity and its purpose; as with blogs themselves, some very logical and commonsense questions jump to mind for most people:

>> Who's going to read this stuff, anyway?

>> What am I supposed to talk about on Twitter?

>> Why do people use Twitter?

>> Isn't Twitter a huge waste of time?

And in the case of people who already have a blog, the big question is, "Do I really need Twitter, as well?"

I hope you can forgive my answer to these questions: It's up to you! People use Twitter for all kinds of reasons. I've seen Twitter accounts devoted to spiritual guidance, sports, sex, marketing, web development, and diaries. You name it, and someone is using Twitter to talk about it. So, explaining why you should use Twitter, and what you might get out of it, is pretty hard to do!

TIP

Although this chapter covers using Twitter from a web browser on your phone, computer, or tablet, accessing Twitter via an app will provide you with a very similar experience. Should you choose to tweet from an app on your phone or tablet, you may want to try more than one app until you locate the one that works best for you.

For most Twitter users, the first goal is communication, quickly followed by reaching out to more people in a format that they can use easily (and for free) and that reaches people very quickly.

Here are just a few ways in which individuals and businesses are putting Twitter to work:

>> **Restaurants:** Advertise specials, let customers know about available tables, and offer coupons.

>> **Pundits:** Post links and resources to support their viewpoints.

>> **Friends:** Coordinate get-togethers and even arrange dates.

>> **Conference organizers:** Remind potential attendees of sign-up deadlines and early-bird pricing specials.

>> **Conference attendees:** Let other attendees know about good speakers (and snacks) and keep those who aren't attending up to date.

>> **Celebrities:** Extend their personal brand and identity by talking about their projects.

>> **Characters from popular television shows:** Carry on dialogue with viewers between episodes — written by the show's writers, actors, or marketing folks.

>> **Political candidates:** Update voters about their policies and appearances.

>> **Emergency services:** Update followers about operations. In 2012, users without access to TV, radio, or landline phones were able to follow emergency responder updates during Superstorm Sandy.

Twitter updates have a lot of potential to inform and entertain. To get a sense of the mechanics of using Twitter, follow these basic steps:

1. **Sign up for a Twitter account and choose a nickname.**

   When you set up your account, you can choose to share your updates — called *tweets* — with anyone (meaning the public) or to restrict access to only the people you choose to allow to follow you.

2. **Customize your icon and profile page to make them reflect your personality or brand.**

3. **Run your contact list through Twitter to see whether any of your friends, family, and colleagues are on Twitter.**

   If any of them are on Twitter, decide whether you want to follow their updates.

4. **Post updates.**

   You can tweet about anything, from news about your plans to any of your thoughts or activities.

Following someone on Twitter is equivalent to making that person into a friend or contact on other social networks; Twitter simply calls those folks who read your updates *followers.* As with other social networks, the number of followers you have indicates your popularity, and a lot of people focus on getting those numbers high.

The really neat thing about Twitter is that you can participate without ever visiting the Twitter website. Twitter is designed so that you can handle the whole thing by mobile phone apps, keeping you updated with a device that you probably already have close to hand.

Getting Started

I'm a big fan of learning by doing, so in the following sections, I walk you through signing up for Twitter and getting started. I get the easy job — getting you started with Twitter. You have the hard job of figuring out what to tweet about!

Signing up for an account

Follow these steps to set up a Twitter account:

1. **Point your web browser to** www.twitter.com.

   The Twitter home page opens.

2. **Enter your first and last name in the Full Name field.**

   You're limited to 20 characters in this field.

3. **Provide an email address to use with your Twitter account in the Email field.**

4. **Create a password in the Password field.**

5. **Click Sign up for Twitter (see Figure 18-4).**

   Twitter loads the Create an Account page, which confirms the information you already provided.

6. **Choose a Twitter username and type it in the Username field.**

   Unlike some social networks, you can change your username later.

   Your username is limited to 15 characters, and while you type in your desired username, Twitter checks to see whether it's available. If you don't get a green OK message, try again until you find an available username.

7. **Click Create My Account.**

   Twitter creates your new account and loads the Who to Follow page. You also receive an email that contains your new account information at the address you used to sign up.

Tweeting

After you sign up for a Twitter account, it's time for the fun part — your first tweet! You can send a tweet pretty darn easily from the website. Follow these steps:

1. Point your browser to www.twitter.com and log in to Twitter if you aren't already logged in.

Twitter loads your personal home page, which displays messages from all the people you're following.

2. Click the blue quill icon in the upper-right corner.

While you type, watch the number at the bottom of the field; it tells you the number of characters still available.

3. Click Tweet (see Figure 18-5).

Twitter posts your tweet into your message stream, where your followers can read and respond to it. If any of them subscribe to your updates with their phones, they receive a text message that contains your tweet.

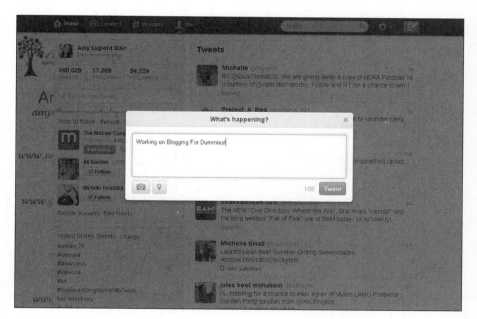

FIGURE 18-5:
You can post a tweet on Twitter very quickly.

Posting a tweet is just the beginning. Other kinds of messages include the following:

>> **@ messages:** When you want to direct a message to a specific person but still include it in your main message stream (which means all your followers, and the public, can see it), start your message with the @ symbol followed by the username of the person. For example

```
@b4dbook i'm reading your chapter on Twitter right now!
```

To view similar tweets aimed at you, click the Mentions tab in the menu of your Twitter page, as shown in Figure 18-6.

FIGURE 18-6:
View public messages directed at you by clicking the Mentions tab.

>> **Direct messages:** You send private, direct messages to a specific Twitter user or group of users rather than to all of your followers. To send a direct message to a user, that user must be following your account or must have elected to receive direct messages from those they do not follow. The default setting is for users to only be allowed to send direct messages to people who follow them. To send a direct message, visit the user's profile page and click

REMEMBER

the Message icon or select the Messages icon from your Twitter navigation bar; it looks like a small envelope.

» Be careful about sending direct messages — you can too easily post things publicly that you meant to be private!

» **Retweets:** Do you see a tweet in your stream that you want to rebroadcast to all your followers? That's called retweeting. To retweet, simply move your mouse cursor over the tweet to make the Retweet link visible. Click the link, and the tweet is automatically sent to your followers. Alternatively, you can copy and paste the text of the tweet into the What's Happening? field, preface it with RT, and even add your own remark, as below:

```
that makes so much sense! RT @dbarefoot On a similar
bent, there's a great quote about creativity being
something plus frequent iteration.
```

TIP

» It's considered good form to include the username of the person you're retweeting.

Exploring the Settings

You can personalize your Twitter home and profile pages in a lot of ways, and you can update your account information, change your username and password, and so on. You can make all these changes on the Settings page, which you access by clicking your profile picture at Twitter.com. The Settings page includes the following areas:

» **Account settings:** Change the email address at which Twitter contacts you and your username.

» **Password:** Change your password. You need to know your current password in order to change it.

» **Mobile:** Set up your phone to receive tweets from Twitter.

» **Email notifications:** Decide whether you want to receive email messages when you get a new follower, receive a direct message, are retweeted or mentioned, or subscribe to the Twitter email newsletter.

» **Design:** Select a new theme for the look and feel of your Twitter pages, upload your own custom background image, or even change the background, text, and link colors.

» **Apps:** View those apps that can currently access your Twitter account.

» **Widgets:** Create and manage your widgets from this location.

Tying Your Blog into Twitter

Many bloggers have set up a system that automatically tweets about their blog posts as soon as they are published. One such tool is called Twitterfeed (www.twitterfeed.com), but many options are available, from plug-ins to tools integrated directly into your blogging or even your favorite Twitter platform.

Setting up such a system is pretty simple, really. After your blog has an RSS feed (see Chapter 16), you simply direct your blog-sharing tool to connect the feed and your Twitter account. Whenever you post a new blog update, a tweet containing the blog post title and URL is added to your Twitter feed.

WARNING

Tweeting about your blog posts can really help to drive traffic to your blog, but some users find the impersonality of this kind of message irritating. Be aware of what your audience is looking for if you decide to go this route.

REMEMBER

Don't forget to ask your readers to follow you on Twitter by sharing a link to your Twitter account!

Getting Started with LinkedIn

LinkedIn (www.linkedin.com) is a social networking tool that focuses on business-oriented networking rather than friend-based networking. Many online professionals have been using it for years as a way to network with other professionals and showcase their own resumes. It turns out, however, that LinkedIn is a fantastic tool for bloggers.

Connecting through LinkedIn

One of the best reasons for a blogger to set up a LinkedIn account is exposure, and no, I don't mean spending too much time out in the cold. Creating a professional-looking LinkedIn account highlighting both your professional and blogging achievements is a great way for people to find you, including future readers and potential clients. (Learn more about monetizing your blog in Chapter 20.) Unlike those surfing Twitter for brief tweets and Facebook for fun pictures, the people spending time on LinkedIn are more likely to come ready to read great, often wordy content.

Remember reading about building your community as well as joining existing blogging communities in Part 3? LinkedIn is a wonderful tool to connect with other bloggers in your niche. Not only can you create connections by linking to each other's accounts, but you can also create and join existing niche LinkedIn groups. This is a fabulous way to grow your network.

Some other great ways for bloggers to use LinkedIn include:

>> Creating personal updates that link back to your latest blog post

>> Sharing posts from other blogs that might relate to your site and your network

>> Showcasing your blog's latest achievements

>> Connecting to other bloggers who are farther along in their blogging journeys

>> Showing potential readers and clients a bit more about you than what you can include on your blog's About page or bio

Creating your LinkedIn account

Like most social media platforms, creating a LinkedIn account is simple, quick, and free. To get started, perform the following steps (see Figure 18-7):

1. **Point your web browser to** www.linkedin.com.

2. **Provide your first and last name.**

3. **Provide an email address.**

4. **Create a password that is six or more characters in length.**

5. **Click Join Now.**

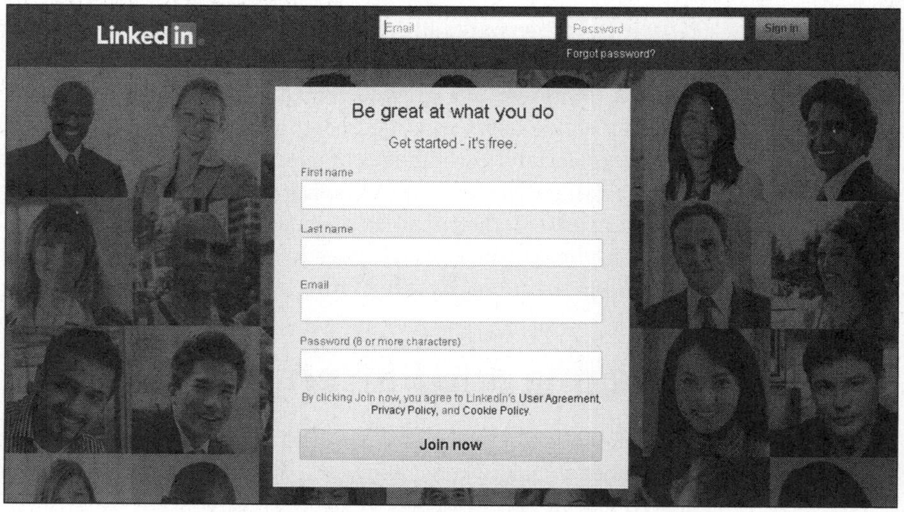

FIGURE 18-7: Creating a free LinkedIn account is quick and easy.

BLOGGING ON LINKEDIN

Although connecting with other bloggers and potential readers and clients through LinkedIn seems like a no-brainer, what you may not realize is that you can actually blog directly on LinkedIn. LinkedIn's blogging platform is called Pulse, located under the Interests menu on your LinkedIn page. Once there, LinkedIn users can choose to publish a post just as they would on their own blog. It's even possible to publish a complete blog post directly to your LinkedIn home page. Even though it may seem counterintuitive for bloggers to post content somewhere other than their own website, posting on LinkedIn may actually be a way to drive readers to your site. Remember that visitors to LinkedIn are looking for information and are ready to spend some time reading content. By posting directly to LinkedIn, you've got an opportunity to show a new audience what you can do. Write a fantastic how-to or list post related to your niche, show off your photography skills with your media selections, or highlight a professional skill you bring to the blogging table. Once LinkedIn readers get to know you through your posts on that platform, they may be ready to make the jump with you to a new platform — your blog!

Ready to learn more about LinkedIn? Check out *LinkedIn For Dummies,* 3rd Edition, by Joel Elad (John Wiley & Sons).

TIP

Getting Pinny with It

If Twitter is the snarky little brother of the social media family, then Pinterest is the crafty aunt who always brings the best desserts to holiday gatherings. Founded in 2010, Pinterest has grown from 5,000 users in its first year to 100 million monthly active users in 2015, according to the social media giant. Pinterest is a visual wonderland with images of everything from DIY dining room tables created from reclaimed barn wood to inspirational quotes superimposed on photographs of ocean sunsets. Described as a visual bookmarking and discovery platform, the site is a virtual pinboard of ideas located on the Internet and shared in user-created Pinterest boards (see Figure 18-8).

Blogging and Pinterest

The connection between Pinterest and blogging is crystal clear and can be significantly beneficial to most bloggers. You'll recall from Chapter 16 that SEO, or search engine optimization, helps blogger content to be seen by the millions of potential readers conducting searches on sites such as Google and Bing each day. Imagine that Pinterest is one more place for potential readers to both find and share your content, but rather than searching on Google or Bing, they're searching on Pinterest itself.

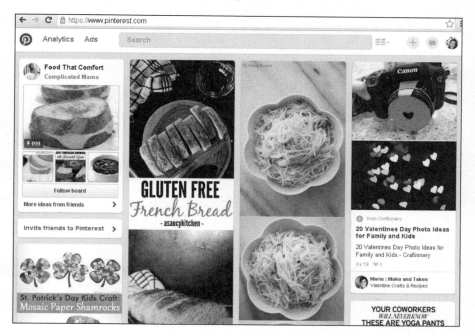

FIGURE 18-8:
Pinterest is an incredibly visual social media platform comprised of themed, virtual pinboards.

In Figure 18-9, I searched Pinterest using the phrase "rainbow birthday cake." Instead of receiving a list of related links as I would on Google, I am served photo after photo of related images. Clicking on these images will take me to — you guessed it — blog posts related to my search!

Creating Pinterest content

So how does an image linked to a post appear in Pinterest in the first place? Unlike Google search results that are provided by Google itself, Pinterest content is populated entirely by other Pinterest users. Each user creates Pinterest Boards, themed categories that contain pins related to that theme. Figure 18-10 shows an example of a populated Pinterest Board, in this case organized around the topic of Fourth of July. Posts on this Board vary in topic from dessert and drink ideas to patriotic outfits for kids.

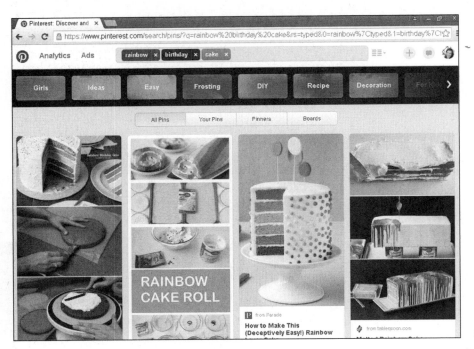

FIGURE 18-9:
Pinterest
searches provide
images that are
all linked to posts
on the web.

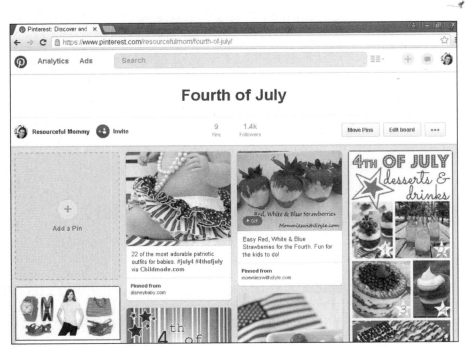

FIGURE 18-10:
This Fourth of July
Pinterest Board is
one example of
how to organize
ideas and images
on this platform.

When Pinterest was first building in popularity, placing images and posts on a Pinterest Board was not as straightforward as it is in 2016. When I first began using Pinterest, I installed a Pin This item on my web browser's toolbar. When viewing a website that I wanted to add to my Board, I utilized this tool. You may notice when browsing the web now that there are various Pin This–type tools throughout online content. These Pinterest social sharing buttons are found everywhere from the beginning of a post to the images throughout the post to the end of the post next to comment and other social share buttons. In a post on my blog, Resourceful Mommy, hovering over each image provides readers with a Pin It option (shown in Figure 18-11).

FIGURE 18-11: Hovering over images on Resourceful-Mommy.com provides readers with the option to pin those images to their Pinterest Boards.

Utilizing Pinterest to grow your audience

As they say, there is more than one way to bake a cake, and there is more than one way for bloggers to tap into the power of Pinterest in growing blog readership. A great place to start is by creating your own Pinterest account and populating your own Boards.

To create a free Pinterest account, perform the following steps (shown in Figure 18-12):

1. **Point your web browser to** www.pinterest.com/business/create.

2. **Provide your email address.**

3. **Create a password.**

4. **Type your blog name into the Business name field.**

5. **Select Professional under the drop-down menu for business type.**

6. **Add your blog's URL in the Website (optional) field.**

7. **Click Create account.**

FIGURE 18-12:
Creating a
Pinterest account
related to your
blog is a quick
process.

Now, I don't recommend that you create Pinterest Boards that are covered in nothing but pins from your own blog. One of the cardinal rules of social media is that you promote others more than yourself. With that said, it certainly behooves you to create Boards related to your content so that you can include your own posts as a small portion of each Board.

Another critical way to tap into the power of Pinterest is to include visually appealing photographs and graphics in each of your blog posts. After all, if you want readers to share your content on Pinterest, you need to include an image that can be pinned. Take some time to search around Pinterest to get an idea of what types of images draw your eye to them most quickly. Are there certain colors that grab your attention? Do you tend to click on images with superimposed headings? Take some time to play around with your blog post images and notice which articles are receiving the most interaction from the Pinterest community.

And remember, all of the tips in this chapter are exactly that — tips. Social media still remains a very personal experience, and everyone will utilize these platforms in a slightly different way. Now get out there and get social!

Chapter 19

Measuring Blog Presence

For a moment, picture your new blog running just the way you want it. The graphics are pretty, you're blogging every day, and comments are rolling in. Everything looks perfect, and you seem to be well on your way to a successful blogging career. But wait! For no real reason, over a few weeks, the number of comments left on your blog each day starts to decrease. Your visitor numbers are down. You don't find an obvious explanation, and you can't imagine why your readership is disappearing so quickly!

If you ever find yourself in this type of situation, you may start to ask yourself questions such as "How many visitors do I have every day, anyway?" or "How many of my visitors have been here before?"

It's time to understand your web traffic statistics. You, as a blogger, may find web stats especially important because, in contrast to the way a static website generates traffic, your audience numbers are affected each time you post.

You must pay attention to how your blog is performing on the Internet, but doing so can be confusing and boring. Spending an afternoon peering at web stats, especially if you don't know what you're looking for, can be a tedious experience. It's like . . . well, it's like watching paint dry. But it doesn't have to be as painful as it sounds. Web statistics are very geeky, but thankfully you can choose from services available to bloggers (and webmasters in general) that allow you to track your blog's success in interesting and informative ways by using a friendly interface.

Exploring the Power of Statistics

Even if you like the way your blog is performing, you should take a look at your blog stats once in a while. Some bloggers look at them daily to see what kinds of visitors appeared on their blogging radar overnight; some bloggers check their stats once a week or once a month. Whichever pattern you choose, keep a good handle on your statistics. Knowing how many visitors you have can help you improve your blog in the future, making it even more popular.

For an example of what a typical web-stats tool looks like, check out StatCounter's measurement of my Resourceful Mommy blog (www.resourcefulmommy.com) in Figure 19-1.

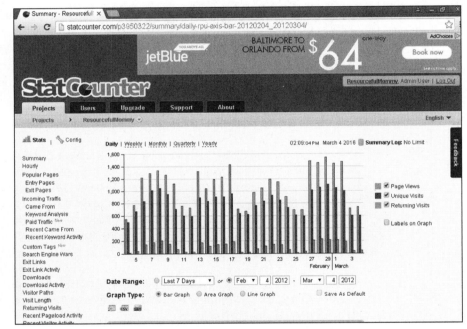

FIGURE 19-1:
Author Amy Lupold Bair uses StatCounter to track Resourceful Mommy's web stats.

REMEMBER

Although tracking your site's statistics is a good idea in case you might sometime require that information, most bloggers are hobby bloggers, not professional bloggers. The bottom line is that you should blog in a way that makes *you* happy, which may mean not worrying about who is coming to your blog and why.

Using web statistics, you can track

>> What countries your web visitors are surfing from

>> How long visitors stay

>> How many visitors check out your site for the first time

>> How many visitors have been to your blog before

>> What pages your visitors start their visit on

>> What pages visitors end their visit on

>> What sites send visitors to you

>> What search words visitors use to find your site

>> What browsers your visitors use

>> What kind of computers your visitors use to surf the web

>> What screen resolutions your visitors set their monitors to

With some of the more advanced web analytics software, you can see what pages are the least popular, find out how search engines handle your blog, and even see what errors or missing pages your visitors get when they try to access parts of your site. (If you have removed an old blog post or renamed a posting, your statistics will tell you which pages are missing.) A lot of bloggers particularly want to know what websites are sending visitors to their blogs so that they can figure out where to invest time and energy in comments and discussion forums.

Knowing even a little bit about your traffic can help you make all kinds of strategic decisions about your blog, from what kind of design to use to the subject of a post.

Blog stats become even more useful when you begin analyzing them. *Web analytics* are the trends that your statistical or log software shows you. Some traffic software helps break down these trends for you, but the most basic software simply displays the raw data about how visitors use your site and lets you draw the conclusions. When people talk about web analytics, they're referring to the process that you undertake when you're looking through those stats and logs to figure out what visitors are doing on your website. Commonly, you look for trends about what content the visitors view, how often they visit, and what other sites direct traffic your way.

Pay close attention to your website logs so that you can chart what your users are doing over time. You can see what your site visitors are reading and what keeps them coming back for more. You can then use this information for a variety of purposes (such as deciding what to blog about). The following examples illustrate how gathering your blog's statistics and interpreting them can be useful:

>> **You notice that you have a large bunch of readers coming from a particular country (see Figure 19-2), and you don't live in that country.**
In this case, you should see what pages those visitors are viewing — and

determine why they're coming to your site. You can then write more to attract additional visitors who have similar tastes. In fact, noticing a trend such as this one might help you focus on a core audience that you didn't even know about. You can even redefine what you do with your blog in the future.

>> **You have ads on your blog (see Chapter 20), and more people are clicking a certain type of advertisement.** If you take the time, you can see what kinds of visitors are clicking advertisements on your site (if you have any ads, of course). You can use information about what ads your visitors click to sell ad space to certain advertisers.

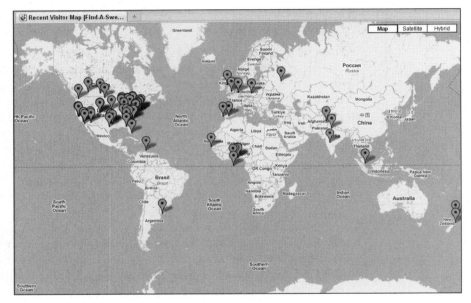

FIGURE 19-2:
Track where your visitors live by using a stat program such as StatCounter.

REMEMBER

You may have trouble staying away from your blog's web stats, and you might want to check them daily. But don't forget that you have a blog to run, which requires that you focus on the quality of the content you produce for your community. Try to avoid an obsession over your web statistics because no amount of tinkering with web analytics can make your blog popular. Your content is the only thing that can accomplish that feat.

Knowing What the Statistics Mean

To understand what you're looking at when you scan your web statistics or server logs, you need to know a series of terms. Most web analytics software uses these terms, but you should always check to see how the software's creators define measurements. Web analytics software tends to use these terms in the same way, but not always. I cover the most vital terms in the following sections.

REMEMBER

You'll run into more terms than the ones I cover in this chapter, but the most important ones for bloggers are *page views, unique visitors,* and *repeat visitors.* Together, these three statistics give you the most accurate picture of how many visitors your blog receives and what they do while they visit.

I also introduce you to what the term *hits* means, which new bloggers often find misleading, and how statistics can help you resolve errors on your blog.

Hits

A *hit* is an official request from a web browser for a file from the web server. The file can be an HTML file or a movie file. Essentially, accessing any file available on a web server to the surfing public counts as a hit.

REMEMBER

Any given web page causes *multiple* hits on the server when it loads, even though it's only one page. Multiple files are actually called to display the page: the HTML file, any associated style documents, and all the image files. If an HTML file has five images, it counts as six hits — one for the HTML file and five for each image.

A lot of people think that hits indicate the number of website visitors or even the number of pages viewed, but hits don't even come close to measuring those kinds of figures. Hits are pretty meaningless if you're trying to understand how many visitors you have, but they can help you get a feel for the traffic load that your site puts on the web server.

Page views

A *page view* is normally defined as a page within a web server log. If the web browser requests an HTML file, the log records that as a single request, even if the server needs several files to display the page. Each time the web browser loads a page of your site, it counts as a page view. Page views are a valuable measurement because you can get a better understanding of how people actually use your site.

In Figure 19-3, you can see an example of how StatCounter displays page view data.

REMEMBER

Advertisers are often very interested in the number of page views on a website (more is better), and most bloggers consider a high page-view number something to brag about.

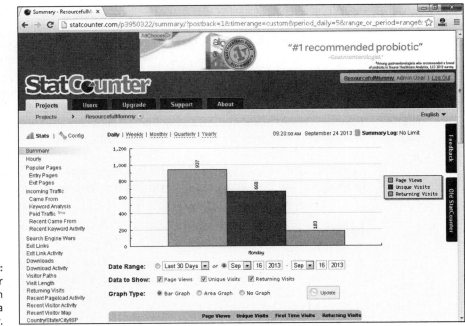

FIGURE 19-3:
StatCounter
breaks down
page loads for a
given day.

Unique visitors

Unique visitors are just what they sound like — individual visitors who come to your website. The analytics software counts them only once, no matter how many pages they view or how many times they visit. When you're looking at the number of unique visitors your blog gets, take a look at what time period the analytics software refers to. Fifty unique visitors in one day is, of course, a much bigger deal than 50 unique visitors in a month.

Repeat visitors

Repeat visitors are blog readers who visit your site on more than one occasion and, usually, visit multiple pages. Pay attention, just as with unique visitors, to the time period this repeat-visitor number covers.

In Figure 19-4, you can see a graph that breaks down the percentages of first-time visitors to repeat visitors on the web statistics tool StatCounter.

Errors

Most stat software tracks *errors,* instances when your visitors get an actual error message when they try to do something on your site or when they try to view a page that doesn't exist anymore (or never did).

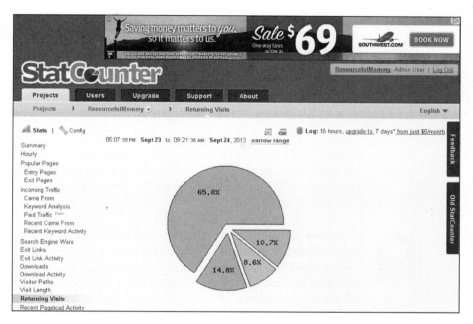

FIGURE 19-4:
Keep tabs on how much of your traffic is new and how much is repeat visits.

A LACK OF STANDARDS

Currently, no official standards govern the world of server logs and web statistics. No large corporations tell anyone how to capture their traffic numbers, what terminology to use, or how to analyze the statistics. The world of web stats has, more or less, grown organically, and a set of rules around the analysis of server logs has emerged from the community.

The various software tools have a lot of inconsistency in what and how they measure statistics. As a result, I commonly use two different programs to measure unique visitors on my own blog, and the two software programs rarely agree about what that number is. It's a frustrating fact of life. (Between you and me, I tend to use the bigger number.)

Knowing about this inconsistency, you might want to consider using at least a couple of web statistics tools (I talk about the options in the section "Getting Web Stats," later in this chapter) and comparing the results that you get. Different web analytics software treat server logs differently, and some software is certainly better than others. Most often, users prefer packages that create charts and graphs, which represent their data visually, making the numbers easier to understand quickly. Because no hard-and-fast rules exist, feel free to do research into what packages can work best for you.

TIP

Track your error logs to find out where visitors are having problems — and be sure to fix the errors.

Getting Web Stats

You can find many statistics software applications that track web traffic available for installation on your blog. But before you get too carried away, check to see whether your blog host offers web traffic–tracking software or gives you access to your server logs.

TIP

If your web host offers stats software, review the offering carefully. You might not need any additional tools, or you might want to supplement the preinstalled tool with one of those discussed in the following sections, if only to check the accuracy of the numbers you're seeing. Keep in mind that different applications can measure statistics differently, so the numbers may not be exactly the same.

TECHNICAL STUFF

Some bloggers like to look at the server logs for their sites. *Server logs* are simple text files that web servers generate to keep track of information about who visits a web server, when they visit, what kind of browser they use, when errors occur, and so on.

Most web hosts provide access to stat software and server logs through an administrative control panel.

In the following sections, I cover the different services and software available. You should be able to find a service that fits your web-stats needs.

Choosing hosted statistics software

Like hosted blog software, the company that creates the hosted web statistics software package also manages that software. Typically, you install the software by adding a chunk of HTML code to your pages, which communicates with the hosted software.

Because you must be able to place some HTML code into your blog software templates so that it appears on every page that you want to track, blog software that doesn't give you the ability to add code will rule out using a hosted statistics solution.

Google Analytics

www.google.com/analytics

Google Analytics has a great interface with many options that you can customize and use to analyze stats to your heart's content. Google Analytics can calculate how many page views and number of visits your blog or site has received. The Google Analytics system (shown in Figure 19-5) is free, but it requires a registered Google Account (which is free, as well).

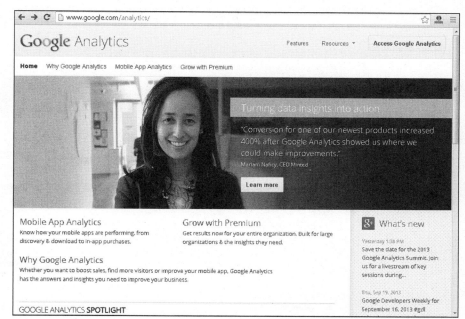

FIGURE 19-5: Use Google Analytics to check out where your website's traffic comes from.

StatCounter

www.statcounter.com

StatCounter is a free, hosted statistics tracker, and new users can figure it out easily, thanks to good organization and explanation in the control panel. Need more features? StatCounter offers paid accounts starting at $5 per month.

After setting up your site in StatCounter, you must insert StatCounter HTML code into your blog templates so that it can track every page. StatCounter measures page views and hits, of course, but much more, too.

Site Meter

www.sitemeter.com

Site Meter has been around since the beginning of stat tracking on the web. This tool provides you with basic details about each visitor who comes to your blog and shows you what the visitor does while he or she is there, even down to what page he or she is on before leaving.

Site Meter (see Figure 19-6) has two levels of service: the free Basic edition and the Premium edition. The Premium edition provides more information than the Basic setup and grants access to a longer history of your statistics, but the free edition is a good starting point for new bloggers. The premium edition starts at $6.95 a month or $59 per year.

FIGURE 19-6:
Site Meter offers two levels of statistics tracking.

Choosing installable statistics software

Web analytics software that you can install on your web server and manage on your own is called *installable* software. If you want to use a specific analytics package that your web host doesn't normally provide, look into whether you can install software on your server. Some hosts can give you suggestions and may even assist you when you install analytics software.

Installed software usually measures the same metrics as hosted statistics software, but it does so by analyzing log files stored on your website rather than gathering information when a visitor hits your site. Some web developers feel that installed software therefore provides more accurate numbers than hosted software, but many other web developers and bloggers hotly debate that opinion.

When you sign up for a web-hosting package, the web host probably has some kind of web statistics available to you. These packages can range from open source software to custom, home-grown solutions.

Check the technical requirements for the package that you want to install to be sure that your server works with it.

TIP

The Webalizer

www.webalizer.org

The Webalizer is an open source application that you install on your server. Because it's free to use, many web hosts offer it as part of their standard web-hosting packages. Originally created in 1997, the Webalizer lets you track hits, page views, geographical origin of your traffic, and other data.

The Webalizer generates easy-to-read pages that show traffic to your site broken down by month, but you can also see traffic figures by day and even by hour. It offers all the usual suspects, from page views to unique visitors to the top referring sites.

AWStats

www.awstats.org

AWStats is a popular web statistics analyzer that you can install on your web server. Its features enable you to track not only visitors but also streaming media, email, and FTP transactions on your server. AWStats requires that you have the Perl programming language installed on your web server to operate. (Most web servers support this requirement.)

AWStats generates graphs and other visual indicators about the activity of your visitors month by month, letting you see the region and cities where traffic originates, as well as the operating systems and browsers that your visitors use, among many other measurements.

Mint

www.haveamint.com

Mint, which began in 2004 as a basic website tracking tool, has matured into a great service. Mint's installable software offers the usual suspects: new and returning visitors, the sites from which they get to your site, search terms that they use to find you, and so on. Mint also looks really cool: It produces fun graphs and charts.

A Mint license costs $30 per site.

Finding Out What Others Are Saying

With web analytics software, you can watch the behavior of your site's visitors, but you can also find out a lot by monitoring mentions of you, your blog, and your topic on the web (especially on your competitors' blogs!) on other websites. Watching what's going on within the blogosphere is a huge task. You can spend hundreds of dollars to have others do it for you, or you can check out some of the simple tools available on the web.

Among the simple blogosphere tools available to you are the following:

>> **Email notifications:** Receive updates via email about content or topics that you want to keep up with.

>> **RSS watch lists:** Keep current on topics by using your favorite newsreader software. (Read more about RSS in Chapter 16.)

You can use these tools in a variety of ways by doing random manual searches and installing software designed to display web information on your desktop.

REMEMBER

The power of RSS and the syndication of news and blog feeds become apparent when you start trying to monitor certain phrases and keywords. RSS is one of the best ways to track what people are saying about your blog and about topics that you're interested in.

Google Alerts

www.google.com/alerts

Google Alerts (see Figure 19-7) provides you with email notifications that it sends to you based on keyword searches of Google's search system. Sign up for an account and then create an alert by entering keywords to be notified about.

To receive any email from the Google Alerts system, you need to enter some keywords. Follow these steps:

1. **Go to** www.google.com/alerts.

2. **Enter the keywords that you want to be notified about in the search text box.**

3. **Select the alert options that you want included in your search from the Show options drop-down list.**

   Your options are How often, Sources, Language, Region, How many, and Deliver to.

FIGURE 19-7:
Google Alerts
sends you email if
it hits your
keywords in
searches.

4. **Type your email address into the Your Email field or select Feed.**

   If you are already signed into your Google account, your Gmail address is
   automatically filled in.

   If you select Feed, you can subscribe to these custom search results using an
   RSS reader. See Chapter 16 for more on RSS.

5. **Click Create Alert.**

   Google begins to track your search and sends you the emails that you
   requested at the rate you want them.

When a keyword gets a hit, you get an email that includes a link to the web page.
Google Alerts can do automatic keyword searches for all kinds of websites, including blogs.

These alerts work best when you create a specific and detailed search. Think about
how you can refine your search to keep your results to a manageable number. For
instance, if you want to track a particular news topic, use several keywords rather
than just one. For example, use `knitting sock yarn hand-dyed`, not just `socks`.

Set Google Alerts to search for your name, your blog name, and any keywords that
you want to be aware of. Use these alerts to find out when people are talking about
you, your blog, or the topics you're covering.

TIP

Twitter

www.twitter.com

Twitter is a social-networking service that allows you to post online messages known as *tweets*. People can then watch your tweets, and you can watch theirs. Your tweets can be anything, from short messages to links to websites or conversations with others. You can also use Twitter to track what people are talking about by searching for keywords and *hashtags* (Twitter users sometimes mark keywords in their tweets with a # to set them off and make it easier to search for them). You can search using the Twitter search engine at the top of the screen on www.twitter.com. You can read more about Twitter in Chapters 17 and 18.

Alexa

www.alexa.com

Alexa is a web analytics service that goes above and beyond to compare your site's popularity to all other sites in the world. That's quite a lot of information! If you'd like to know how many sites are linking back to your blog, for example, Alexa is the tool for you.

IceRocket

www.icerocket.com

Track mentions of specific keywords on blogs, Twitter, Facebook, and more using IceRocket. This easy-to-use service delivers results on currently trending topics, as well, making it a good resource if you're trying to decide what to blog about on a slow day. IceRocket offers:

» Twitter topic search tool

» Blog topic results based on IceRocket search terms

» Trends over time — the percentage of blog posts in the last month, two months, or three months mentioning any term

6

Getting Business-y with It

Finding out how to monetize your blog through advertising, affiliate programs, and sponsorships

Making blogs work for your business or organization

Chapter 20

Making Mad Mad Money

You've gotten to know the basics of blogging, you've built your online community, you've mastered the art of creating pinnable images; now it's time to consider turning your blog into an income source. Long gone are the days of bloggers needing to explain the value of their online platforms. Companies are well aware of the value of online influencers, and the sky's the limit for ways bloggers can convert their time online into substantial income.

In this chapter we'll take a look at common ways to monetize blogs, but keep in mind that creativity is king in the online world. Let this chapter inspire you rather than confine you.

Finding Out How Advertising Works

Advertising on your blog has never been easier. Many different advertising systems offer bloggers a free way to place ads on their blogs, and businesses have picked up on the fact that blog advertising can really work. Putting an ad or two on your blog can help you easily earn a little money doing something you enjoy. Many bloggers turn a pretty penny, and some even earn a living from advertising.

Ever since websites came into existence, you could find online advertisements. From the first web banners of the early Internet to today's contextual advertising systems, ads have run the gamut from wildly successful to a waste of precious bandwidth.

In some cases, the effectiveness of ads has more to do with the readers than anything else. Some types of blogs attract readers likely to look at and click through ads, whereas other blogs' readers seem to not see the ads at all. In fact, some blog readers may find the existence of ads on a blog downright offensive!

REMEMBER

The amount of money you can make from hosting advertisements on your blog is directly related to your blog traffic. Don't have enough traffic to woo advertisers? Take a look back at Part 5: Marketing and Promoting Your Blog.

Banner ads (rectangular ads usually placed along the top or bottom of a site) used to dominate ad slots on the web but became less important because people often just tuned them out. Then, pop-up, animated, and blinking advertisements generated a few clicks and ultimately managed to generate a massive backlash. Many of these moving, beeping, and blinking ads just irritated users instead of successfully advertising a product or service.

TIP

Some blog monetization has nothing to do with traditional website advertising. Read on to learn more.

Today's contextual advertising tools are actually intelligent; ads are matched by subject to the words and phrases that you use on your blog. Generally, this approach gives you ads that better suit your readers' interests, making those readers more likely to click the ads.

First, decide whether your blog is meant for an advertising campaign. Many blogs can benefit greatly from advertisements. However, you should think about a few things before diving in:

>> Does your blog have a design that's ready for ads?

>> Does your blog software support the advertising system you choose?

>> Will advertising earn you any money?

>> Will your audience put up with ads?

Answering these questions isn't easy; in fact, you might find it impossible unless you jump in. Try using some advertising and observe the results.

Planning for advertising

You can use several kinds of advertising methods to turn a blog into a place where you can make a tidy profit. The last few years have seen an explosion of companies that want a piece of the action in the blogosphere, and these companies have come up with creative ways to make ads easy to use, simple to implement, and appealing to your readers.

If you're a new blogger or just new to advertising programs, you can easily latch onto the first advertising system that you find and commit to using it. Although this system may serve your needs well, you might want to take a look at some of the different ad systems available and find out about how advertising tends to work in the blogosphere before you start using ads.

REMEMBER

While you do your research, keep in mind that if you decide to make that leap into monetizing your blog, you should choose software that allows you to control your advertising so that it doesn't overwhelm the blog audience that you worked so hard to build.

A multitude of advertising companies offers bloggers simple solutions to monetize websites. Most of these programs work in similar ways but have unique delivery methods. Many bloggers also choose to work with a specific ad network, which serves ads directly to their bloggers' sites. As a blogger, choosing an advertising program that works for your audience can make the difference between an increase in readers and turning off your existing traffic.

Looking at the formats

You can deliver ads to a blog audience in four different ways. Additional methods are available, but most don't work very well in a blog. The most popular advertisement formats for blogs are

>> **Text-based ads:** These ads are text-only and feature a link or links to the advertiser's website or service. Each ad is very plain, and most advertising systems limit your ability to customize their look and feel.

>> **Graphical banner and button ads:** Banner and button ads can be static, animated images, or even video. These ads usually have preset sizes, but you can customize them to fit your blog design.

>> **RSS ads:** RSS ads can include text or images, and they're linked to the advertiser's website straight from your RSS feed. If you want to find out more about RSS, see Chapter 16.

>> **Pop-up ads:** Pop-ups tend to be everyone's least favorite type of ad, but oddly enough, pop-up ads that open in a new window are still quite successful at getting people to click an advertiser's website. The readers might be fairly irritated by the time they get to the site, but they do click.

TIP

The Interactive Advertising Bureau makes recommendations each year about ad sizes and standards. You might find the recommendations useful in planning for ads. Visit www.iab.com/guidelines/iab-display-advertising-guidelines/ to see the options.

Most ad programs today — with the exception of sponsorships — use *contextual advertising,* which coordinates ad display with related editorial content. So, a blog post about skiing might include ads for ski shops and resorts. A blogger who posts about blogging, for example, ends up with ads for blog software and tools.

Contextual ad systems search your blog for keywords that match products the advertisers have in their inventory. These ads then appear beside the topic keywords and, in theory, apply in the context of the web page on which they appear.

Contextual ads about blog polling tools appear on the left side of the Colorado Moms blog, as shown in Figure 20-1.

FIGURE 20-1:
Contextual advertising puts blogging tool ads next to a post on the same subject.

Assessing business models

Money can flow from the advertiser to the blogger in different ways. Always read the terms of service for an ad program because each advertising company has a different idea about how to compensate bloggers. The usual business models for online ads are

>> **Cost per impression:** In this model, advertisers pay for the number of times a computer loads a page that displays the ad. The advertiser might prefer that a reader click its ad, but it recognizes that simply appearing on a blog that users access also has value.

>> **Cost per click or pay per click:** The blogger makes money only when a reader clicks an ad and goes to the advertiser's website. This type of ad is very common in contextual ad programs, as well as on search engines in the sponsored results section.

>> **Cost per action:** The advertiser pays only when the reader actually takes action after he or she views and clicks the ad on the blog. This required action can include anything from signing up to receive more information to actually purchasing a product.

>> **Sponsorships:** When an advertiser wants to be actively associated with the content of your blog, it might offer to sponsor the blog or some part of the blog. A sponsorship usually includes premium advertisements and exclusive ad placement, and the blogger sometimes even thanks the sponsor in the editorial content of the site. See "Seeking Sponsorships," later in this chapter.

WARNING

A lot of bloggers have had the same great idea about the ads on their blogs: "I'll just click these myself and send my cost-per-click rates through the roof! I'll make millions!" Unfortunately, the advertising companies have figured out this little scheme, and they refer to it as *click fraud.* Advertisers spend good money to have their ads displayed, and companies that run advertisement programs go out of their way to make sure that clicks on those ads are legitimate clicks. Make sure that you understand what happens if you click ads on your own blog before you do it: Some programs penalize or even ban bloggers who engage in click fraud.

Getting Advertising Going

Most bloggers choose to incorporate advertising programs by signing up with a company that serves as a middleman between the blogger and the advertiser. This company typically negotiates rates with the advertiser, tracks ad performance, and pays the blogger for advertising placement.

Although you can cut out the middleman and sell your own ad space, many bloggers find that they don't really want to spend their time dealing with the negotiation, tracking, and technical overhead.

But even the most time-pressed blogger can likely find the strength to listen when an advertiser contacts that blogger directly and offers to sponsor the blog. These arrangements are typically more lucrative for the blogger (and the advertiser, presumably), and the two parties negotiate this relationship on a case-by-case basis, depending on the audience, product, blog traffic, and other factors.

After you decide on formats, placement, and business models, it's time to put ads on your blog. The good — and bad — news is that you have dozens of options to choose from. In the following sections, I show you a few well-regarded advertising programs to consider.

Google AdSense

www.google.com/adsense

AdSense is Google's contextual advertising program, and it's really the biggest player in the contextual advertising arena. When you sign up for Google AdSense, you choose what kinds of ads you want on your blog, from text to images to videos. You can see examples of the Google AdSense formats in Figure 20-2.

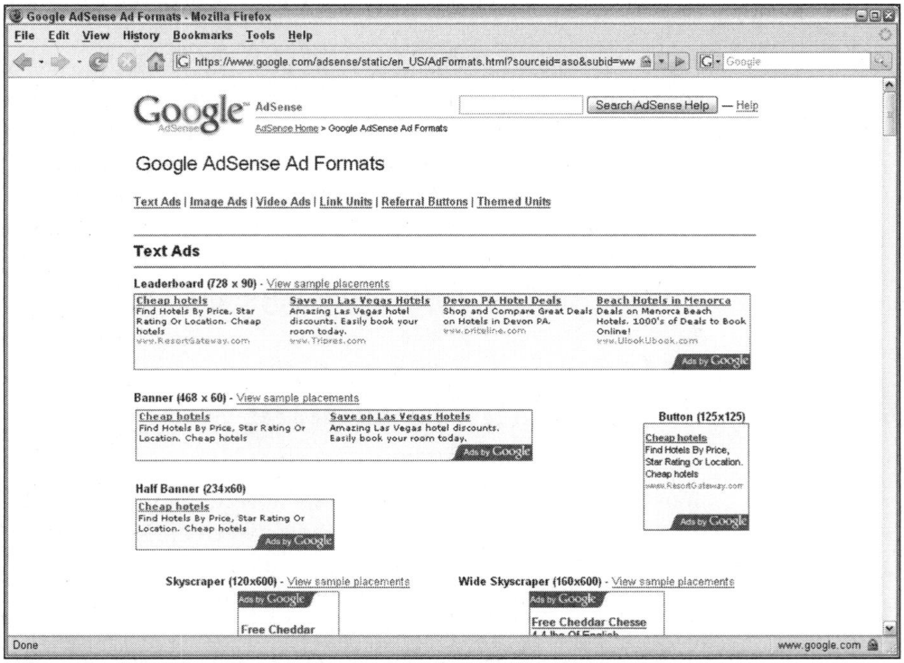

FIGURE 20-2: Google AdSense puts advertisers on your blog and money in your pocket.

Advertisers pay Google money when your blog visitors click the advertisements displayed beside your content, and you receive a portion of those payments. Successful bloggers who have a lot of traffic can earn a living from Google AdSense, but income varies greatly, depending on the size of your audience and how well your blog topics match the advertisers who contract with Google.

Matomy SEO Media Group

`www.matomyseo.com/r/publishers`

Matomy SEO provides context-based ad links within your blog content, providing you with a monetization option that matches the content already existing on your site. There are no fees attached to payment for online publishers approved to join the Matomy SEO Publisher community.

You can display Text Link Ads on the same page with Google AdSense, Yahoo! Publisher Network, and other contextually served ads.

SiteScout

`www.sitescout.com`

SiteScout is an advertising marketplace similar to the others mentioned in the preceding sections. Bloggers can choose between text, banner ads, full-page *interstitials* (splash pages containing a full-page advertisement), inline ads, and image ads. Interstitials are high-paying ads that take over the entire browser window when a user clicks to move from one page of your website to another; they usually feature a Skip This Ad link or button.

Putting Ads on Your Blog

To get these ads onto your website, the programs you sign up for usually provide you with a bit of code that you insert into your website templates. Some programs have step-by-step instructions for popular blog software packages, but be aware that you might also need to consult your blog software documentation for help with putting your ads where you want them.

First, decide just where you want the ads on your page. The best thing to do when you're thinking about introducing ads into your blog design is to make sure the ads aren't overpowering.

WARNING

Don't damage your reputation or credibility by overloading the site with ads or by associating ads too closely with your blog posts and content. Aside from pop-up ads, nothing is more annoying than having a blog design that's created around ads rather than a blog that's designed to include ads.

At the same time, you need to place ads in spots where readers can see them. Bloggers have discovered a few truths about ads, although your results might differ:

» **Ads at the top and bottom of each page do poorly.** Readers often ignore and rarely view advertisements along the top or the bottom of a blog because the site content usually appears in the middle of the screen. While users scroll their windows to view site content, they may never see these top and bottom advertisements at all.

» **Ads in the sidebars perform well but might interfere with navigation.** The left side of the website is a traditional place for ads. However, it's also a prime place for navigation tools, and your website design might require that you locate such tools higher than the ads you want people to view. As for the right side, not only are navigation tools sometimes placed here, but the bulk of blog content tends be aligned to the left side of the screen. Some users might cover the right side with other windows and therefore miss these right-side advertisements entirely.

» **Ads within the content itself get clicked.** Some blogs have their ads placed within their content, so visitors don't miss the ads. But you need to be careful when you use advertising within your content. Remember that you want to make the content king, not the ad.

TIP

Try out ads in different places on your blog and see how your audience reacts, as well as how your earnings do. You might need to try several different locations before you find one that balances your readers' needs with your advertisers'.

Putting Ads in Your RSS Feeds: Feedblitz

Active bloggers debate about whether RSS feeds should contain ads. Traditionally, bloggers have used RSS as a way to share information, and only later did it become a place to put advertisements. You might want to consider using RSS ads because many of your blog readers might use RSS readers to consume the content of your blog.

RSS ads are simply banner or text advertisements that appear below or above the content displayed in your RSS reading program. The ads are usually smaller than typical banner ads on the average website because they're meant to fit within the RSS feed.

FeedBlitz (www.feedblitz.com) rose in popularity in the blogging community when the demise of Google Reader sent bloggers scurrying away from Google's RSS service, FeedBurner. Like FeedBurner, FeedBlitz allows bloggers to publish their blog content in RSS form that can be read on a reader or via email.

Getting Paid to Post

As alluded to earlier, monetizing your blog doesn't have to mean filling up your text or even your sidebar with ads. Many blogs make the majority of their blog-related money through sponsored post campaigns. For many bloggers, sponsored post campaigns means receiving money to post content related to a company or a product. Some bloggers also post product reviews and consider the product they've received to be compensation. Blogging for money can also lead you down the path of the professional blogger, where you write posts for other blogs.

Placing products on your blog

Some bloggers fear that the influence of advertisers and content sponsors might take over the traditionally independent voice of the blogosphere. When advertisers offer money or goods to bloggers to share information about their products and services in a blog, it might not result in an honest review of the business. So, if you're paid to post information about someone else, make sure that you retain your right to post your own, honest opinion.

REMEMBER

If you post sponsored content or reviews of products sent to you for free, you are required by the FTC (Federal Trade Commission) to disclose that at the beginning of your blog post. Learn more at www.ftc.gov.

Many bloggers hear from PR firms and companies daily with requests for sponsored content placement and product reviews. However, a variety of companies also connect bloggers and brands.

The companies in the following list all offer in-network bloggers the opportunity to participate in everything from sponsored content to product reviews to even spokesperson campaigns. In fact, many bloggers have used their sites as a launching point to build a related career — such as spokesperson work or paid speaker — and the blog networks below are often instrumental in making that happen:

» MomSelect (www.momselect.com)

» TapInfluence (www.tapinfluence.com)

- » Global Influence Network (www.globalinfluencenetwork.com)

- » One2One Network (http://one2onenetwork.com)

- » The Motherhood (www.themotherhood.com)

- » Clever Girls Collective (www.clevergirlscollective.com)

TIP

Many advertising networks such as Federated Media and BlogHer also place sponsored content campaigns on blogs within their network, combining two revenue streams for bloggers within their networks.

Blogging professionally

You can offer your blogging services to those who might want them by making a small business for yourself as a professional blogger. Believe me, companies are often looking for competent writers whom they can hire to contribute content to their blogs. To offer your service, check the blogger-wanted ads on job boards and see whether you're interested in writing about any topic. Also, be sure to post about your availability on your own blog's sidebar and in your blog itself.

A site where you can start your search for blogging jobs is Jobs.Progblogger (http://jobs.problogger.net). This popular website provides help to bloggers so that they can monetize their websites. The job board is highly active, and blogger jobs often appear here.

REMEMBER

When you begin blogging professionally, you need to keep track of any progress you make. Typically, this tracking includes either the number of posts that you create or the number of site visitors over a period of time. You can organize this information in various ways, but the tracking needs to prove that some interaction occurred between you and your readers.

Tying in Affiliate Marketing

If you ever blogged about a product that you really like and just knew that you were helping the company that makes the product make a sale, you can now make some money from that sale with affiliate marketing.

Popular retailers have set up affiliate marketing programs, most notably Amazon. com. You sign up with an affiliate program, and when you blog about one of its products, you include a piece of identifying information that the company gives you. You earn cash when readers of your blog click the product and buy it.

If you find yourself blogging about items that others might buy as a result of your recommendation, check to see whether the company that makes the product has an affiliate program, and sign yourself up.

In short order, your blog can contain links to books, DVDs, or other products that provide you with a commission on each product bought through a link from your website.

Amazon Associates Program

`https://affiliate-program.amazon.com`

Amazon is the most recognized affiliate program available, and it's arguably one that you likely benefit from using because many bloggers mention books and DVDs that they've enjoyed.

Amazon Associates works by letting you create specially formatted links that you can use on your blog to drive traffic to the Amazon website. Anything that a visitor who clicks your link purchases earns you a percentage of the sale as a referral fee.

Rakuten Affiliate Network

`http://marketing.rakuten.com/affiliate-marketing`

Rakuten Affiliate Network, formerly called LinkShare, is another affiliate program that calls itself a pay-per-action marketing network. You can place both text and graphical ads on your blog and make money from any sales that come from readers' purchases.

Seeking Sponsorships

You can get *sponsorships* in two ways: by receiving requests from companies and by seeking them out yourself. Such sponsorship can mean one of two things:

>> Sponsors might pay you to put their ads on your website.

>> Sponsors might simply provide you with free goods or services in return for advertising on your website.

You need to think carefully about whether to take on a sponsor because you might not want to agree to the requirements, such as the following:

>> **Prominent placement or exclusivity:** A sponsor is different from the usual ad on your website because sponsors like a prominent placement on your blog — possibly including the exclusive right to advertise on your blog.

>> **Acknowledgment:** A sponsor might ask you to use the phrase "This blog sponsored by . . . " or some variation of it to let your readers know that a specific company is funding your blog. You may also want to thank your sponsor occasionally to generate extra goodwill.

>> **Time commitment:** Sponsorships often run for a set length of time, usually much longer than a standard ad runs. Sponsorships of several months to a year aren't unheard of.

Getting sponsors interested in your blog is probably the hardest advertising strategy, though it's also the most lucrative. To find a sponsor, you need to "sell" your blog, from the design to the content. Make the sponsor want to post its advertisements on your site — not someone else's. When you're seeking sponsors, keep your blog dynamic, on topic, and well written.

One of the best things sponsors do for your blog is legitimize your work. Many bloggers might be viewed by the public as "just another blogger" within the static of the Internet. But, if you have sponsors that believe in what you're doing, you can attract other professional relationships, such as speaking engagements or press interviews. If you're regarded as an authority, you can build a stronger brand.

Negotiating a sponsorship experience

Sponsors can be demanding advertisers, and they can restrict how you develop your monetization plan by changing the way you advertise on your site. Some sponsors demand *exclusivity* — which means that they're the only business of that type that advertises on your site, forcing you to turn away other potential sponsors. Others might demand that you always write about their products or services in a positive way. Dealing with sponsors can be a true balancing act. But the rewards can be worth the work.

Here's my recipe for a successful sponsor/blogger relationship:

>> **Be clear on your topic.** Know who you are and what you're writing about. If you have a blog that isn't clear about its subject, when you're seeking sponsorship, potential sponsors may be unable to understand why they are a good match for your blog. Sponsors want a very clear idea about the content you're creating and what you can do for them.

Keeping your blog on topic is especially important when sponsors are actively using their brand identities on your site. Make sure that they're aware of everything you might write about so that they don't have any surprises or objections to editorial content.

>> **Be clear about what you're promising.** Be sure that both you and your sponsor understand exactly what influence and control — if any — the partnership offers the advertiser. Thoroughly outline how you'll handle both content and advertising placement of the sponsor; the advertiser should be upfront about its expectations of you.

>> **Know your audience.** Educate yourself on your audience if you're seeking paying sponsors for your blog. With increased sponsorship, you absolutely must address the question of who your audience is. You need to document the activity in your community, track your comments, and analyze the information from your web statistics. (Check Chapter 19 for information on web statistics and traffic software.)

TIP

Create a report of your statistics to prove to any sponsors that you have the numbers you claim. Don't use any guesswork when creating this report. Your sponsors want to see solid numbers and data to back up your claims. Sponsorship arrangements often require you to create statistics reports. The simple fact is that if you want to make money, you have to gather data.

You can collect data from your audience in the form of contests, polls, and other interactive experiences. Ask your audience members who they are — and if you approach it in a professional manner, they might be happy to reveal a little bit about themselves.

>> **Banner placement and visual cues.** If you've been placing advertising on your blog for awhile, you already have a good idea where ads appear to good effect on your site, and you probably also know what types of ads work best. So, you can demonstrate the benefits of placement and ad types to any potential sponsors.

However, if you've never had ads on your site when you first seek a sponsor, be prepared to offer ideas and suggestions for adequately highlighting the sponsor's ads and branding. You can even provide a design mock-up or some kind of visual representation. Or you might even consider creating a demo website that actually shows the ads in the positions and formats that you think can work.

>> **Limit other monetization methods.** Some bloggers find that if they use other advertising systems at the same time as a sponsor, it dilutes the effectiveness of the sponsorships. Many sponsors ask to be the exclusive advertiser on your site or that you limit what other kinds of advertising and advertisers you use while they sponsor you. This request isn't unreasonable, especially if you have a lucrative sponsorship agreement that compensates you for the loss of those ad spots.

Setting boundaries

Jumping to the professional level in the blogging world poses a few potential pitfalls and requires ongoing reinvention on your part. Set up and keep to a few simple rules about what your professional limits and intentions are, and don't be afraid to write those rules down in a document that you share with sponsors and your readers.

Also, be ready to say no. Some sponsors might want more than you're willing to give. Yes, you may be able to earn some money from your blog, but don't forget the reason you're blogging in the first place. Your blog is your territory, not your sponsor's. You're renting the sponsor space on your site, giving it access to your audience. You aren't signing up for someone to tell you what to do. You already have parents for that!

REMEMBER

Don't jump at every offer that comes in the door. You may find this advice difficult to follow when you're seeking your first sponsor, but you need to maintain a high level of professionalism — not just for yourself but also for your audience. In the same way that you protect your audience from nasty comments and spam, you need to be sure that you give them an appropriate experience with your sponsors and advertisers. Protect the integrity of your blog and avoid sponsors that demand more time, editorial control, or space on your blog than you're willing to give.

Accepting Gifts, Not Obligations

Many companies offer news media access to products and services to generate press attention, and increasingly, bloggers are being offered the same goodies. After all, some blog topics are so specific that companies absolutely know that the blog's readers will be interested in their products. For example, a blogger who writes about cell phones might be targeted by a mobile phone company and offered a free product or money in exchange for some kind of online review or feedback.

This kind of exchange can be a tricky situation because some bloggers regard the gift as some kind of bribe or obligation to write something positive about the product in question.

In fact, that perception isn't correct. I know bloggers who accept products for review on the condition that they say what they really think about it, and most companies are perfectly satisfied with this kind of arrangement. In addition, most bloggers who do these kinds of reviews are very upfront with their readers about how they obtained the product in question and what agreement they have with the company that provided it.

If you're getting these offers, you can probably benefit from establishing such a policy. Most bloggers don't want to be seen as taking bribes or favors from companies that just want the bloggers to say nice things about them. Your policy needs to lay out how you plan to deal with such situations.

Here are three things to consider when you start to get product-review offers:

>> **Be clear about what you'll do with the product.** Tell the product maker that you won't write a positive review if the product doesn't deserve it. Make sure that you're very specific about what you'll provide in return for the gift (if anything).

>> **Be prepared to return gifts.** A lot of bloggers, especially the incredibly geeky ones, would love to receive a gift from a company that has the latest and hottest product. However, if the company has unreasonable demands or demands that don't match the blogger's vision, the blogger might choose to simply return the gift.

>> **Donate what you receive.** You can avoid an ugly scene with your audience or any sponsors of your blog by taking the gifts you receive, writing your review, and then giving the items away. You can send them to your favorite charity or hold a contest for your audience. Donating your freebies generates all kinds of goodwill from your community while avoiding any accusations of bias.

Keep to the core of what makes your blog great. If you get an offer for a free product, think about it first — don't accept it right away. You can even go to your community members and see what they think if you require advice. Whether you accept ads or sponsorships, and how you implement them, really depends on you. And remember, if you've received payment or a product, you are legally required to disclose that information in each post.

Viewing Your Blog As an Influential Platform

While the majority of this chapter focuses on ways to earn money on your blog, your blog may actually catapult you to earning opportunities off of your website or even offline completely. Many of today's top bloggers earn revenue in relationship to their blogging rather than through their blogging. Once you've built a large audience with great content and social media engagement, the sky truly is the limit. Some other ways bloggers earn revenue include:

- » Event appearances
- » Brand spokesperson contracts
- » Book deals
- » Television and radio appearances
- » Event and conference hosting
- » Product creation and endorsement
- » Creating and holding workshops
- » Consulting
- » Speaking engagements

Chapter 21

Blogging for Companies

As a business owner or entrepreneur, you're probably wondering whether blogging can help you be more financially successful or allow you to promote your company in some way. Many of today's technically savvy businesses have started blogs and found them to be terrific tools for reaching out to customers, generating buzz about a service or product, building goodwill, or just informing customers about what they're up to.

If you're thinking about adding a blog to your outreach efforts but aren't entirely confident that it'll be worth the time and effort, you aren't alone. Many companies have difficulty seeing the value in blogging. Some professionals worry about diverting time away from more crucial workplace tasks, whereas others worry about opening themselves up for public criticism.

And the truth is that even though blogging can provide a business with a really incredible tool, it isn't right for *every* business. Nonetheless, in this chapter, I do my best to persuade you that blogging can work for you and your company, whether you're a lone-wolf entrepreneur just starting out or a Fortune 500 executive with more marketing staff than you know what to do with.

TIP

If this chapter piques your interest, check out *Buzz Marketing with Blogs For Dummies*, by Susannah Gardner (John Wiley & Sons, Inc.), which covers in depth what I can only touch on in this chapter.

Putting Blogs to Work for Your Business

A stigma still lingers somewhat around blogs. Blogs, for a lot of folks, equate with the worst kind of narcissistic navel-gazing. Those kinds of blogs do exist, of course, but in reality, the blogosphere contains so much more than that. Hundreds of nonprofit organizations, small-business owners, consultants, newspapers, and schools have moved into the blogosphere.

Why? Blogs are simple to set up, easy to publish, and have a proven track record for increasing search engine traffic to a website. For a company in which time is of the essence and accessibility is a necessity, blogs are a low-investment way to accomplish a lot. Don't believe me? Then perhaps you'll believe General Motors, McDonald's, Microsoft, Amazon.com, *The New York Times,* and Southwest Airlines; all these companies have added blogs to their business practices.

Considering the benefits of a business blog

For a business or organization, you can use blog software to release company public-relations documents to the public, or you can go further and introduce blogs as part of your external communications to your customers and potential customers. Some companies use blogs internally to coordinate work teams or communicate across distances. Here are a few of the ways businesses are using blogs:

>> Generating conversation and buzz about the company and its products or services

>> Reaching out with information and support to current customers, even resolving issues traditionally handled by phone-based customer service

>> Creating new pathways to interact with the public about an industry or issue, including gathering feedback and input to guide future product development

>> Defusing negative criticism or press by publicly addressing problems

>> Demonstrating expertise and experience to potential customers

>> Directly driving sales or action

>> Collaborating across teams, branches, regions, or staggered shifts

When it comes to business, the main thing that a business blogger should consider is that blog software, implemented properly, can allow companies to improve their communications and organization with very little overhead. In some cases, blogs have even saved businesses money by delivering documents and data online that were previously delivered via snail mail.

Businesses haven't been the only beneficiaries, either. Customers have benefited from increased access to news, information, support, and dialogue with companies that have blogs.

Making blogs work for you can be simple if you have a communication strategy that's flexible and can evolve when your blog takes off. Blogs can generate sales and establish strong communication directly with customers, and marketing experts believe blogs are a friendly method of making customers happy.

Checking out businesses that blog

You know that blogging is important. You already know that it gives you a very good way to generate talk about your company. Do you need a little more convincing? Well, the following sections discuss how some other companies are blogging.

Hewlett-Packard

`http://community.hpe.com/`

You've probably owned a Hewlett-Packard product at some point in your computing life. Hewlett-Packard has built computers, printers, cameras, and high-end computer servers for years, building up incredible expertise across a range of consumer products. You can see that knowledge in the HP blogs, which claim to convey the "unvarnished thoughts of HP employees." Topics range from computers to the Cannes Film Festival to gaming, and the bloggers come from all areas of the company's structure.

Wells Fargo

`http://blog.wellsfargo.com`

What could a bank possibly blog about, you ask? Apparently, banks can discuss a whole lot with their customers. Student loans, small business, and stock markets are all topics discussed on the Wells Fargo Blogs site. Wells Fargo Blogs gives multiple contributors a public voice in a variety of blogs, from The Student LoanDown to Guided by History.

Dell

`http://en.community.dell.com/dell-blogs/default.aspx`

The Dell community of blogs feature posts written by Dell employees and experts about topics ranging from new technology to upcoming ways to connect with Dell through social media.

Disney Parks Blog

`http://disneyparks.disney.go.com/blog/`

Disney Parks and Resorts as well as the Disney Cruise Line use the Disney Parks Blog (shown in Figure 21-1) as a platform to share Disney news as well as behind-the-scene first looks to fans. Rather than employing just one or two bloggers, Disney Parks Blog allows a variety of Disney Cast Members to share the projects on which they're working. This blog also gives Disney fans a rare opportunity to communicate directly with Disney.

FIGURE 21-1:
The Disney Parks Blog gives Disney fans rare access to behind-the-scenes information and conversations with Disney Cast Members.

Deciding whether to blog

Blogging for business reasons is a sensitive topic both in and out of the blogosphere. Old-school bloggers don't like seeing blogging turned from a personal outlet into a professional one, and many businesses worry that the informality of a blog looks unprofessional. And that isn't all: Some businesses also have concerns about employees who have personal blogs on which they might talk about their work or appear to be representing the company.

Blogging isn't for every corporate culture. If your company has traditionally had an open hand with communication and outreach, blogging is going to be a great tool for you. But if you have a reserved corporate culture, blogging might be too much of a stretch beyond business as usual. Still, many companies that might seem an odd fit for blogs for marketing or outreach have been happily surprised at the results they've obtained.

Businesses that need to keep information or trade practices confidential, or that stand to lose by having an open–door policy, probably shouldn't blog. For instance, some government agencies and law firms are limited by the very nature of their businesses in what they can communicate. You know best whether your corporate culture or industry can benefit from the use of a blog.

TOP FIVE REASONS WHY BLOGS WORK FOR BUSINESSES

Here are the most important reasons that blogs work so well as a business and marketing tool in today's Internet-enabled world:

- **Cost:** A lot of blogging software packages are open source and available at no cost, but even those that have licensing fees are very reasonably priced. Hosted services can also provide you with an inexpensive platform to begin business blogging.

- **Communication:** A blog allows you to communicate with potential and current clients in a direct and informal way. You can chat and communicate about your product or service without pressuring your client. You use a business blog to make sure that your potential or existing clients get the facts about your product without a heavy-handed sales pitch.

- **Research:** Many companies want to break into new markets and new demographics. Blogging allows for collaborative discussion that can help you gather valuable information about how to position products and services.

- **Feedback:** Find out what you're doing right and wrong in your business or with your products by just asking outright on your blog. Discover how to improve what you're currently doing or how you can deal with existing problems — and get points for effort while you do.

- **Reputation:** Do away with that corporate-giant personality that most companies can't help but convey. Blogs can put a human, personal face on what has usually been a monolithic surface. If you let the public see how you respect and regard them, you reap the benefits of being honest and open. Smaller businesses and consultancies benefit from the publicity around their names and opinions.

REMEMBER

At the very least, however, track your company and what's said about it in the blogosphere. Just because you ignore blogs, that doesn't mean they ignore you! Chapter 19 explains how you can keep tabs on what others say about your business online.

TIP

If you're still on the fence about starting a blog, try one with a set endpoint, for an event or a product launch. After the event occurs, you can end the blog's life span gracefully and have some real data to use in assessing whether blogging was a worthwhile endeavor for you. Also, take a look at your competitors — are any of them blogging? If so, does the blog appear to be reaching visitors effectively? Are readers leaving comments? Watch how these competitors are making use of a blog and give some thought to whether you might be able to do something similar (but more effectively).

Planning for Business Blog Success

Blogging for a business comes down to planning. Don't let the ease of getting started with the technical side of blogging seduce you into jumping in without preparing. You need to decide what your goals are, figure out whom you want to actually write the blog, map out the topics that you plan to discuss, and plan how you might integrate direct action or sales.

Setting goals

Before you jump into blogging for your business, you need to set goals that define how you can know whether your blog is successful after you launch it. Decide what you want the blog to help you accomplish. Do you want to replace some of your existing customer service efforts with the blog? Are you launching a new product that needs publicity? Whatever your direction, plan your purpose prior to launching the blog.

REMEMBER

So many things could go into a blog, but you also have a business to run. Decide how much time you want to devote to writing and maintaining your blog. Blogging is part of your business, but it can't take away from time you need to devote to other tasks.

You might choose to define success by

>> Increasing traffic to your website

>> Reaching a certain number of blog comments on a daily basis

> » Seeing more conversation about your company/products/services in the media or on other blogs

> » Earning money from product sales or blog advertising

You might want to define success for your blog in other ways, so don't think you have to use any of these suggestions. A blog is such a flexible medium that yours might accomplish a goal I can't even imagine!

Choosing a blogger

Businesses have developed two approaches to company blogs: blogs written by one person and those written by multiple people from all over the organization. Either approach is valid, as long as everyone posting to the blog has a clear idea of the goals, ideas, and style of the blog.

TIP

If you create a blog that has multiple contributors, put a single individual in charge of content on a regular basis and encourage others from the organization to chime in when they have something to say. The responsibility for the blog is in one person's hands, but the door is open for wide participation.

Occasional writers are welcome, but don't suddenly give employees brand-new job duties that they can't meet. Having multiple voices in a blog can also help you to convey the culture of your company overall, giving readers a taste of what people at all levels of the organization think about and do.

If you spread the writing around, you might be able to create a blog that has a huge amount of content and satisfies a very large readership. The multiple-voice perspective might also awaken ideas in the other writers and generate internal conversations.

TIP

No matter who blogs, you must decide internally whether someone needs to vet posts before actually posting them, and who should do the vetting. It's a good idea to have someone who isn't blogging keep an eye on things, just to get a second opinion.

When you're considering just who should blog on behalf of the company, give some thought to

> » **Writing ability:** You need a blogger who's an effective writer and who also *likes* to write. Some companies choose to hire a blogger from outside the company who has experience and the ability to communicate effectively about topics related to that company.

> » **Position within the company:** Who's the right person to reach out to the public? CEOs offer one perspective, as do those on the factory floor. Try to

match the goals and style of your blog with the right people within your company, and don't be afraid to give unexpected staffers a try. You might be surprised at how interesting readers find a behind-the-curtain approach.

>> **Knowledge and expertise:** Be sure to choose a person who has sufficient knowledge and expertise to be interesting and engaging on the subjects the blog discusses. Preferably, you want people who really know what they're talking about and have information to share.

>> **Time commitments:** Choose a blogger who has the time to put into the site. Don't overload already busy staff with this new job requirement.

After you choose a blogger, you have a few more folks to identify. Don't forget to plan whom you want to review comments, deal with spam, and fix technical issues.

Deciding what to write

While you think about topics for the blog, consider how informal or personal you want to make your blog style. Although the occasional personal post can help to humanize your blog, don't be tempted down the journaling path: You're creating a business blog, so look for creative ways of covering your industry.

The goal of many business blogs is to establish (or maybe reestablish) the business as a leader in its industry. Think about how to demonstrate expertise while staying interesting and readable: You need to show that you know your stuff without becoming a stuffed shirt! Use the blog to persuade people that they should trust you without coming right out and telling people, "I'm trustworthy!"

Whoever blogs for your business needs to have a keen understanding of the goals and culture of the company, as well as know how much information to put on the blog without going too far. Many companies set up rules about topics that are appropriate for the blog as well as define what information they want to keep confidential.

Here are some general guidelines to keep in mind for your blog content:

>> **Keep it true.** Double-check blog posts for accuracy before making them live. Like a newspaper or any other publisher, follow a process to make sure you're publishing facts and not fiction. You can include opinions on your business's blog as long as you label them as just that.

>> **Keep it relevant and real.** Be as open and honest as you can in your blog. This approach to transparency can make some in your company nervous (hi, corporate lawyer!), but the more successful business blogs provide insight or communication from real people. Some even give the public access to the viewpoints and words

of high-level staff the readers would normally never meet or talk to. Furthermore, whoever blogs should stay on topic and keep posts related to the subject of the blog, no matter how interesting that TV show was last night.

» **Keep it informative and educational.** One problem that many companies encounter when they start to blog is the fact that their blogs are (ahem) boring. You might have great information, but if people don't also find it interesting to read about, you can't get readers to stick around long. Try to write posts that educate with a light-hearted manner and that focus on information and news that are useful to those reading it.

» **Keep it positive.** Steer away from discussing your competition in your blog. If you can say something nice about another company, don't hesitate, but you probably don't want to point out just what other companies are doing wrong. That kind of approach can turn your blog into a giant argument, scaring off less-opinionated customers who might otherwise be interested in your products and services.

» **Keep using keywords.** Part of the plan of a business-related blog is to make sure the blog is useful to readers, but for that plan to work, you have to get readers from the search engine to your blog. Use your knowledge of your industry and topical news to use keywords that people are likely to use in search engines when they look for the subject of your blog or your business.

TIP

Pay special attention to the words that you use in the titles of your blog posts: Search engines often weight these words most heavily, so hit the highpoints in your titles. Informative is better than cutesy!

» **Keep linking.** Business blogs should also link to related articles and websites. You can link to resources on your business's own website, but don't hesitate to point folks to good information that isn't on your website. If you're a source for information that they need or can get them to the information they need effectively, you don't lose them for long.

Also, look for chances to link the blog to itself! A lot of bloggers are clever about linking to old posts on their own blogs so that new readers know where to go deep within the blog archives. This kind of linking can increase traffic and also inform and educate your readers.

» **Keep posting.** Post on a regular basis and don't stop. Don't worry about an absolutely right number of posts per week, but most experts agree that two to three posts a week is enough to keep your blog active and useful without overwhelming your readers. Other bloggers post less frequently, and others post multiple times a day. Do what works for you and for your readers, but be consistent so that your readers know what to expect from you. If your blog has long silences followed by short bursts of posting, you create a recipe for low readership numbers.

Generating sales or action

Asking potential customers to check out your services after they read something on your blog can turn those readers into actual customers. If you see a logical link to a product or service that you offer, it only makes sense to let people know. But you need to do more than simply push sales. You tread a fine line between a blog that points out possible purchases, along with providing content, and one that isn't anything more than a big ad.

REMEMBER

Keep one idea in mind: Meet the needs of your readers. If you can put yourself in the shoes of a blog visitor, you might be able to successfully discriminate between a reasonable link to a product sale and one that's too blatant.

Some blogs don't try hard to get people to pull out their wallets. Instead, the blog's purpose might be to gather feedback and get people to participate in an event or contest. Again, try to be genuine and inviting, rather than pushy. Get readers involved and invested in your goal.

Maggie Whitley Designs (www.maggiewhitley.com) is a site that skillfully pairs a personal blog with a home business. Maggie — known to her fans and customers as Gussy — candidly shares the ins and outs of her daily life with her husband, Zack, their growing family, and even their dog, Bauer. However, Maggie Whitley Designs, formerly known as Gussy Sews, isn't all about Maggie discovering the joys of motherhood. One click on Shop Gussy (www.shopgussy.com) takes you to the flip side of this blog — the store. Here you can purchase the wares of the family you've fallen in love with through Maggie's blog, from zip pouches to totes and bags. Genius! (See Figure 21-2.)

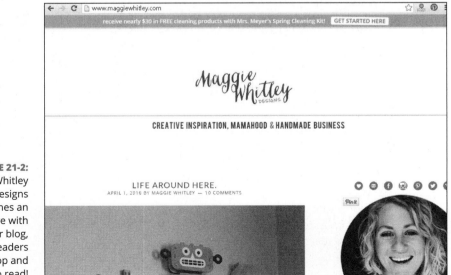

FIGURE 21-2:
Maggie Whitley Designs combines an online store with a popular blog, bringing readers to shop and shoppers to read!

Delivering with Technology

You might be thinking about how you, as a blogger, can make connections with potential customers by using your blog. Words are a great start, but technology can also be your friend! A lot of the standard blog bells and whistles are designed to get people involved or to make it easy for them to consume your blog.

Use the tools in the following sections to get readers to return to your blog again and again.

Enabling comments

Comments are a double-edged sword for companies that start blogs. On the one hand, they do a great job of starting conversation and interaction. On the other hand, they can be a source of a lot of work because you have to keep them free of spam or inappropriate conversation. Many businesses are tempted to start a blog and keep comments turned off, but that cuts out a huge part of the benefit of a blog: hearing from your readers and interacting directly with them.

My advice? Turn on the comments! But take precautions by setting up a good policy about what kinds of comments are acceptable and implement some of the very good spam-fighting tools discussed in Chapter 10.

Creating RSS/web feeds

Before the advent of web feeds, blog readers had to remember to visit the blog periodically to see whether the blogger had posted a new entry. This dangerous method made it easy for people to forget to visit. Web feeds, or RSS feeds, give you a way to let people know quickly, easily, and automatically that you have new content available on your blog. Blog visitors simply subscribe to the feed by using a newsreader, which tracks the feed and updates it every time you update the blog, giving instant notification to the reader.

Users can set up web feeds, usually formatted as RSS (Really Simple Syndication), quickly and easily. In fact, most blog software packages automatically include an RSS tool, so you can set it up once and never think about it again.

I talk more about web feeds in Chapter 16.

Podcasting

Podcasting, which joined the blogosphere several years ago, has proven to be a powerful blog ally. *Podcasting,* the recording and distribution of audio and video files to subscribers, has a tremendous potential to give your business blog a boost by providing multimedia presentations to your readers. You can add personality and a face to your blog. Posting interviews, discoveries, tutorials, and other adventures that your company has had can boost your visibility higher than a text-only blog can.

You can read more about creating a podcast in Chapter 13.

Starting a wiki

Wikis are collaboratively built websites that any visitor can edit. Although this collaborative format may unfortunately allow for misinformed information, businesses and organizations have found that wikis can complement blog sites nicely. Blogs allow for comments, but a wiki can provide a little more flexibility because visitors can both post pages and leave updates in a wiki, contributing to everything from documentation to news coverage.

Wikis are terrific collaborative tools, and if you've been trying to figure out a good way to share knowledge within an organization, you might want to use this approach. Many companies have found wikis useful for group learning purposes, such as building documentation or setting up procedural tasks. One of the most well-known examples of a successful wiki is Wikipedia (`www.wikipedia.org`), an online encyclopedia to which anyone can contribute content or edit existing content. You can even find it available in multiple languages.

Joining a social network

Adding your company to a variety of social networks, which has moved from an option to a necessity, can also help to boost your visibility in the blogosphere. Using these mediums properly can add a viral component to your communication strategy. (*Viral* marketing is advertising that consumers actually spread themselves. For example, when you forward a funny video created by a company, you've spread the "virus.")

A lot of social networks exist, so be sure to choose those that are most pertinent for your industry and approach, not those frequented by 14-year-old girls (unless that suits your business!). LinkedIn (`www.linkedin.com`) and Facebook (`www.facebook.com`) are good places to get started.

Be sure to check out the social media platforms where your customers are spending much of their online time, namely Twitter and Facebook. Ready for the next step? Head over to Google+ and Instagram. And if you have a product and want customers, run, don't walk to Pinterest. I introduce social networks and what they're all about in Chapters 17 and 18.

Advertising on Blogs

Traditional marketing strategies include advertising, and blogs are no exception. But these aren't your father's ads: Blog advertising runs the gamut of everything from text links to full sponsorships.

In the past, taking out a typical advertisement meant that you'd go to the local newspaper, select an ad size, and choose a section in which you wanted your ad to appear. Maybe people saw the ad, maybe they didn't, but you got charged by how many newspapers were printed, not how many sales you made.

Online advertising offers more accountability to the advertiser: Because of the way websites work, you can track how many times readers' computers load an ad, when a reader clicks it, and what the person does after he or she clicks that ad. Because advertisers like this kind of measure of effectiveness, printed material has seen a significant decline in the purchase of ad space, whereas online advertising has grown hugely. You can use several methods to get your name or even your blog URL seen on other websites and blogs.

Going contextual

Contextual advertising is the practice in which an ad-serving tool matches the advertisements based on the content that appears in the blog. For example, a blog about candy would have ads for candy, and a blog about movies would show ads for upcoming films. If the website visitors are interested in the content of the website, they're likely also interested in goods and services related to the topic of the website, and thus they're more likely to click the ads.

The first major player in the contextual advertising game was Google AdSense. The program was popular from the start, and after a few rocky periods of users abusing the system, it has proven to be quite a moneymaker for successful bloggers. Many professional bloggers make their living almost entirely on the income received from Google AdSense revenue. Search-engine marketer Alexandre Brabant uses Google AdSense on his company website, eMarketing 101 (www.emarketing101.ca). The Google AdSense program ads appear below the navigation bar of his site, as shown in Figure 21-3.

Here are two ways that you can get involved with Google's contextual advertising tools:

>> **Sign up to put ads on your blog or website.** Use the Google AdSense program (www.google.com/adsense). Chapter 20 introduces this program.

>> **Submit your blog or website for display.** The Google AdWords program (www.google.com/adwords) lets you present your blog or website in the ads displayed on other websites.

TIP

If you want to find out more about leveraging Google AdSense for your blog or business, check out *Google AdWords For Dummies*, by Howie Jacobson (John Wiley & Sons, Inc.).

Yahoo! and several other companies also have contextual advertising programs. Do a web search for *contextual advertising programs* to see what's on offer.

You can add contextual advertising to your web (RSS) feed or put yourself into other web feeds by using the FeedBurner Ad Network (http://feedburner.google.com).

Advertising via ad networks

A number of advertising middlemen can help successful bloggers put ads on their blogs. In most cases, you can choose between text and graphic ads in a set of standard web-advertising sizes. You create the ad, the ad network serves it up, the blogger posts new content, and his or her visitors see your ad.

If you want to advertise on some of the most successful blogs around, check out one or more of these ad networks:

>> **Blogads (**www.blogads.com**):** Offers ad placement on more than 3,500 blogs and allows you to choose an audience to target (for example, parents or news junkies).

>> **ClickZ (**www.clickz.com**):** Offers ad placement on the ClickZ family of news, opinion, and entertainment sites.

>> **Crisp Ads (**www.crispads.com**):** Offers advertising across blog categories (such as autos and food) or on specific blogs. More than 10,000 blogs are enrolled.

>> **FeedBurner (**http://feedburner.google.com**):** Offers placement on blogs and in RSS feeds; choose from categories of blogs and/or target specific times of day or geographic regions.

Each of these services offers you an array of popular blogs and ad formats to choose from, organizes the deal, and handles the transaction. Rates are negotiated based on the level of advertising, the blogs that you're placed on, and how many times your ads are viewed or clicked.

Sponsoring a blog

For a splashy way to be seen on a blog or website, consider sponsoring the site. Sponsorships for popular blogs have gained a lot of notoriety in the blogosphere. Some bloggers call accepting sponsorships "selling out," but others regard it as a great way to get paid to do what they love. Sponsorships tend to get you coverage on other blogs, even if it's just speculation about the amount you paid to sponsor a blog, but as they say, "Any publicity is good publicity."

Sponsorships usually entitle you to occupy any and perhaps all advertising slots on a blog, and they often earn you mentions in the text of the blog, as well. Few blogs actually advertise that they accept sponsorships, largely because sponsored blogs are still fairly rare. If you want to sponsor a blog, contact the blogger directly with an inquiry. He or she can let you know whether the blog is open to a sponsorship, and you can go from there.

Sponsorships can be expensive to do. Be prepared to negotiate with the blogger about the length of your sponsorship and the amount of money you're willing to pay, but think bigger than you would for advertisement. In some cases, sponsors assume the operating costs of a blog, in addition to paying the blogger for his or her time and audience exposure.

As a sponsor, you're entitled to more than just a prominent ad placement (though you should get that, too!). You can consider requesting *exclusivity* — that you're the only advertiser in your industry on the blog, the only sponsor, or the only advertiser. You can request mentions in the copy of the blog, or any other arrangement you think is good for both you and the blogger. For many sponsors, having a prominent logo placement and label at the top of every blog page, and no other advertising on the blog, fills the bill.

Topics to discuss with any blogger you're considering sponsoring include the following:

REMEMBER

>> **What topics the blog covers:** Know what kinds of content the blog you're sponsoring typically has and what kind of language it uses. Because readers associate your brand with the blog, you need to be comfortable with the way the blogger expresses him- or herself, as well as what subjects the blogger may raise.

You might also want to discuss how you plan to handle situations in which the blogger has blogged about a topic with which you have a problem. Understand that the blogger is likely to resist giving you editorial control, and be clear about what, if any, say you want to have in the content of the site.

>> **How you want the blog to acknowledge your sponsorship:** Be sure to establish how the blogger will place your brand on the page, and when and where he or she will mention your business and link to your business's website.

>> **How other ads or monetization occur on the blog:** Talk with the blogger about other ways that he or she earns revenue and decide what, if any, of those systems can remain in place during the term of your sponsorship. Be prepared to compensate the blogger for any revenue that he or she usually earns that you request he or she remove from the site. For example, if the blogger commonly uses Google AdSense advertising that you don't want to appear on the blog when you sponsor it, ask for accounting statements showing the value of those ads to the blogger.

7

The Part of Tens

Chapter 22

Ten Ways to Grow Community

Every online community needs leaders or facilitators to keep the discussions lively, upbeat, and on topic. Taking on the role of community leader or even founder can be a tough job, and sometimes the rewards come slowly. Don't let these realities discourage you, though. Encouraging growth in any community requires a certain level of patience, persistence, and attention — but when it works, it really works.

This chapter offers ten simple tools for developing your blog from your soapbox into a real community, with true interaction between you and your readers, and among the readers themselves.

If you're lucky, in the process of getting people to read and comment on your posts and on each other's comments, you even discover how to convert readers into community evangelists who can make the community larger, more fun, and more active.

Write Often

Get writing! (Or podcasting, or posting photos, or whatever it is you're doing on your blog.)

Establish a regular schedule for maintaining your blog. A schedule really helps readers know what to expect and when. A regular schedule can even build anticipation and excitement. Be open to ideas, provide a welcoming environment, and keep yourself on topic so that interested, engaged readers get what they're looking for when they visit.

Listen and Respond to Readers

One of the best things that you can do for the community is to make sure that everyone's having the best time he or she can. How do you know whether your readers enjoy their time on your blog? Why not just ask?

Give people a way to let you know whether the community aspects of your site work for them by including a Contact Me page. But if you really want to hear about how things are going, try just posting a blog entry asking people for their thoughts and constructive criticism about what you're doing.

You may not even need to open the lines of communication with your readers. In fact, they may already be reaching out to you! If someone asks you a question, either in the comments or through email, make sure to reply. Acknowledge what the person says in your reply and take the time to answer properly, even if only to thank him or her for the comment. Thoughtful responses to questions and comments about your blog can do as much to build your community as original blog posts can.

Keep on top of what people are saying within your blog domain and don't be a stranger to those who like what you do. Embrace their enthusiasm for your blog. Give them a reason to keep coming back. Interaction can make those who might shy away feel that they're really part of the community that you're developing.

Visit and Participate

Join other communities. It's that simple. If you want to build a community around your blog, you need to participate in others. Find blogs that are related to the topic areas of your blog. Jump in to the conversation by offering a different perspective or some feedback to the blogger or to the folks who leave comments. Mentioning your site on other blogs is fine, as long as you make sure that your comments relate to the subject at hand and add to the conversation.

REMEMBER

Building community is just as much about supporting other bloggers as it is looking for support for your blog. Jeremy Pepper's blog (`www.pop-pr.blogspot.com`), shown in Figure 22-1, includes a list of PR blogs and resources for his readers, supporting his audience as well as other public relations blogs.

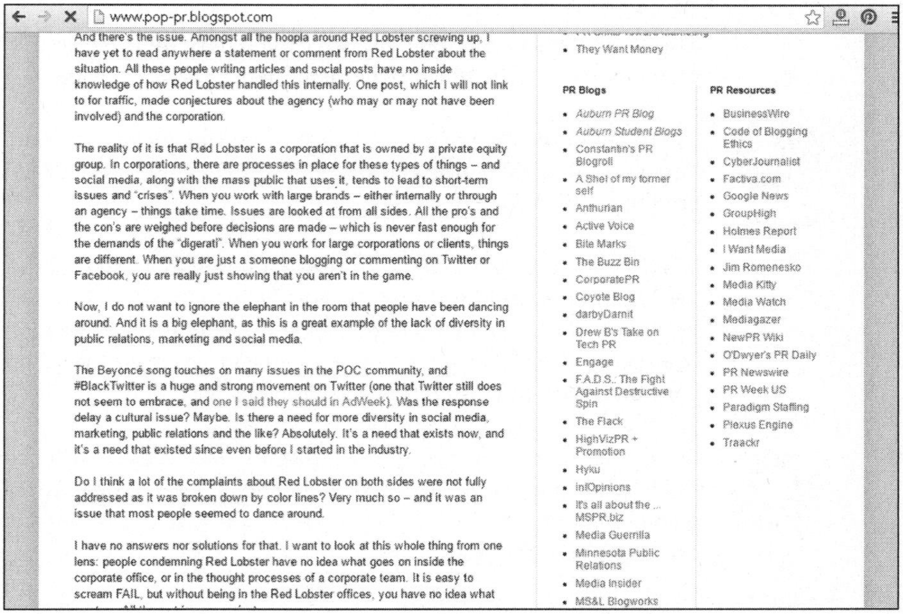

FIGURE 22-1:
Support other members of your blog community to build your own audience and community.

Also, don't just write and leave. Keep active in the communities in which you're a member and use that time to connect with others. Take what you can from the community, but also give back what you think can benefit everyone as a whole. Remember that participating in these communities might even give you ideas for your own blog, so you're likely to benefit in several ways from the time you spend on these blogs.

You can also share links between your blog community and related blogs that you want to support. Offer to set up a type of network where you can share content between sites. Anything is possible; you only need to ask.

Guest Blog and Invite Guest Bloggers

If your blog readership is up and running and you're attracting a significant number of daily readers, you can request that members of your community help you out by guest-blogging on your site. Depending on the software you're using, you can either set up secondary blogs or allow guest bloggers to post to the main blog of your site. Getting other perspectives and comments from your community "experts" is incredibly cool, and you might be able to build a series of posts from other bloggers into your site.

This kind of blogging trade-off can let you have multiple voices fill out the content on your site and provide a richer experience for your readers.

REMEMBER

These relationships are great to have when you get sick or want to take a vacation. Tap your guest-blogging community for help covering your blog when you aren't around to do it.

It's also a great idea to look for opportunities to write on other websites as well. See whether other blogs might need a little help with a few additional posts. Also, help keep the conversations going on other blogs that you enjoy. Each time you comment on another blog, you get exposure to a few more potential readers for your own blog and build links back to your blog.

TIP

Be sure to have a guest blogging policy in place for your site, covering topics such as length of post, topics to be covered, and payment. Make sure that the site you're guest blogging for has a policy as well, and that you understand the rules before committing to the post.

Communicate via Email and Newsletters

As spam-ridden as electronic mail can be, you can still use it to stay in contact with your community. Offering newsletter delivery through email of some or all of your blog content to your readers can attract users who aren't comfortable with some of the fancier technologies, such as RSS. Try these three tactics:

>> Offer readers the chance to subscribe to bonus content that does not appear on your blog.

>> Allow your users to sign up for email notifications when you post something new to your blog.

>> Let your readers sign up for an email newsletter that recaps recent blog posts of interest.

Many blog software programs have built-in Tell a Friend or Email a Friend functionality. If you turn this feature on, every blog post includes a small icon or link that, when clicked, lets your reader fill out the name and email address of a friend and send an email notification about your blog post to that friend. It's like free marketing. Figure 22-2 shows this Email a Friend option on Vera Sweeney's blog, Lady and the Blog (www.ladyandtheblog.com).

FIGURE 22-2:
Email sharing tools allow readers to clue in friends about your great blog post.

You can easily reach users who have mastered email but aren't up on newsreaders and RSS by setting up your blog to allow users to sign up for email notifications when you post a new blog entry. Allowing them to sign up and also remove themselves from your email system puts them in control of the situation, which means that you don't contribute to the spam problem. The FeedBurner site (http://feedburner.google.com) lets you set up an email notification/subscription tool.

Taking the time to create some kind of additional email newsletter can also get people interested in your website. You can take a little time at the end of each calendar month to pick out your best or most popular blog posts. You can include the links to your blog posting, or you can copy and paste the blog post into an email and send it off. You may even want to highlight the top blog posts of some of your friends!

You can create this kind of newsletter in several ways, but it's most effective if you sign up for an email service provider such as Constant Contact (www.constantcontact.com), Topica (www.topica.com), Emma (www.myemma.com), or MailChimp (www.mailchimp.com), to name a few. These services can handle subscription requests, unsubscribe requests, and changes of email addresses, all without needing you to do anything. In addition, most of them offer you the capability to track click-throughs on links in your newsletters and track whom you email and when.

TIP

You can find a few free mailing-list options out there, but most of them involve a monthly fee. Shop around to find one that fits your price range.

Get Social

One of the best ways to build your blog's community is to plug in to communities that already exist, including social media platforms. Social media sites like Twitter, Instagram, Pinterest, and Facebook are home to millions of potential blog readers who may want to make your site one of their favorite online destinations.

If you haven't already created social media accounts related to your blog, it's time to get started. Turn back to Chapters 17 and 18 for information on Twitter and social media in general. Find the niche groups that apply to your own interests and begin connecting. Look for Facebook groups that may be a fit, including local blogger groups or promotions groups in which members share each other's blog content.

TIP

Hoping to build your online community by leveraging the communities of others? Be sure to promote and support others more than you ask for help yourself. You want to be a positive force online, not a negative one!

Involve Your Readers

What does your community like to read? Do the members like your posts about your personal life, or are they more interested in what you're doing in your daily job? Or do they want your opinion about some other topic that you've discussed?

Watch to see what element of your content is most popular and what gets the most comments and responses. Consider periodically polling your readership or using a survey creation tool such as Survey Monkey (www.surveymonkey.com) to find out what your readers would like to see on your blog.

Knowing what's popular in your blog can help you when you write later on because you can draw on this knowledge to create more posts that get responses. Keep an eye on those posts that get lots of comments, and understand their appeal to your audience as you make decisions about what to post about in the future. You can find out more about understanding your audience in Chapter 10, and get some help with content in Chapter 9.

You may also want to involve your readers by asking a leader in your online community to be in charge of responding to comments or leading forums. Check out Chapter 15 to learn more about online forums. Guest posts are another great way to allow your readers to become more involved in your blog so that they begin to feel a connection to your online community.

Connect Offline

It may sound counterintuitive to work on building an online community by connecting offline, but making connections in real life rather than just on your computer screen can go a long way in building your online community.

Do you have a local readership that is growing in leaps and bounds? Consider holding a local meet-up, even reaching out to a local restaurant to suggest a sponsor partnership. You may also want to find local blogger groups or social media clubs holding events and make plans to attend. The blogging community is notably supportive, and connecting with your fellow bloggers offline is likely to help you build your online networks as well.

Finally, look into blog conferences, typically held around the country throughout the year, and find an event that may be a fit for you. Not only will you learn tons of tips and tricks that will help your blog in general, you'll also make connections with bloggers who have their own well-established communities who may just want to get to know your blog next.

Go Mobile

A 2015 Pew Research Center report (www.pewinternet.org/2015/04/01/us-smartphone-use-in-2015/) found that nearly two-thirds of Americans are now smartphone owners, with 10 percent of smartphone owners having no other way to access the Internet in their homes. With the rise of readership on mobile devices, it's critical that your blog be mobile ready.

Many WordPress themes are mobile ready, but for those of you whose platforms or themes are not mobile compatible, it's important to take the steps necessary to make accessing your blog on a mobile device possible. To find out whether your blog is mobile compatible, check out Google's Mobile-Friendly Test (`www.google.com/webmasters/tools/mobile-friendly`), which allows you to test your blog for mobile compatibility.

Some bloggers choose to create a second version of their blog, created just for mobile. It probably makes more sense for you, however, to either select a mobile-optimized blog theme or install a plug-in to bring your site up to speed for mobile access.

Diversify

Unless you are writing a hyper-niche blog, it's a good idea to mix things up every now and then to reach new audiences and build your community. Consider periodically creating new content themes in your editorial calendar from time to time to pull in readers looking to read about different topics. For example, do you write mostly about crafts for kids? Consider branching out and occasionally posting recipes that are family friendly and get the kids involved in the kitchen. Maybe you write mostly about travel. Have you thought about also starting a series for readers looking to get the most out of their local attractions? The bigger your potential audience, the bigger your audience's potential!

Chapter 23

Ten Things All Bloggers Should Do

The 22 chapters before this one cover every blogging topic that you might imagine, from choosing your site's URL to monetizing your writing. Now you may be asking, what else is there? Beyond the topics covered in depth throughout this book, you can tap into a vast variety of tips and tricks that can take you to the next level or even help you settle in happily where you are right now. In the interest of space and time, I cover ten of these pointers in this chapter and leave you with your blogging career to discover and enjoy the rest.

Discover Your Voice

Are you the life of every party? When people describe you, do they begin with the word "funny"? Or do you consider yourself to be quiet and reflective? Perhaps you're known within your circle of friends or family as the go-to person for useful information or helpful tips.

Your blog is an extension of you, and discovering your blog voice is a bit like discovering yourself. Many bloggers struggle in the first weeks (or months or years!) to find their blogging voice. It's also quite common for bloggers to travel far down their blogging path before deciding to change their writing style.

As you begin thinking about your blogging voice, ask yourself what you want your readers to know and feel about you. Do you want your blog to mimic an informational website, perhaps sharing product reviews or the latest news? Or would you like to treat your site as an online journal, sharing every bit of yourself?

It is not at all uncommon for bloggers to struggle as they find their blogging voice and gain the courage to write freely. However, after you've discovered your voice, blogging will become magically easier and suddenly more enjoyable.

Stoke Your Muse

When I began my personal blog, Resourceful Mommy (www.resourcefulmommy.com), I was a full-time stay-at-home mom parenting a 2-year-old and a 4-year-old. My days were filled with playdates and diaper changes. Much of my early writing focused on the products that got us through our days, the questions I had as a young mother, and the concerns I had about life after full-time mothering as my oldest headed off to kindergarten.

Eight years later, my life is radically different, and naturally, my writing is as well. For example, we spend far more time traveling with our now easy-breezy older kids, so you're likely to find more traveling tips and tricks than ways to get your little one down for a nap. Also, rather than write about what I want to be when I grow up — or at least as my kids begin to — I now own a full-time business and write for a living.

Even though much has changed in my life, what hasn't changed completely is my blogging muse. My children have always been a main inspiration to me and a source of much of my content fodder. Similarly, as my husband and I journey through our second decade of marriage, our relationship inspires many post ideas. Finally, time for introspection remains a primary muse as I set out to write honestly and thoughtfully about my life.

Were I to focus only on my blog and not remember to take time for my family and myself, my muses would be neglected and, consequently, my content would suffer. As you work hard to bring your blog to the place you want it to be, don't forget to take time to stoke the muse that inspired you to write in the first place.

Survey Your Readers

Although I touch on this topic briefly in Chapter 22, it is worth revisiting the idea of surveying your readers from time to time. Unless you are blogging solely for you and care nothing about growing or fostering your readership — which is absolutely fine, by the way — you should take time periodically to connect with your readers to get their thoughts on your blog.

Some bloggers like to keep an open, ongoing survey that is always available, not unlike a feedback box in a place of business. A link to such a survey can be included at the end of posts, within your RSS feed (see Chapter 16 for more about RSS), or even as a widget in your sidebar. You may choose to check in with your bloggers once or twice a year instead, devoting an entire post to reader outreach.

Typical reader questions may include:

>> Age

>> Location

>> Education level

>> Gender

>> Favorite post topics

>> Interest in blog giveaways and contests

>> Preferences for blog subscription method

TIP

Creating such a survey is a rather easy pursuit, with tons of free surveying tools available. One popular tool is Survey Monkey (www.surveymonkey.com), which allows users to create basic surveys at no cost. For those of you with a Google account, you may want to consider creating a simple questions form on your Google Drive (www.drive.google.com). Each new form allows you to embed a link for your readers to complete the form, and your Google Drive keeps track of your readers' responses.

Find Your Tribe

You've likely caught on by now that the blogging world not only requires participants to learn a new technological skill set but also introduces them to a whole new language. One of these fun terms is *tribe*, or simply put, the readers and fellow bloggers to whom you most relate.

I was very fortunate and found my personal tribe on Twitter very early in my blogging career. Although we've gone from using Twitter as our main form of communication to checking in with each other daily in our closed Facebook Group, we continue to be there for one another as a source of everything from helpful hints to a safe place to vent.

Finding your tribe can be a tough and lonely road, but after you've plugged in to the online community that is right for you, it will take your blogging experience to a new, more enjoyable level. Take your time finding the community that is best for you, and be sure to look both inside and outside your content area while on your journey. Whereas I consider myself a journaling blogger, some of my closest blogging friends are frugal-living bloggers. It may be that finding the bloggers who share similar thoughts about blogging, social media, or life in general leads you to your tribe.

REMEMBER

Don't count your readers out when searching for your tribe! What are some of the other blogs that your most frequent readers also enjoy? (This is where a reader survey comes in handy!) Do your readers participate in online forums? Do they also blog? Don't be afraid to think outside the box when trying to join the right tribe for you.

Know Your Traffic Sources

If you're interested in tracking your website statistics, you've likely spent some time reading Chapter 19. There are many reasons to know how many visitors your blog receives, from being able to report to advertisers to simply knowing that you're not sending your content out into the abyss. However, even if you truly don't care about the number of readers your blog draws, you still may want to know your traffic sources.

I don't spend much time monitoring how many page views I receive on my personal blog, but I do love to take a look periodically at my traffic sources. For starters, it's nice to know whether that sidebar ad you've placed on a friend's blog is actually driving new readers to your site, or whether that free guest posting you've been doing is truly building your audience.

It's also useful to your future content creation to know whether some content is drawing more readers than other posts. For example, did you write a deeply personal post and later find that the post was included in an around-the-web post on another blog? When you take a look at what terms are driving search engine–related traffic, are you surprised by what is bringing readers to your site?

This information may inspire future editorial calendar (where you schedule future blog posts) ideas! You may also want to go back to old posts that are still receiving search engine traffic and update these posts with links to more recent posts. Using tracking programs (described in Chapter 19) to look thoughtfully at your traffic sources may give your blog — and you — a needed boost, even if traffic is the least of your blogging goals.

Set Goals

Speaking of blogging goals . . . have you set yours?

Joining the blogosphere can be an overwhelming experience. You have a laundry list of decisions to make, from your blog name to your site platform to your interest in making money from blogging. The idea of sitting down and listing specific goals for a pursuit that is still relatively new may feel like the proverbial straw that broke the camel's back.

When I first entered the world of blogging, I found myself looking at each new opportunity through the lens of what that opportunity would do to get me where I was going. This helped me decide what guest blogging opportunities to take, for example, and focus my limited time.

Blogging goals don't have to be complicated, and they're certainly open to revision as your blog grows and changes. Some simple goals may include:

>> **Grow readership:** Would you like someone other than your mother and spouse to read your blog? Set a specific goal such as 50 new readers in the first month.

>> **Follow a blogging schedule:** How often do you hope to post? Once a week? Once a day? More? Less?

>> **Utilize social media:** Yes, social media use may fall under your goals for your blog!

>> **Find a guest blogging opportunity:** Do you have a favorite blog that also happens to allow guest posts? Becoming a guest blogger on that site is a worthy goal!

>> **Monetize:** If you are simply blogging for yourself or as a hobby, making money from your blog may not even be on your radar. However, for many bloggers, it is a main goal for their blog to provide at least enough income to offset the costs of the hobby or part-time job of blogging.

Define Success

Setting goals for your blog is an important task for all bloggers — even veteran bloggers like myself — but that doesn't mean that this step should be skipped. All bloggers should take the time to define their version of success.

Even as my personal blog met a series of goals that were important to me, I continued to receive feedback from those around me regarding ways I could do more or be better. The problem with that input is that it ignored my personal definition of success. It turns out that my sometimes modest traffic was meeting my goals, and the amount of sponsored posts I wrote actually exceeded my plans for my blog.

By taking the time to define your version of success for your blog, not only will you know when you've achieved success, you'll also build a shield against that green-eyed monster, jealousy, as you look at the blogs around you.

Create a Monetization Plan . . . or Not

My initial monetization goal at the launch of my blog eight years ago was to eventually find freelance writing assignments to supplement my family's primary income. I never could have imagined that my blog would lead to writing books such as this or working with global brands in social media.

With that said, it was still important for me to think critically about blog monetization before getting too far along my own blogging path. Despite the unexpected twists and turns — most of them positive — my blog's monetization plan guided me through decisions at every step along this journey.

Some questions to consider when creating your own monetization plan may include:

>> Do you plan to seek ads for your blog? What type of ads will you allow?

>> Would you like to work with individuals and companies to place ads or do you prefer to apply to an ad network? For more information about advertising on blogs, visit Chapter 20.

>> How do you feel about accepting money to post content on your blog?

>> Do you hope to use your blog as a platform to seek other jobs such as paid writing or speaking opportunities?

Prepare to Grow

The first time someone asked me to write somewhere other than my own blog, I turned to my husband for help with making the decision. He asked, "What will that do to get you where you hope to go?" and the truth is, I had no idea at that point where I was hoping to go. As with many things in life, blogs often grow and change in spite of rather than because of the goals we set.

A blogger who begins with a journaling blog on a free platform such as Blogger (for more on Blogger, stop by Chapter 4) may end up choosing to move to a self-hosted platform with a dedicated server due to amount of traffic or depth of content. In fact, some blogs that began with a single writer have grown over the years to become multiple-writer sites, with the original author acting more as an editor-in-chief than a lone author.

If massive growth falls under your definition of success, you should certainly decide now how you want that to occur. But even if you don't anticipate blog growth, it is still a worthwhile use of your time to think about what you'd like a growing and expanding blog to look like should that day come.

Know When You're Done

I recently read a great blog post — naturally! — about life after blogging. Although blogging has been around in one form or another for quite some time now, in the expansive timeline of the world of communication, blogging is still a baby. It will be quite a while before there are as many former bloggers as there are active bloggers.

Even so, the day will likely come when the cons of blogging outweigh the pros. Perhaps your blog chronicles your battle against cancer and you've reached remission. It may be time to thank your readers for joining you on your journey and then no longer post. Or maybe you're a parenting blogger whose children no longer allow you to write about their lives. It may even be that you've made blogging a profession and the time to retire has arrived.

Whatever the reason, it's important for bloggers to know when they're done, even if that means that they're just done with that particular blog. After all, blogging, at its core, is meant to be enjoyable, and when it isn't anymore, you might need to reevaluate or move along to new pursuits.

Index

community standards
  comments, 178–180
  forums, 257–258
Connected Accounts menu
  (Squarespace), 140–141
Constant Contact email service
  provider, 356
contact forms, 60
content
  anonymous blogging,
    198–199
  business blogging, 340–341
  creating for Pinterest,
    297–300
  first-person writing, 166–167
  importing to Squarespace,
    139
  knowing your audience,
    160–165
  links, 168–170
  overcoming writer's block,
    170–172
  overview, 159–160
  quality writing, 166–168
  updating, 15, 166
contextual advertising, 320,
  345–346
contrast, adjusting (photos),
  217
Contributor account
  (WordPress), 112
control panel (blogging
  software), 58
copyright, 166
cost per action, 321
cost per click, 321
cost per impression, 321
couponing/deal blogs,
  151–152
cPanel database management
  tool, 108
CPU resources (web hosting),
  53

craft blogs, 148
Creative Commons license,
  215, 229–230
Crisp Ads ad network, 347
cropping photos, 216–217
CSS (Cascading Style Sheets),
  131
customizing. *See also* editing
  Blogger blog
    Layout area, 96–98
    overview, 91
    Template Designer, 93–96
    templates, 92–93
  footers, 28
  header, 28
  logos, 28
  sidebar material, 28
  Squarespace blog
    linking social networks,
      140–141
    sidebar, 142
  Tumblr blog, 127–129
  WordPress design, 117–118
Cyberduck, 106

D

dad blogging, 147–148
Dashboard
  Blogger
    Basic Settings area, 88–89
    Email settings page, 90
    overview, 78–79, 87–88
    Who Can Comment
      options, 89–90
  Tumblr, 129–130
  WordPress
    Appearance menu, 114
    Comments menu, 114
    Links menu, 113
    Media menu, 113
    Pages menu, 114

    panels, 115
    Plugins menu, 114
    Posts menu, 113
    Settings menu, 114
    Tools menu, 114
    Users menu, 114
date-based archives, 18–19
Deckard, Andrea, 151
deleting comments, 181–182
Delicious social bookmarking
  website, 280–281
delivering podcasts, 234
Dell, 335
Derivatives Allowed license,
  230
design blogs, 152
designing blogs, 27–28
diary blogs
  The Bloggess, 8
  life bloggers, 151
  overview, 9–10
digital cameras
  midrange, 207
  mobile, 207
  overview, 206–207
  point-and-shoots, 207
  SLRs, 207
disclosure statement, 41
disk space (web hosting), 52
Disney Parks Blog, 335–336
DISQUS tool, 177
diversification, 358
DIY blogs, 152
domain
  naming, 46–49
  registering
    GoDaddy, 50
    Hover, 50–51
    Namecheap, 50
    Network Solutions, 50
    overview, 49

privacy
  Privacy Mode (web browser),
    200
  protecting, 43–44
ProBlogger blog, 170–171
product placement, 325–326
product-review offers,
    330–331
professional blogging, 326
professional social networks.
    See LinkedIn
profiling audience, 164–165
promoting. *See also* marketing
    and promotion
  podcasts
    FeedBurner, 234–237
    iTunes, 237–238
    podcast directories, 239
    vlogs, 247–248
pseudonyms, 196
public domain photos,
    215
publishing
  Blogger posts
    comments, 86
    launching, 86
    previewing, 84–85
    scheduling, 85–86
  podcasts
    assigning metadata, 231
    delivering, 234
    format, 232
    storing podcasts, 232–234
  Tumblr text posts, 126
Pulse platform, 296

Q

Quick Draft panel (WordPress
    Dashboard), 115
Quiz Meme, 172
quizzes, 172
Quote post (Tumblr), 126

R

Rakuten Affiliate Network, 327
Ravelry, 197, 278
Real Life with Sarah blog, 41
Really Simple Syndication
    (RSS) feed
  creating, 268–269
  defined, 222
  generating traffic through,
    267–268
  news agencies, 266
  overview, 265–266
  terminology, 266
  uses for, 269
  XML, 265–267
reblogging (Tumblr), 127
recent posts, 17–18
recycling posts, 170–171
registering domain
  GoDaddy, 50
  Hover, 50–51
  Namecheap, 50
  Network Solutions, 50
  overview, 49
  Panabee, 51
relationships, effect of
    blogging on, 41–42
Remember icon, 3
repeat visitors, 306–307
reputation, protecting, 43–44
Reputation.com, 44
Resourceful Mommy blog,
    299, 302, 360
rich media (forums), 256
RiseUp webmail service, 196
Rowse, Darren, 170–171
RSS (Really Simple Syndication)
    feed
  creating, 268–269
  defined, 222
  generating traffic through,
    267–268

news agencies, 266
  overview, 265–266
  terminology, 266
  uses for, 269
  XML, 265–267
RSS feed link, 21

S

Sabin-Wilson, Lisa, 99, 118
Savings Lifestyle blog, 151–152
Scary Mommy blog, 175
scheduling posts
  anonymous blogging,
    198
  Blogger, 85–86
  time of day, 162
Scheer, Robert, 150
*Search Engine Optimization For
    Dummies* (Kent), 262
search engine optimization
    (SEO)
  blogging software, 58
  defined, 261–262
  keywords, 262–263
  spiders, 262
  tools for, 263
Search feature, 16
security
  anonymous blogging
    IP addresses, 199–200
    software, 200–201
    staying up-to-date, 201
  protecting privacy and
    reputation, 43–44
Selfish Mom blog, 179
SEO (search engine
    optimization)
  blogging software, 58
  defined, 261–262
  keywords, 262–263
  spiders, 262
  tools for, 263

U

UBB.Threads forum software, 253

unconferences (camps), 118

uniform resource locator (URL), 77

unique visitors, 306–307

Unordered List tool (Tumblr), 124

updating content, 15, 166

Updyke, Andrea, 17

uploading

images to Squarespace, 137–139

WordPress files, 105–107

URL (uniform resource locator), 77

user registration, protecting against spam with, 188–189

Users menu (WordPress Dashboard), 114

V

Valade, Janet, 107

Vanilla Forums software, 253

vBulletin forum software, 253

video podcasts, 224–225

Video post (Tumblr), 126

View blog button (Blogger Dashboard), 78

Vimeo, 244

Vine, 244, 279

Vintage Revivals blog, 148

viral marketing, 344

vlogging

editing vlog, 246–247

equipment, 245

Facebook Video, 244

Maker.tv, 244

overview, 241

promoting vlog, 247–248

reasons for, 242

setting for, 245–246

Vimeo, 244

Vine, 244, 279

YouTube, 243–244

W

Warning icon, 3

Wayback Machine, 33

web feeds

advertising on, 319, 324–325

automatically tweeting blog posts, 294

as blogosphere tool, 312

business blogging and, 343

creating, 268–269

generating traffic through, 267–268

news agencies, 266

overview, 265–266

terminology, 266

uses for, 269

XML, 265–267

web hosting

buying

Bluehost, 55

Doteasy, 55

Hostgator, 55

overview, 53–54

Siteground, 54–55

CPU resources, 53

disk space, 52

overview, 51–52

researching, 52–53

WordPress, 103

web statistics and analytics

blogosphere tools, 312–314

errors, 306

hits, 305

lack of standards for, 307

overview, 301–302

page views, 305–306

repeat visitors, 306–307

server logs, 308

services and software for

hosted, 308–310

installable, 310–311

unique visitors, 306–307

usefulness of, 302–304, 362–363

Web Style Guide, 170

The Webalizer, 311

Webby Awards, 150

weblog, 16

Wells Fargo, 335

Whalen, Kelly, 169, 264–265

whitelists, 190

WhitHonea.com blog, 148

Whitley, Maggie, 342

Who Can Comment options (Blogger Dashboard), 89–90

Wikipedia, 344

wikis, 344

Windows Movie Maker, 246, 247

wireframe, 96–98

WordCamp, 118

WordPress

Administrator account, 111

Author account, 111

Contributor account, 112

creating post, 115–117

customizing design, 117–118

Dashboard

About the Author

Amy Lupold Bair: Named one of the most powerful women in social media by *Working Mother* magazine, Amy Lupold Bair is the owner of Resourceful Mommy Media, LLC (www.resourcefulmommymedia.com), a social media marketing company that includes the blogger network Global Influence as well as her own site, Resourceful Mommy (www.resourcefulmommy.com). She has loved the Internet since she first heard the whir-whir-click of a dial-up modem, her first home online was a Geocities community, and she still maintains a Prodigy email account for sentimental reasons. Amy's primary digital addiction is Twitter, where she is always available in 140 characters or fewer as @ResourcefulMom, although her use of Instagram is climbing the social media ladder and is nearly on par with her Dr. Pepper obsession. Over the years, she has contributed to a variety of sites including Lifetime Moms and the Disney Voices team at Babble.com. Amy is also the author of *Raising Digital Families For Dummies* (John Wiley & Sons, Inc.). Prior to her career as a social media consultant, writer, and speaker, Amy taught middle school English and drama. She and her social media–averse husband live in the D.C. suburbs where they are raising their two bloggers-in-training along with three social media–savvy pets.

Dedication

This book is dedicated to my friends in the blogging community for their incredible friendship, encouragement, inspiration, and trailblazing. The sticker on my laptop says "All my friends live in here," and although that may not be quite true, it is certainly where I've found some of the best friends of my life.

Author's Acknowledgments

Thank you first and foremost to John Wiley & Sons for giving me this opportunity and making me part of the *For Dummies* family. It is an absolute pleasure and a highlight of my blogging adventure. Special thanks to Ellen Gerstein, who changed my life with the best Twitter direct message ever, as well as to Amy Fandrei, who continues to keep this very grateful blogger around. Thank you as well to my project manager, Maureen Tullis, my copy editor, Scott Tullis, and the entire *For Dummies* team.

I am grateful, always, for the love and support of my husband, Jason, and our children, Emma and Noah. I am also thankful for Winnie the Wonder Pup, the home office dog who has been by my side every step of the way. Mom and Dad, thank you for not rolling your eyes too often when I told you I was becoming a blogger and for getting me through many crazy deadlines over the past eight years. Thank you to my Celebrate Recovery family for your encouragement and support. It is far easier to enjoy this writer's life without hurts, habits, and hang-ups weighing me down. "As iron sharpens iron, so one man sharpens another." —Proverbs 27:17

Publisher's Acknowledgments

Acquisitions Editor: Amy Fandrei

Project Editor/Copy Editor: Scott Tullis

Technical Editor: Paul Chaney

Editorial Assistant: Kayla Hoffman

Sr. Editorial Assistant: Cherie Case

Production Editor: Selvakumaran Rajendiran

Project Manager: Maureen Tullis

Cover Image: scyther5/Shutterstock

Apple & Mac

iPad For Dummies,
6th Edition
978-1-118-72306-7

iPhone For Dummies,
7th Edition
978-1-118-69083-3

Macs All-in-One
For Dummies, 4th Edition
978-1-118-82210-4

OS X Mavericks
For Dummies
978-1-118-69188-5

Blogging & Social Media

Facebook For Dummies,
5th Edition
978-1-118-63312-0

Social Media Engagement
For Dummies
978-1-118-53019-1

WordPress For Dummies,
6th Edition
978-1-118-79161-5

Business

Stock Investing
For Dummies, 4th Edition
978-1-118-37678-2

Investing For Dummies,
6th Edition
978-0-470-90545-6

Personal Finance

Personal Finance
For Dummies, 7th Edition
978-1-118-11785-9

QuickBooks 2014
For Dummies
978-1-118-72005-9

Small Business Marketing
Kit For Dummies,
3rd Edition
978-1-118-31183-7

Careers

Job Interviews
For Dummies, 4th Edition
978-1-118-11290-8

Job Searching with Social
Media For Dummies,
2nd Edition
978-1-118-67856-5

Personal Branding
For Dummies
978-1-118-11792-7

Resumes For Dummies,
6th Edition
978-0-470-87361-8

Starting an Etsy Business
For Dummies, 2nd Edition
978-1-118-59024-9

Diet & Nutrition

Belly Fat Diet For Dummies
978-1-118-34585-6

Mediterranean Diet
For Dummies
978-1-118-71525-3

Nutrition For Dummies,
5th Edition
978-0-470-93231-5

Digital Photography

Digital SLR Photography
All-in-One For Dummies,
2nd Edition
978-1-118-59082-9

Digital SLR Video &
Filmmaking For Dummies
978-1-118-36598-4

Photoshop Elements 12
For Dummies
978-1-118-72714-0

Gardening

Herb Gardening
For Dummies, 2nd Edition
978-0-470-61778-6

Gardening with Free-Range
Chickens For Dummies
978-1-118-54754-0

Health

Boosting Your Immunity
For Dummies
978-1-118-40200-9

Diabetes For Dummies,
4th Edition
978-1-118-29447-5

Living Paleo For Dummies
978-1-118-29405-5

Big Data

Big Data For Dummies
978-1-118-50422-2

Data Visualization
For Dummies
978-1-118-50289-1

Hadoop For Dummies
978-1-118-60755-8

Language &
Foreign Language

500 Spanish Verbs
For Dummies
978-1-118-02382-2

English Grammar
For Dummies, 2nd Edition
978-0-470-54664-2

French All-in-One
For Dummies
978-1-118-22815-9

German Essentials
For Dummies
978-1-118-18422-6

Italian For Dummies,
2nd Edition
978-1-118-00465-4

e **Available in print and e-book formats.**

Available wherever books are sold. **For more information or to order direct visit www.dummies.com**

Math & Science

Algebra I For Dummies,
2nd Edition
978-0-470-55964-2

Anatomy and Physiology
For Dummies, 2nd Edition
978-0-470-92326-9

Astronomy For Dummies,
3rd Edition
978-1-118-37697-3

Biology For Dummies,
2nd Edition
978-0-470-59875-7

Chemistry For Dummies,
2nd Edition
978-1-118-00730-3

1001 Algebra II Practice
Problems For Dummies
978-1-118-44662-1

Microsoft Office

Excel 2013 For Dummies
978-1-118-51012-4

Office 2013 All-in-One
For Dummies
978-1-118-51636-2

PowerPoint 2013
For Dummies
978-1-118-50253-2

Word 2013 For Dummies
978-1-118-49123-2

Music

Blues Harmonica
For Dummies
978-1-118-25269-7

Guitar For Dummies,
3rd Edition
978-1-118-11554-1

iPod & iTunes
For Dummies, 10th Edition
978-1-118-50864-0

Programming

Beginning Programming
with C For Dummies
978-1-118-73763-7

Excel VBA Programming
For Dummies, 3rd Edition
978-1-118-49037-2

Java For Dummies,
6th Edition
978-1-118-40780-6

Religion & Inspiration

The Bible For Dummies
978-0-7645-5296-0

Buddhism For Dummies,
2nd Edition
978-1-118-02379-2

Catholicism For Dummies,
2nd Edition
978-1-118-07778-8

Self-Help & Relationships

Beating Sugar Addiction
For Dummies
978-1-118-54645-1

Meditation For Dummies,
3rd Edition
978-1-118-29144-3

Seniors

Laptops For Seniors
For Dummies, 3rd Edition
978-1-118-71105-7

Computers For Seniors
For Dummies, 3rd Edition
978-1-118-11553-4

iPad For Seniors
For Dummies, 6th Edition
978-1-118-72826-0

Social Security
For Dummies
978-1-118-20573-0

Smartphones & Tablets

Android Phones
For Dummies, 2nd Edition
978-1-118-72030-1

Nexus Tablets
For Dummies
978-1-118-77243-0

Samsung Galaxy S 4
For Dummies
978-1-118-64222-1

Samsung Galaxy Tabs
For Dummies
978-1-118-77294-2

Test Prep

ACT For Dummies,
5th Edition
978-1-118-01259-8

ASVAB For Dummies,
3rd Edition
978-0-470-63760-9

GRE For Dummies,
7th Edition
978-0-470-88921-3

Officer Candidate Tests
For Dummies
978-0-470-59876-4

Physician's Assistant Exam
For Dummies
978-1-118-11556-5

Series 7 Exam For Dummies
978-0-470-09932-2

Windows 8

Windows 8.1 All-in-One
For Dummies
978-1-118-82087-2

Windows 8.1 For Dummies
978-1-118-82121-3

Windows 8.1 For Dummies,
Book + DVD Bundle
978-1-118-82107-7

_e_ Available in print and e-book formats.

Available wherever books are sold. **For more information or to order direct visit www.dummies.com**

Take Dummies with you everywhere you go!

Whether you are excited about e-books, want more from the web, must have your mobile apps, or are swept up in social media, Dummies makes everything easier.

For Dummies is the global leader in the reference category and one of the most trusted and highly regarded brands in the world. No longer just focused on books, customers now have access to the For Dummies content they need in the format they want. Let us help you develop a solution that will fit your brand and help you connect with your customers.

Advertising & Sponsorships

Connect with an engaged audience on a powerful multimedia site, and position your message alongside expert how-to content.

Targeted ads • Video • Email marketing • Microsites • Sweepstakes sponsorship

21 Million Monthly Page Views & 13 Million Unique Visitors

Custom Publishing

Reach a global audience in any language by creating a solution that will differentiate you from competitors, amplify your message, and encourage customers to make a buying decision.

Apps • Books • eBooks • Video • Audio • Webinars

Brand Licensing & Content

Leverage the strength of the world's most popular reference brand to reach new audiences and channels of distribution.

For more information, visit www.Dummies.com/biz

Dummies products make life easier!

- DIY
- Consumer Electronics
- Crafts
- Software
- Cookware
- Hobbies
- Videos
- Music
- Games
- and More!

For more information, go to **Dummies.com·** and search the store by category.

FOR DUMMIES

A Wiley Brand